Marginal Narratives and the Question of Human Rights in Asian Pacific Literature

Sk Sagir Ali · Avijit Basak
Editors

Marginal Narratives and the Question of Human Rights in Asian Pacific Literature

Springer

Editors
Sk Sagir Ali
Midnapore College
West Bengal, India

Avijit Basak
Department of English
Maharaja Manindra Chandra College
Kolkata, West Bengal, India

ISBN 978-981-97-4546-3 ISBN 978-981-97-4544-9 (eBook)
https://doi.org/10.1007/978-981-97-4544-9

This Springer imprint is published by the registered company Springer Nature Singapore Pte Ltd.
The registered company address is: 152 Beach Road, #21-01/04 Gateway East, Singapore 189721, Singapore

Preface

Asia does not exist. This might sound strange, but along with Africa, Asia of popular culture, movies, and arts is an invention of Western discourse, where the cartographic dwarfing of these two continents represent how monolithically they have been constructed in Imperial imagination to justify the missionary zeal of colonialism through misappropriation. The late counter-discourses to this monolithic dwarfing also challenge the sweeping generalizations of values that we have inherited from our colonial legacies. We are gradually, but surely, awakening to the urgent demand of Asian perspectives to be a major organ in global narratives. But Asia is also a continent of contradictions, of inter-cultural and counter-cultural tensions where its violent pasts reappear in modern attires to exert its legacy. Asia is an independent and a dependent continent where international politics is a matter of incredible exploitation and violation. Any attempt to understand Asia needs the commitment of a polyglot. Asia is not one, neither it is meant to be. The lexicon of traumas, therefore, needs heteroglossic approach in cohabitable conditions. This book, *Marginal Narratives and the Question of Human Rights in Asian Literature* is an exercise in accommodating multivocal perspectives, beginning from introductions to the scholarly essays that make up the most important corpus of the text. This is part intentional and part unavoidable because Asia itself is a mosaic of intertextuality and transitional narratives. Part I of the Introduction, entitled "The Ghosts of Imperial Wounds: Asia, Human Rights, and the Grammatology of Plurisemiosis," written by Avijit Basak, argues for an immediate change in the narratives of Human Rights as a decolonial measure and highlights the need for the codification of Asian idioms of traumas and brutalities, frequently inherited from its colonial past. Part II of the Introduction, entitled "Asia as Method: Decoding Human Rights and Power Dynamics in Asian Historical Tapestry and Contemporary Realities" by Sk Sagir Ali complements and counters Basak's contention by highlighting the shifting curves of Human Rights narratives in the wake of 9/11 arguing for an ever-awake democratic space and power to dispense the rights of the powerless. These two introductions, intentionally kept separate to emphasize different and overlapping perspectives, aim to prepare the readers for the dazzling array of demands, interpretations, and viewpoints that the esteemed contributors to this book have advanced and formulated.

West Bengal, India Sk Sagir Ali
Kolkata, India Avijit Basak

Contents

1 **Introduction Part I** ... 1
Avijit Basak

2 **Introduction Part II** ... 13
Sk Sagir Ali

Part I Human Rights Narratives, Literary Activism, and Nationhood in Asia

3 **Voices of Resistance: Kaifi Azmi's Exploration of Reason, War, and Revolution** ... 27
Mohammad Asim Siddiqui

4 **Refugee Chronicles: Khaled Hosseini's "Sea Prayer" and the Struggle for Human Rights** ... 41
Nisreen T. Yousef

5 **Wartime Rape: The Figures of the 'Birangana' and the 'Comfort Woman'** ... 51
Sanchali Sarkar

6 **Sovereign Verse: Jacinta Kerketta's Literary Activism in Rights and Welfare** ... 63
Subhayu Bhattacharjee and Sinor Lama

7 **Behind Bars: Systematic Violence and Human Rights in *the Plague upon Us*** ... 73
Sk Sagir Ali

Part II Cinematic Echoes: Mnemoculture and the Visual Discourse of Human Rights in Asia

8 Frames of Memory: Mnemoculture in Human Rights Films on Cambodia and Vietnam 85
Farddina Hussain

9 The Spectral as the Political: Dystopia, Myth, and Horror in Patrick Graham's *Ghoul* 95
Rishiraj Pal

Part III Borderless Struggles: Narratives of Marginality and Social Injustice in Asia

10 Borders and Boundaries: Resituating *the Tiger Claw* in the Current Times 105
Indira Chakraborty (Bhattacharya)

11 Marginalised Lives in Assamese Literature: Saga of Loss and Longing in Assam's Chars 117
Parvin Sultana

12 Dead Horses Tell no Tales: Agrarian Revolts, Farmer Suicides and the Right to Cultivate in Neoliberal India 129
Syamantak Shobhan Basu

Part IV Activism, the limits of agency and the Pursuit of Social Justice in Asia and the Pacific

13 Hunger's Cry: Bijon Bhattacharya's "Nabanna" and the Bengal Famine of 1943 151
Subhajeet Singha

14 Dalit Negotiations: Yogesh Maitreya's Perspective on University Spaces and Human Rights 161
Ambalika Biswas

15 On the Margins of Respectability: The Disempowered *Devadasi* in Muvalur Ramamirthammal's *Web of Deceit* 173
P. Muralidhar Sharma

16 Telling, Writing and Translating: Narratives of Reclaiming People's Rights 185
Mrinmoy Pramanick

Editors and Contributors

About the Editors

Sk Sagir Ali is Assistant Professor at the Department of English, Midnapore College, West Bengal. His published works include the edited books, *Religion in South Asian Anglophone Literature: Traversing Resistance Margins and Extremism* published in 2021, *Literature and Theory: Contemporary Signposts and Critical Surveys* published in 2022, and *War on Terror: Nation, Democracy and Liberalisation* published in 2023 from Routledge (Taylor and Francis). His articles appear in journals of repute like Journal of Global Postcolonial Studies from the University of Florida Press, South Asia: Journal of South Asian Studies, Social Identities: Journal for the Study of Race, Nation and Culture, Journal of Muslim Minority Affairs, Postcolonial Text and in other journals. Ali has lectured extensively at several colleges and universities, namely SNDT University, Mumbai, ISPELL India, Dhurpguri Girls college and at American Comparative Literature Association. And of late, Ali has been named as the Chief Series Editor of the Book Series, *Peripheral Lives in Asia: Reimagining Nationalisms, Citizenship and Precarity in the 21st Century* with Routledge, UK. He has been editing a special issue on "Migrant Portrayal: Precarity, Displacement, and Human Rights in South Asian Narratives" with Journal of Postcolinial Writing (Taylor & Francis).

Avijit Basak is Assistant Professor in the Department of English, Maharaja Manindra Chandra College, under the University of Calcutta where he has been working since 2015. He is presently pursuing Ph.D from Presidency University on Holocaust literature. He writes both in English and Bangla, and his works have been published by Burdwan University Press, Routledge, and Baibhashik amongst others.

Contributors

Syamantak Shobhan Basu, MA, MPhil is a PhD student in Literary Studies at the University of Illinois in Urbana-Champaign. He is interested in studying the intersections between technology, nationalism, neoliberalism and global capital. In particular, he is interested in the proliferation of nationalism in India with the advent of internet and social media technologies. He is also interested in popular culture and its role in network formations. Outside of academia, he is a poet and fiction writer.

Subhayu Bhattacharjee is Assistant Professor, Deptt of English, Mirik College, Darjeeling. He is also a doctoral fellow in Cultural Studies at the University of North Bengal, India and had been previously enrolled as UGC JRF in IIEST Shibpur, Kolkata. He has published in international journals of repute such as Glocalism: Globus et Locus (Milan), Sanglap (UGC CARE, MLA), Hyper Cultura (SCOPUS), New Global Studies (Walter De Gruyter) .

Ambalika Biswas teaches English Literature at the Department of English, Rabindra Mahavidyalaya, Champadanga, Hooghly. She has also taught in Royal Thimphu College, Thimphu Bhutan, under the Royal University of Bhutan from 2011 to 2013. Her areas of interest are Gender Studies, Dalit Literature, and Indian Literature.

Indira Chakraborty (Bhattacharya) is Assistant Professor in English in the Department of English, St. Xavier's University, Kolkata. She has completed her PhD from Visva Bharati University, Santiniketan. Her areas of interest include Canadian Diasporic Literature, Migration Studies, Digital Humanities and New Literatures. She has published articles in various edited volumes and journals and also has teaching experience and research exposure in various institutions.

Farddina Hussain is Associate Professor at the Department of English, Gauhati University and her areas of interest are human rights, gender studies, Posthumanism and visual arts. She has published several research papers in journals and also attended conferences abroad to present her views on cinema, posthumanism and graphic narratives.

Sinor Lama (co-author) is Assistant Professor, Department of Geography, Mirik College, Darjeeling. He is also a doctoral scholar researching on cultural anthropology of the North East.

Rishiraj Pal is Assistant Professor of English at the Centre for Distance and Online Education, Rabindra Bharati University, Kolkata, and a doctoral candidate at the Department of English, Visva-Bharati, Santiniketan. He has presented his research on James Joyce at various international symposiums held in Singapore, Rome, Georgia, and Dublin. He was awarded a Rosa Maria Bollettieri scholarship to attend Trieste Joyce School at the University of Trieste, and a full scholarship to attend Dublin James Joyce Summer School at University College Dublin. He is currently editing a volume on Sexual Cultures.

Mrinmoy Pramanick teaches in the department of comparative Indian language and literature, University of Calcutta. His areas of interest are translation studies, language and community, migration—refugee and border, and dalit literature. He finished a major project on Indian exodus from South East Asia and worked on a project on Bengali Dalit Oral narratives. He translated Sharan Kumar Limbale's *Dalit Sahityache Soundarjya Shashtra*and Ganesh Devy's *Off Many Heroes* into Bengali. His translation of Kalyani Thakur Charal's poems into English *I Belong to Nowhere*, published by Tilted Axis, London. He edited *Dalit Sahitya Charcha, Lekhalekhir Pathshala, and Kathay Kathay Limbale, Oh Priest Give Me the Seeded Banana, Memoir of Sundarban: A Journey from an Island.*

Sanchali Sarkar is a Doctoral Researcher at the Chair of Critical Development Studies at the University of Passau, Germany. Her doctoral project focuses on gender and mobility. She is also working as a guest lecturer at the Department of English at Basanti Devi College (post graduate section), Kolkata. She received a Humboldt grant in 2023 to take part in the Gender and Law workshop organized by Freie University Berlin, Germany. She was also a guest researcher for the 'South Asia work-in-progress' retreat in 2022 at the Max Planck Institute for Social Anthropology (Halle) in Germany. She received the prestigious AUFF Grant in 2018 to work as a Predoctoral Research Fellow at the Department of Global Studies, Aarhus University, Denmark. She is currently co-editing a volume on 'queering urban spaces'.

P. Muralidhar Sharma is Assistant Professor in the School of English, Gangadhar Meher University, Sambalpur. His areas of research interests include Literature and Performing Arts, Indian Literature in Translation, and Postcolonial Studies. His research papers have been published in journals of academic repute like South Asian Review, Margins, Caesurae, among others. His PhD thesis, entitled 'Mapping the Cultural Space of Women Performers: Devadasis and Courtesans in Indian Fiction' looked at the intersections between disciplines as diverse as Literary Studies and Dance Studies. He is currently editing a volume on Literary Cultures and Socio-political Movements.

Mohammad Asim Siddiqui is Professor of English and Chair, Department of English at Aligarh Muslim University, Aligarh. A literary critic, translator and editor, Siddiqui's recent publications include *Shahryar* (Sahitya Akademi: 2021), co-authored books *Jahan-e -Syed* (Bennett, Coleman & Co. Ltd.:2017) and *A History of Aligarh Muslim University* (Bennett, Coleman & Co. Ltd.:2021), translation of *Qurratulain Hyder* (Sahitya Akademi 2023), numerous research articles and translations in books and journals, and regular columns and reviews on art and culture in *The Book Review*, *Biblio: A Review of Books*, *The Hindu*, Scroll.in and many other magazines, newspapers and news portals. A Fulbright Fellow at NYU in 2007, he has published, among others, with Oxford University Press, Cambridge University Press, Routledge, Bloomsbury, Sahitya Akademi and Orient BlackSwan.

Subhajeet Singha is Assistant Professor and Head of the Department of English, Deshapran Mahavidyalaya, under Vidyasagar University, West Bengal.His area of research includes Postcolonial Studies, Renaissance Literature, 19th Century Historiographical Studies of Bengal, Famine Studies.

Parvin Sultana currently teaches Political Science in Pramathesh Barua College in Assam. Her research interests include gender, migration and minority politics in Assam. Her articles have been published in journals like *Economic and Political Weekly*, *Social Change of Sage*, *Oxford Journal of Policing* etc. She also regularly reviews books for *The Book Review Journal*. Apart from academic writing, she writes regularly on various socio-political issues for various newspapers and webzines in Assam.

Nisreen T. Yousef is Associate Professor of Contemporary British and American Literature. She currently works at Middle East University, Amman, Jordan. Her research interest revolves around Colonial and Postcolonial Literature. Dr. Yousef was awarded her PhD from the University of Leicester/ UK.

Chapter 1
Introduction Part I

The Ghosts of Imperial Wounds: Asia, Human Rights, and the Grammatology of Plurisemiosis

Avijit Basak

1.1 Introduction

The elementary question that drives this book is to address the question of Human Rights from Asian perspectives, or an attempt to do so in this post-human and post-truth time. Human Rights, as they exist today, aspire to universalization, diluting cartographic and cultural differences, seen through a lens of imperialist reckoning. This macronarrative blurring must be discarded in favour of micronarratives that not only celebrate diversity, but also grieve for the crimes that took place in the name of civilizational utilitarianism. This book is aimed at creating such a discourse which tries to locate traumas in local experiences which might have similarities with the familiar memory of Western eco and biopolitics, but urgently need academic interventions not to get lost under the economy of colonial solipsism. The ellipsis of Asian injuries, in its Derridean sense, is both written off and under erasure. It is time to turn the table assertively, not only as an important step towards decolonization but also to claim the most powerful "logic of supplementarity", as Derrida conceives it in *Of Grammatology* (1997, 215) that destabilizes the stable notion of a universal Human Rights. Intruding in the narrative from the outside, it would force the vanguards of such ideas to rethink and reshape their ideological bias for a more embracive effort. Justice is infinite, and so are rights. They can never be fully fleshed out, but it is in limitless attempts to right the wrongs perpetrated on the vulnerable marginal, and precarious people that the notions of Human Rights can thrive. The answer lies in plurality and continuity. One important problem that scholars, historians, and philosophers from the Third World face is the lack of Asia-centric trauma theories, not least because of the incredible heterogeneity of the region. Therefore, most of

A. Basak (✉)
Department of English, Maharaja Manindra Chandra College, University of Calcutta, Kolkata, India
e-mail: avijit.basak@hotmail.com

S. S. Ali and A. Basak (eds.), *Marginal Narratives and the Question of Human Rights in Asian Pacific Literature*, https://doi.org/10.1007/978-981-97-4544-9_1

the attempts to narrate different Asian grievances must rely on a mimesis of Western trauma theories. However, this mimesis can be a political act of founding a diegesis of indigenous trauma theory. The translation of trauma in different cultures can transcend the primary aporia of imperialism to open up dispersive avenues of language acquisitions to ask for participatory representation in the discourse of Human Rights. Mimesis and emblematic evocations can act as *pre*-text, a paratext, to the narrative that is to come, supplementing, appropriating, and respooling indigenous grieves as texts, embedded in collective and cultural memories.

United Nations defines Human Rights as "rights inherent to all human beings, regardless of race, sex, nationality, ethnicity, language, religion, or any other status. Human rights include the right to life and liberty, freedom from slavery and torture, freedom of opinion and expression, the right to work and education, and many more. Everyone is entitled to these rights, without discrimination." It further claims that international human rights law is one of its "great achievements" expounding it as "a universal and internationally protected code to which all nations can subscribe, and all people aspire. The United Nations has defined a broad range of internationally accepted rights, including civil, cultural, economic, political and social rights. It has also established mechanisms to promote and protect these rights and to assist states in carrying out their responsibilities,"[1] We are, of course aware of the fact that a universal concept of Human Rights is as untenable as Feminism or Postcolonialism conceived in singularity. Like the later two theoretico-praxis Human Rights must thrive in plurality and the political, embedded in cultural polyphony and polysemy. Thus, even though the essays included in this book try to capture the essential multipronged approaches, it is just *an* intervention, hopefully a significant one, in the increasing dialogic growth of Asian frames of references to critical schools.

Any overture to Human Rights and its historical background makes us look back to WWII. Even though at the end of the Great War the foundation of the League of Nations was the first attempt to oversee any possible violation of peace, it was only with the United Nations, established in 1945, that any sustained and stable attempt to keep peace internationally began. However, as time passed the fissures and fault lines of such an institution became more and more apparent. Depending on a number of powerful nations for its funding and peacekeepers, along with a Security Council overwhelmingly Euro-American, and Christian in operation, made the entire process of *world*-peace a matter of interpretation and interest. A major institution like International Court of Justice, which started functioning in 1947 and affiliated to the UN, is begrudged by Northeast Asia as Koh and Phan note in their essay "The Asian Way to Settle Dispute" (2016, 5). Even though they believe that South East Asia has a better track record to seek legal help from the ICJ, out of the 190 cases that have been entered in the General List of ICJ till 4th July 2023,[2] Strachan observes in "Resolving South East Asian Territorial Disputes: A Role for the ICJ" that it has dealt with South-Asian territorial disputes only 3 times till 2009. Owada reminds us in "The Experience of Asia With International Adjucation" (2005) that this is the same number that PCIJ, Permanent Court of International Justice, a precursor of ICJ, handled from 1922 to 1946 for the entire Asian region (10). According to Owada the reason behind such a low participation is a product of a lack of trust (15) even though the situation is changing gradually. Though Owada, and Koh and Phan sound optimistic about the recent upsurge of legal interventions to solve certain international Asian issues, we cannot but ponder over the fact-finding of Simon Chesterman who shows in "Asia's Ambivalence about International Law and Institutions: Past, Present and Futures" (2016) that only 8 Asian countries, covering 15% of the total states, have accepted the jurisdiction of ICJ as compared to 30% of Eastern European States, 41% of African States, and 69% of Western European and Other States Group (WEOG) (961). ICJ, Permanent Court of Arbitration (PCA), and the International Criminal Court (ICC) are located in the Hague whereas International Tribunal for the Law of the Sea (ITLOS) is in Hamburg, even though Singapore has been nominated as a venue for ITLOS cases in 2020. It is clear that these important organs of Human Rights are not equipped to be aligned to an Asian frames of references, neither can we expect them to be nuanced to cultural and historical imperatives to do so. In fact, as Aristyo Rizka Darmawan has rightly pointed out in "International law takes a step towards Asia" (2020), centuries of exploitation under the practice of colonialism is a crucial reason behind the scepticism that Asian nations exercise in dealing with international law. It is a matter of irony that the UN considers decolonization as a global issue,[3] its role is majorly limited to declaratory proclamations. Darmawan further notes how, keeping with the general trend, only 6 Asian nations out of 40 sought legal help from ITLOS. Darmawan opines that countries like India see international law as "a tool for justifying centuries of colonialism", even though India was the first Asian country to appear before the ICJ as Respondent in 1955 (Owada 15).

Colonial legacy, exploitative violence, traumatic memory, and experiential hesitation confine and characterize the Asian outlook to a "universal" codification of international laws to protect human rights. The essential and essentialized traits of Eurocentrism of such a codification is a well established fact. Martti Koskenniemi has surveyed in "Histories of International law: Dealing with Eurocentrism" (2011) the evolutions of international law as a western humanist attempt to contain and explain certain rights as universal without taking cognizance of the fact that African and Asian experiences are vastly different from theirs precisely because of colonial and local structures. Thus, the logocentric formation of international law is oblivious of its own historicity which needs to be re-evaluated and deconstructed. This idea of deconstruction does not of course argue for an obliteration, but for an accommodation of a plurilateral understanding of differences. Koskenniemi points out how Ernest Nys has traced the ways the origin of international law is embedded in European Renaissance values (153), harking back, especially to the Peace of Westphalia (1648) inheriting all the problematics, both political and religious, of the time. That the genesis of international law coincides with the expansion of European colonialism is not an accident (155), giving the legal experts leeways to generalize the non-Europeans as "too different" to be alike, thereby excluding them from the purview of international law (156). The advancement of the idea of a civilized West *vis-a-vis* a brute East was implied in such a formulation (158), binaries which are still conspicuous in the mainstream narrative in any case of humanitarian crisis. Koskenniemi rightly observes that the recognition of "a combination of solipsism and imperialism is quite important in understanding the way knowledges operate to create communities of power claiming a universal . . . view of the world" (170). The nineteenth century saw the expansion of international law, arbitrarily imposed on the colonies only to protect the whites, bolstering the "hegemony" of European nations, only challenged in the later half of the twentieth century (154). In fact, international law may act to silence colonial violence because of its "intertemporal" approach, excusing crimes like the practice of slavery because no such law to sanction existed back in those days benefitting colonial masters, as Jörn Axel Kämmerer notes in his entry "Colonialism" to *Oxford Public International Law* (2018). In similar vein, he points out, due to the imperial nature of international law "States with populations who were victims of colonial oppression would be bound to accept rules which were made without their participation, and which were disadvantageous to their indigenous populations." However, the legal parlance associated with concerns of righteousness, like modernity, globalization, rule of law, or humanitarian intervention, is, Koskenniemi says, "profoundly Eurocentric", Europe being the cognitive and cartographic pivot. This argument undercut the UN's attempt to form a dynamic international human rights law through UPR or Universal Periodic Review[4] of the human rights record of the participatory nations as the parameters are set according to a mostly westernized understanding of justice controlled by legacy psychology. Not only that, often the UN's expression of outrage and condemnation is worded in a Western understanding of international issues. For example, the current page on the Un website specifically, and rightly, condemns Hamas's attack on Israel on October 7th of 2023, and has described Israel's response as attacks on "targets."[5] Hamas's assault was brutal, causing death of 1405 Israelis, and the kidnapping of about 200 Israeli citizens; however, in retaliation Israel has killed 1500 Hamas members, and over 6000 Palestinians including 2500 children as observed by Talmiz Ahmad in "Partisan diplomacy and regional insecurity" (2023). Israel has not only besieged the city of Gaza, it has also destroyed hospitals, and religious sites, killing reporters, and UN employees. UN's guarded response is disturbing, to say the least. The quotation from the UN Secretary General on the homepage does not even name Israel and its blockade and occupation of Gaza hampering humanitarian aid to be accessed by the war-ravaged citizens.[6] This imperial bias is invariably either overt or covert. A historiography of international law would suggest that "Europe rules as the silent referent of historical knowledge" (Koskenniemi 155) inflecting its past and the futural. The modern manifestation of international law with a jurisdiction over human rights along with other area of interests are products of Euro-American culture leading Tony Anghie to conclude that imperialism is still persistent (Koskenniemi160). The utilitarian myth and narrative of a Euro-genetic universal system of thought will only enable Europeans to control and exercise it (160). Thus, the very project of modernizing human rights, undertaken by international law (159), and humanitarian intervention is still very much circumscribed in the classical notion of "protection and obedience" as Koskenniemi seconds Anne Orford (171). Kämmerer's "Colonialism" is a trenchant critique of the illegal practice of imperialism and neo-colonialism showing how erstwhile colonies have been grievously harmed by this illegal forceful occupation often executed through brute force and genocide. With decolonization international law, *prima facie*, becomes international in true sense, but the visible trauma, both psychological and territorial, makes public international law, according to Kämmerer, postcolonial in nature. The Third-World approaches to international law (TWAIL) is decolonizing international law through condemnation and assertion—a demand of retroactive reparation for socio-economic loss and justice for human loss is gradually becoming palpable in legal discourse. Kämmerer shows how a number of legal disputes have been raised against the formal colonial masters by the decolonized nations for reparation and restitution. However, there is no example from Asian nations against their former European masters in Kämmerer's text.

This resistance to fully welcome the precept of international law, what it represents and how it exercises has led to at least two problems in Asia. Asians are largely unaware of their rights and are equally ignorant of the platforms to seek help from. Secondly, Asian nations have failed to formulate an alternative legal framework, coherent, equitable, and accepted by all the votaries, to protect their citizens from exploitations, both external and internal, challenging the colonial make of the current international law. Taking full advantage of these two shortcomings, Asian nations have even perpetrated unspeakable crimes against humanity on their own people, ironically, frequently, employing colonial laws and practices to justify their actions. India's seditious act (Indian Penal Code 124A) and Pakistan's Blasphemy laws (Pakistan Penal Code, Chapter XV, Sections 295–298), for example, are both colonial in origin, inducted in 1860, and have been used to target intellectuals and minorities with full force. This of course does not mean that the third world should embrace a Euro-centric narrative of universal justice; instead, it highlights the need for an Asian discourse and understanding of human rights as dynamic and evolving pivots . The epistemological problem with this is whereas European nations and the Anglophone America have broadly inherited their philosophical route from the common source of Classical philosophy and literatures, in Asia such a singular archive does not exist. The philosophico-legal traditions are exceptionally diverse, and not infrequently unfamiliar, and mutually exclusive even in Asia. There has hardly been any effort to codify and synthesize an "Asian perspective". A lack of legal awareness along with the absence of parlances associated with human rights from public discourse has created a void forcing people from marginalized and oppressed background to fend for themselves or be dependent on people who continue the epistemological violence of foreign cultural imposition or work within the colonial legal frame. This compulsion is still a major factor in a country like India in its neo-colonial manifestation. Utsa Patnaik, in her article on the farmers' protest in India has shown (2024) how the 'industrial North' still dictates how the 'global South' should deal with its farm produces to suit their needs. She exemplifies this with the Agreement on Agriculture (AOA) passed by the World Trade Organization that came into effect in 1995. It allowed the industrial North to subsidize agriculture, while restricting the global South to do the same for their farmers, leading to unfair trade practices and a lack of option to help reduce the burden of the farmers of the developing nations. Similar hindrances along with governmental apathy and short sightedness, she argues, are directly and indirectly responsible for over 150,000 debt related suicides in India in the last thirty years. Such unimaginable horror stuns not only as incomprehensible bureaucratic chicanery, but also as sheer absence of understanding and empathy. In this atmosphere of paranoia that triggers the brutal trauma of colonial and neo-colonial injustices, the sporadic success of human rights activists can at best be viewed as a pyrrhic victory. Therefore, the need of the hour is to either accept the fact that Asia exists in the intersection of multiple cultures demanding individual process and that Asian problems need Asian parlance to address human rights, thereby negating the humanist and neutral claim of a universal human rights. The colonial legacy of the very people who advocate universalism from Europe compels us to relentlessly question their intention in search of infinite justice.

The preservation and celebration of human rights need an appropriate vocabulary to shape its juridical mechanism. Crimes without precedent need to be named and explained so that they can be debated and judged in accordance with gravity. A great example of this is the way judges and legal workers formulated terms like "genocide" and "crimes against humanity" to define what the Nazis did to the European Jews in the 1940s. The killings of six million Jews in the Holocaust provoked the question of justice to address the crime of mass-murder. Yet, when some of these Nazis were caught, experts were idiomatically not equipped to characterize such a humongous massacre of people. Philippe Sands, who specializes in international law and has extensive experience with international courts, has shown in *East West Street* (2016) how those two juridical terms originated in this context, which also defined the way international law handle such crimes in modern times.[7] This personal memoir charts the induction of "genocide" and "crimes against humanity" in the now canonized Nuremberg trials which was an essential step towards phrasing a crime in legal argot so that people talked about it, making the crime visible in the public sphere through journalistic and scholarly interventions. Such an effort is hardly visible in the Asian context where archiving, historiography, and theoretical and philosophical crossovers are either in its nascent phase or charged in sentimental reception and contradiction. How scholarly and epistemological interventions can change public perception regarding the wrongs perpetrated against them can be exemplified through the African approach to colonialism and decoloniality. Starting from Fanon[8] through Ngũgĩ wa Thiong'o[9] to Achille Mbembe[10] they have passionately and rigorously exposed western interventions as a sham and trenchantly critiqued colonial projects as crimes against humanity. Unsurprisingly, one of the few books that deal with colonialism and international law, and lays bare the understructure of empire and the myth of humanitarian interventions, also moors on the African experiences. In *Decolonizing Human Rights* (2021) Abdullahi Ahmed An-Naim calls "humanitarian interventions" as "deadly mirage" because such a military intervention "kills its pretended beneficiaries without bringing them any benefit" (50), whether it is in Iraq or Afghanistan or Yemen (51). An-Naim's project intersects and complements Mbembe's *Necropolitics*, in that both of them trace the neo-colonial narratives covering the skeleton of empire in such interventions. In her biography of Joseph Conrad, Maya Jasanoff wryly observes that the colony in the Congo Free State was established, fronting a welfare commercial enterprise, by assuring "the highest standard of what would later be called 'human rights,' backed by the leaders of the emerging international community and the conventions of international law"

(2017, 178). The African critiques of European Imperialism do not shy away from borrowing western scholarship to build a local narrative, but they never lose the sight of such narrative's trajectory, routed as they are in colonial hegemony, making necessary adjustment, critique, qualifications, and even appropriations. A critique of west-tinged theory also becomes the subversive act of postcolonial epistemology. The Empire writes back, and in this epistemological fight it is not afraid to use weapons of foreign origin making necessary adjustments, rewriting and restructuring them as a step towards counter-discourse. Thus, decolonial epistemology may begin as an act of catachresis as "cultural translation" as Bao proposes in "Queer as Catachresis: The Beijing Film Festival in Cultural Translation" (2017, 80) that challenges and subverts master narrative exposing its bias. This is what Gayatri Chakravorty Spivak has called performing "affirmative sabotage"[11] maintaining a "critical intimacy"[12] with western rhetoric.

Who speaks for Asian traumas? This is a question that haunts this book. The spectre of unresolved injuries, of mind and body, of the fractured and schizoid identities, we believe, should cause the anguish that Derrida traces at the root of writing, at the crossroads of a lack of /in speech and a sense of responsibility, in his book *Writing and Difference* (2005, 8–9). Literature is as good a starting point as any in starting a conversation. This introduction in no way implies that history and historiography have fallen short of expectation, however, it argues that a tangible discourse on trauma has not been vocabularized as yet in the Asian context. Israel–Palestine conflict, for example, has introduced, much like genocide and crimes against humanity, a new acronym, WCNSF,[13] which means Wounded Child No Surviving Family in Gaza. There is a lot of discussion surrounding this coinage and mental health experts are concerned regarding the trauma that this war and siege inflict on children leading them to self-harm and contemplate suicide.[14] Such coinages, to highlight a specific plight of a terrible persecution are rare in Asian context, with even lesser public visibility. Cotemporal with the Holocaust in the Europe, the Bengal Famine of 1943 where millions of people died because of colonial antipathy has not garnered the same amount of critical-philosophical attention. Not only the colonial rulers directly responsible for these crimes against humanity and genocide went unpunished, but we have also not yet reached a consensus regarding the number of people died and affected due to it. We are still negotiating with the associated trauma which is all but forgotten from semantic field. Colonial historiography and parochial narratives have harmed in more ways than one to write cogently on the trauma of Bengali people. The same goes for the Jallianwala Bagh massacre (1919) which has not garnered enough attention in the trauma episteme of Indian postcolony. It has now achieved a mythical status without much testimonial analyses of the aftermath of the event. We do still talk about the "Holocaust of Indian Partition", as used by Madhab Godbole (2006) in his book on the bifurcation of the subcontinent in 1947, in an attempt to invoke analogous discourse with the European tragedy. A semantic of our traumas is still idiomatically uncodified. Similar examples can be cited from other nations as well. Whether it is Japan's role in WWII, or its occupation of Nanking; the Chinese treatment of Uyghur Muslims and Tibetans; the Pakistani Army's brutal treatment of

Bangladeshi women in *Muktijuddha*; Sinhalese massacre of Tamils, and the consequent civil war; or the pain of the Partition causing a violent infighting among people who lived together for centuries—everywhere in Asia we find unique narratives of trauma in search of closure, both verbal and psychological. In India, though not confined to it alone, we have the questions of Kashmir, the abrogation of Article 370, the misuse of UAPA and AFSPA, the Manipur riot, oppression on religious and sexual minorities, and caste-violence that generate media traction and intellectual theses, but they are not yet enough to be discursively available and visible in the public sphere within the codified framework of respective collective trauma and memory. In the wake of the citizenship act in India which led to an atmosphere of anxiety and uncertainty, and provoked a huge nonviolent protest, people committed suicide, or seriously considered it out of paranoia and foreboding.[15] Most of these issues could have been resolved by dialogues and intercultural understanding, and yet issues persist for their teleological gains. What is common in these examples is that even though these experiences are varied and distinct, we only have western formulations to figure them out. Silence is complicity and it needs to be dismantled with a panorama of narratives. Yet, England does not talk about its colonial exploits to their citizens, with a sense of entitlement still prevalent in their school curricula. Similarly, Japan is silent on its remorseless crimes during WWII. Frequent travel to and interaction with trauma and traumatic sites is a necessary step towards syntactical representation and working through guilt and injury. Neiman in *Learning from Germans: Confronting Race and the Memory of Evil* (2020) points out how Germans have developed a plethora of phrases (17) to interact and exorcise with their Nazi past to make amends where museums and other public structures work as memory triggers in the public space which America is yet to do regarding the practice of slavery (29). On the other hand, Ian Buruma has shown, contrasting the German attempts to come to terms with its past to Japan's complicit and conspicuous silence to engage with perpetrator's guilt and trauma in his book *Wages of Guilt* (2009).[16] Such interpellatory constraints to address psychosomatic stress dilute the immediacy and urgency of the experiential trauma , impelling us to think in colonial terms.

The schizophrenic "double bind" Spivak talks about following Gregory Bateson in *An Aesthetic of Education in the era of Globalization* (2013, 4) of colonial trace embeds our current pedagogy around Human Rights where justice depends on Euro-centric frames of references in this globalized world. Yet we must develop indigenous terminologies and cultural inflection points, "productively undoing" (Spivak 1) the inherited episteme not only due to the exigency of codifying trauma in our local experiences, but also to gradually decolonize our mind from colonial glosses that to a large extent still characterize our response to the various wounds inflicted upon us from different corners. While discussing the "mourning work of postcoloniality" and accountability, we find echoes of Neiman in Spivak when she proposes that in "the aporia or double bind, to decide is the burden of responsibility" (109). Anguish and responsibility translate the work of mourning into an ethical praxis of rights. One line of trauma can trigger and define other branches of similar experiences across nations and cultures, as Michael Rothberg argues in *Multidirectional*

Memory: Remembering Holocaust in the Age of Decolonization (2009)[17] but at the same time the uniqueness of different experiences must be emphasized by the people analyzing them even when we find interexperiential similarities, as Neiman reminds us, following Todorov (Neiman 28).[18] Multidirectionality, or equivalency, is a matter of responsibility (Neiman 29) culminating in developing a glossary of uniqueness, invoking which a justice could be solicited, independent of a western understanding, and validation of the event, negotiating similarities and differences. This is one of the ways to fight the universal imaginary. Life less grievable, and therefore expendable, is a narrative around the world because war, overt and covert, is a profitable business.[19] Exploitation and deprivation of the precarity are essential qualities of neo-colonial neoliberal narratives, and what better way to unspool such narrations to expose the underlying colonial bias and epistemic violence behind the powers that be than in literary writing back through affective sabotage and critical intimacy? Literature, like history and philosophy, can be an ethical exercise, unfolding truths behind myths in public memory and culture, and upholding justice and the infinite demands of the subalterns as trauma subjects.

Notes

1. https://www.un.org/en/global-issues/human-rights#:~:text=Human%20rights%20are%20rights%20inherent,and%20education%2C%20and%20many%20more.
2. https://www.icj-cij.org/cases.
3. For the declaratory steps taken by the UN see https://www.un.org/en/global-issues/decolonization.
4. For the functioning of UPR see, https://www.ohchr.org/en/hr-bodies/upr/upr-home.
5. https://www.un.org/en/situation-in-occupied-palestine-and-israel.
6. The UN secretary António Guterres's quote reads: "I reiterate my utter condemnation of the abhorrent acts of terror perpetrated by Hamas on 7 October—and repeat my call for the immediate, unconditional and safe release of hostages held in Gaza... The parties to the conflict—and, indeed, the international community—face an immediate and fundamental responsibility: to stop the inhuman collective suffering and dramatically expand humanitarian aid to Gaza... The way forward is clear. A humanitarian ceasefire. Now.".

   Here it would be remiss if I do not talk about different steps under the aegis of the UN like UNRWA for Palestinian refugees, which have been doing remarkable humanitarian works with local help. However, financial downscaling, prejudice, and political volatility severely affect the synchronal impact of such initiatives.
7. Sands, Philippe. *East West Street: On the Origins of Genocide and Crimes Against Humanity*. London: Weidenfield and Nicolson, 2016.
8. Fanon, Frantz. *The Wretched of the Earth*, Translated by Richard Philcox (New York: Grove Pres, 2004), for example, argues for a revolutionary overthrow of the colonial power in the face of overwhelming odds, where violence is treated as a counter-measure to colonial brutality ("On Violence" pp.1–62). This Algerian philosophy of liberation is antipodal to one of the main strains of Indian struggle for freedom, non-violence, espoused by Gandhi. Fanon's text is one of the paradigmatic explorations of African anticolonial consciousness for Mbembe.
9. Thiong'o, Ngũgĩ wa. *Decolonizing the Mind*. London: James Currey Ltd, 1991. In this book Thiong'o unravels the ways European cultures have destroyed African Cultures through coloniality and argues for an immediate restitution of Afro-centric frame of reference where Europe will feature in the margins as auxiliary. Importantly, the essential argument is not for

an Africa-only policy in the cultural space, but for an Africa-centric retrieval and celebration of multiplicity.

10. Mbembe. Achille. *Necropolitics*. Translated by Steven Corcoran. Durham: Duke University Press, 2019. This book not only shows how Slavery and similar colonial enterprises were draconian in nature, but is also a thorough exposition of war on terror and Israel –Palestine conflict, all of which, more or less, fruits of expansionist mindset. This multi-cultural and multi-continental approach is a key epistemological engagement as far as cultural negotiations with the western insights are concerned.
11. Spivak develops the concept of "sabotage" in *An Aesthetic Education in the Era of Globalization* (Cambridge, Masachusetts: Harvard University Press, 2012). "Affirmative sabotage" finds a more eloquent formulation in her video lecture "Global Marx, class and politics." *Rosa-Luxemburg-Stiftung* https://www.youtube.com/watch?v=Ac4Ge3s1vCc.
12. "Critical Intimacy: An Interview with Gayatri Chakravorty Spivak." Interview by Steve Paulson. *Los Angeles Review of Books*, July 29th 2016. < https://lareviewofbooks.org/article/critical-intimacy-interview-gayatri-chakravorty-spivak/ >
13. https://www.middleeastmonitor.com/20231107-gaza-coins-a-new-acronym-wcnsf-wounded-child-no-surviving-family/.

    Palestine-Israel conflict has given rise to a number of associated expressions like BDS movement, Nakba, Intifada, sumud etc. on the Palestinian side. For a study of the later three experiential codifications of trauma see https://thefunambulist.net/magazine/redefining-our-terms/nakba-sumud-intifada-a-personal-lexicon-of-palestinian-loss-and-resistance.
14. "Children's Mental Health in Gaza Pushed Beyond Breaking Point After Nearly a Month of Siege and Bombardment", 7th November 2023. < https://www.savethechildren.net/news/children-s-mental-health-gaza-pushed-beyond-breaking-point-after-nearly-month-siege-and >
15. https://cjp.org.in/tag/nrc-suicides/
16. Buruma, Ian. *The Wages of Guilt: Memories of War in Germany and Japan*. London: Atlantic Books, 2009.
17. Rothberg, Michael. *Multidirectional Memory: Remembering Holocaust in the Age of Decolonization*. Stanford: Stanford University Press, 2009.
18. Godbole's book wishes to do exactly this, where the memory of the Holocaust is invoked to compare the trauma of the Partition. In her book Neiman argues for a case of continual engagement with trauma, whether as a survivor or perpetrator. The consequent development of experiential vocabularies is an important part, for Neiman, such an engagement to exorcise such ordeals. This comparative approach, even though problematic and often equally Euro and Anglo-centric can also be found in Isabel Wilkerson's *Caste: The Lies That Divide Us* (Lonodn: Allen Lane, 2020) which includes the very unique Indian experience in the wider Euro-American ambit of racism and the Nazi discrimination against Jews.
19. For a thorough discussion of grievable life and precarity, in the context of war, especially war on terror, see Judith Butler's *Frames of War: When Is Life Grievable* (London: Verso, 2009) and *Precarious Life: The Powers of Mourning and Violence* (Lonodn: Verso, 2004).

References

Ahmad T (2023), "Partisan diplomacy and regional insecurity". <https://frontline.thehindu.com/world-affairs/palestine-gaza-war-israel-hamas-west-asia-uncertainty/article67466744.ece> Accessed on 19/11/2023

An-Naim AA (2021) *Decolonizing Human Rights*. Cambridge University Press, Cambridge

Bao H (2017) "Queer as Catachresis: The Beijing Film Festival in Cultural Translation." In: Chris B, Luke R (eds) *Chinese Film Festivals: Sites of Translation*. Palgrave Macmillan, New York, pp 79–100

Chesterman S (2017) "Asia's Ambivalence about International Law and Institutions: Past, Present and Futures". *Eur J Int Law* 27(4):945

Darmawan AR (2020) "International law takes a step towards Asia." *The Interpreter*. Lowy Institute, 30th June, 2020. https://www.lowyinstitute.org/the-interpreter/international-law-takes-step-towardsasia. Accessed on 19/11/2023

Derrida J (1997) *Of Grammatology*. Translated by Gayatri Chakravorty Spivak. Johns Hopkins University Press, Baltimore - - -. (2005) *Writing and Difference*. Translated by Alan Bass. Routledge, London

Godbole M (2006) *The Holocaust of the Indian Partition: An Inquest*. Rupa, New Delhi

Jasanoff M (2017) *The Dawn Watch: Joseph Conrad in a Global World*. William Collins, London

Kämmerer JA (2018) "Colonialism". *Oxford Public International Law*. Oxford University Press. N.P. https://opil.ouplaw.com/display/9780199231690-e690?rskey=tSOeFO&result=1&prd=OPILhttps://doi.org/10.1093/law:epil/9780199231690/law. Accessed on 19/11/2023

Koh T, Hao DP (2016) "The Asian Way to Settle Dispute." chrome-extension://efaidnbmnnnibpcajpcglclefindmkaj/https://cil.nus.edu.sg/wp-content/uploads/2010/08/Tommy-KohHao-Duy-Phan-The-Asian-Way-To-Settle-Disputes-21-Dec-15-Final.pdf. Accessed on 19/11/2023

Koskenniemi M (2011) "Histories of International law: Dealing with Eurocentrism." *Rechtsgeschichte Legal History*. https://doi.org/10.12946/rg19/152-176. https://www.researchgate.net/publication/254885929 Accessed on 19/11/2023

Neiman S (2020) *Learning from Germans: Confronting Race and the Memory of Evil*. Penguin Books, London

Owada H (2005) "The experience of Asia with international adjucation." *Singapore Yearbook of International Law*. <Chrome-extension://efaidnbmnnnibpcajpcglclefindmkaj/http://www.commonlii.org/sg/journal/SGYBkIntLaw/2005/3.pdf> Accessed on 19/11/2023

Patnaik U (2024) "It's a battle against servitude." *Frontline* 41(5):20–24

Spivak GC (2013) *An Aesthetic Education in the Era of Globalization*. Harvard University Press, Cambridge

Strachan AL (2009) "Resolving South East Asian territorial disputes: a role for the ICJ." *IPCS Issue Brief*. New Delhi: South Asia Research Programme, No. 133. chrome-extension://efaidnbmnnnibpcajpcglclefindmkaj/https://www.files.ethz.ch/isn/109205'B133SEARP-AnnaICJ_(Read-Only).pdf Accessed on 19/11/2023

Web links

https://www.un.org/en/global-issues/human-rights#:~:text=Human%20rights%20are%20rights%20inherent,and%20education%2C%20and%20many%20more

https://www.icj-cij.org/cases

https://www.ohchr.org/en/hr-bodies/upr/upr-home

https://www.un.org/en/situation-in-occupied-palestine-and-israel

https://cjp.org.in/tag/nrc-suicides/

Chapter 2
Introduction Part II

Asia as Method: Decoding Human Rights and Power Dynamics in the Asian Historical Tapestry and Contemporary Realities

Sk Sagir Ali

2.1 The Invention of Human Rights Discourses: Frames of Marginality in the Post-9/11 World

Throughout history, Asia has endured numerous atrocities against humanity, yet Western media and canonical academia have largely overlooked the region's experiences, hindering collective learning from past transgressions and perpetuating the likelihood of their recurrence. In this context, the understanding of human rights remains insufficiently explored and comprehended. Frequently, human rights issues are reduced to mere rhetorical tools by political entities. This disregard for the gravity of human rights has led to the negligent infringement of fundamental rights within marginalized and vulnerable communities, with little accountability for such actions. A pervasive and corrupt social structure further obstructs legal opposition to these violations.

In light of the significant challenges facing many Asian nations, including unprecedented financial, political, and majoritarian complexities, it becomes imperative to examine the historical and cultural roots of these issues. A heightened critical focus at this juncture can shed light on the problems exploited by the establishment to oppress and eliminate those deemed undesirable. This scholarly endeavor addresses the noticeable gap in academic engagement with these issues from a theoretical standpoint.

Furthermore, the Eurocentric conception of human rights has contributed to the negligence of alternative socio-epistemic perspectives necessary for understanding

S. S. Ali (✉)
Department of English, Midnapore College, Midnapore, West Bengal, India
e-mail: skali661@gmail.com

S. S. Ali and A. Basak (eds.), *Marginal Narratives and the Question of Human Rights in Asian Pacific Literature*, https://doi.org/10.1007/978-981-97-4544-9_2

and situating human rights issues in Asia. This neglect perpetuates a biased understanding of human rights and limits the effectiveness of efforts to address violations in the region. The essays in this volume challenge the politics of the establishment by denouncing its supremacist gaze and by illuminating the politics of the governed. By interrogating Western-centric narratives and advocating for a more inclusive approach to human rights discourse, this scholarship aims to foster greater awareness and accountability regarding human rights violations in Asia.

Human rights studies have become more important since the events of September 11, 2001, when public opinion changed about the US's involvement in the War on Terror and the ensuing worldwide worries about the mission's human cost. A general narrative of war, revolution, stories in images, borders and boundaries, famine, dystopia, myth, horror, agrarian revolts, farmer suicides, wartime rape, statist narratives on welfare, writing, translating, carceral, systematic violence, and marginalized lives in the literature highlight the connections between literature and human rights. Literature, social history, current affairs, and insights from the social sciences collectively contribute to our comprehension of the strategies employed by the affluent and powerful to perpetuate the existing status quo, often at the expense of the broader populace, leaving them traumatized and impoverished. Through a comprehensive examination of texts, historical teachings, and current events, this work seeks to advance a more nuanced understanding of these relationships.

In a timely intervention into the ongoing discussion about human rights and literature, Lynn Hunt's (2007) *Inventing Human Rights* develops the connection between the novel and the development of human rights by arguing that empathy fostered by the novel is essential to creating the humanitarian feeling that she claims is essential for human rights. Human rights are portrayed in Hunt as a Western literary tradition-derived "invention" (15–35). As a historian, Hunt argues that for individual rights to be conceptualized as human rights in the late eighteenth century, the epistolary novel had to take part in a major reorganization of compassion. On the other hand, in comparison to Joseph Slaughter's (2007) thorough theoretical examination of the Bildungsroman, her explanation of the structure and functioning of the epistolary novel seems strained. Along with thoroughly examining a few carefully chosen novels from Europe, Latin America, Africa, and the South Asian diaspora, Slaughter attributes the critical practices of postcolonial theory to this long-standing awareness of the ideological components of the Bildungsroman. A bracing argument that narrative fiction serves as a "cultural surrogate" (2007, 93) for the absent warrant and executive sanction of human rights law emerges from his thorough examination of the world novel's engagement with Bildungsroman through the lenses of political, literary, and cultural theory (2007, 20–30). It accomplishes this by endowing the concept of an international human rights order and the authority of human rights legislation with a culturally symbolic legitimacy, both in terms of content and form. To Elizabeth Anker (2012), human rights discourses that uphold Western values are problematic. Recent theoretical works have called for a closer look at the issues when the postcolonial Bildungsroman becomes involved in neo-imperialist and globalization programs. In *Writing Human Rights*, Crystal Parikh explores the sorts of subjectivities and communities envisaged in this subgenre of minor literature, focusing on human rights through "ethical deliberations staged in narratives authored by contemporary American writers of color" (Parikh 2017, 2). As Slaughter, she also elevates the Bildungsroman to the status of a transnationally mobile human rights form that is "endlessly transposable across the globe" and particularly relevant to American writers of color insofar as they use it to create the figure of the human rights subject (Parikh 2017, 21–20). The paradigm of self-development that the form of Bildungsroman explores is crucial to understanding the subject's own recognition of the circumstances propelling life and social perplexities. In her essay, "Teaching the Legal Imperialism Debate over Human Rights," Anker contends the relationship between legal personhood categories and the question of who is considered human. She draws attention to the growing emphasis on the postcolonial world in human rights discourse, which conflates humanitarianism and human rights action with Western foreign aid programs. She assesses postcolonial nation states' adherence to human rights as a gauge of their civilizational advancement (2015, 39). She suggests, among other things, introducing students to the human rights argument surrounding cultural imperialism and situating texts within a colonial history (2015, 41). Moreover, she demonstrates literature's capacity to evoke readers' empathy and have a substantial impact on human dignity and humanitarian action (Slaughter 2007, Hunt 2007, Anker 2012, O'Gorman 2015). Challenging the Western conceptualization of human rights also serves as a direct critique of the violent consequences precipitated by the discourse surrounding "rights restoration" in the aftermath of the 9/11 episode.

In the context of globalization, scholars in literary history demonstrate a heightened propensity to delve into the intricacies of the political language of human rights across diverse cultural milieus, contrasting with the stance adopted by political theorists and activists. While the latter often advocate for cultural relativism and decry cultural imperialism as a barrier to human rights discourse, literary historians, emboldened by the phenomenon of globalization, transcend the dichotomy of particularity and universality. Instead, they engage in an exploration of the nuanced expressions of human rights discourse within varied cultural frameworks (Cmiel, 2004, 119–120). The *Routledge Companion to Human Rights and Literature* (2016), edited by Sophia McClennen and Alexandra Schultheis Moore, and *Theoretical Perspectives on Human Rights and Literature* (2012), edited by Elizabeth Swanson Goldberg and Alexandra Schultheis Moore, have both played a significant role in setting the boundaries of the inter-discipline and exploring the conceptual overlaps and contradictions that underpin the field, and identifying promising areas for academic and scholarly inquiry. Goldberg and Moore define the scope of their edited volume by highlighting the primary focus of their contributors. They also draw attention to how literary interpretations of human rights discourses (fictional, poetic, testimonial, legal, political, economic, journalistic, and cinematic) can highlight the limitations of these discourses and the creative potential of alternative frameworks (3).

2.2 Asia and the Tropes of Human Rights Studies: An Epistemic Break in the Conventions of a Concept

This edited volume on *Marginal Narratives and the Question of Human Rights in Asian Literature* elucidates what it is to be human in and through its chapters on the vast array of narratives and storytelling traditions. This is necessary as, according to human rights scholar Anthony Langlois, "human rights … are rights, generated by narratively rationalized metaphysical beliefs, beliefs, which inform us as to what the metaphysical category 'human person' means" (2005, 383). The volume will examine the role that literature and the arts have played and continue to play in promoting the ideological framework of the discourse surrounding rights. It focuses on the relationship between storytelling, literary representation, cultural narratives, and human rights, as they are understood in law, address, and practice in the Asian perspectives. Asian marginal narratives are often perceived as the boundaries of what it means to be human in a world of limitless possibilities, despite the multifaceted processes fostered by unequal power relations interacting across four main dimensions—economic, political, social, and cultural—and at different levels—including individual, household, group, community, country, and global levels. In the corpus of present human rights literature, envisioned futures of Asia that defy our assumptions about it force us to face uncomfortable but important issues. The marginal location of Asian narratives and human rights are intimately related since scientific advancement significantly influenced the European Enlightenment and the transition from religious to secular ethics, establishing the foundation for the Western liberal understanding of human rights accompanied by the subtle relegation of Asiatic frameworks to the cornerstones of world history. With "the rise of personal story politics and memoir culture in the 1970s and 1980s [that] coincided with mass movements for decolonization, civil rights, women's rights and sexual freedoms," the social ontology of human rights brought about by decolonization challenged human potential and pushed it to the limit challenging our assumptions and making us rethink how we connect as a race, with the environment, and with other sentient beings with different anatomies. These evolving challenges present new paradigms within which human rights need to be redefined to "decreate" (Baxi, 2014: 2) the contemporary human rights narrative entangled in the coloniality of power. This perspective on human rights appears contradictory because here colonialism implies "the continuity of established patterns of power between coloniser and colonised—and the contemporary remnants of these relationships—and how that power shapes our understanding of culture, labour, intersubjectivity and knowledge production" (Mohamed et al. 2020, 663). However, the fight for human rights seems grounded in anti-colonialist ideals. Human rights institutions should not be seen as a standalone issue inside a local community but rather as a component of European systems of governance, social engineering, and economic tools of inequality made essential by European state actions. Furthermore, Western countries have unparalleled power to set international policy. Western nations must guarantee that human rights standards are adhered to by everyone. They bear personal responsibility for their military actions as well. The rationale and incentives behind human rights violations are the same as those supporting violations in Western societies: a distinct international system intended to accomplish particular goals, none of which advance or protect human rights (Souaiaia 2021, 159).

2.3 The Limits of the Universal "Self": Redefining the Global in Terms of the Regional

In his book, *Which Rights Should Be Universal?*, William J. Talbott argues that this is not necessarily a morally imperialist position because not all rights should be granted to everyone. The primary argument against the universalization of human rights concepts is that it would allow for the crime of cultural genocide and give moral imperialism legitimacy. To close the gap between moral universalists and cultural relativists regarding human rights and to broaden the discussion of human rights beyond the confines of a single academic discipline and society, we put our work front and centre with these seemingly unrelated but thought-provoking works. To do this, the book integrates established knowledge from pertinent disciplines to examine the discovery-rooted argument and the flexibility of practising traditions while concentrating on the origins and characteristics of the circumstances that demand a forceful engagement with the concept of human rights and its offshoots (Talbott 2007).

The interests of Asian minorities have traditionally been overlooked and underestimated since nation states are more concerned with promoting homogenous identities in the modern era, which has resulted in a highly uneven world community. The idea of "the right to have rights," in particular, has come to represent or support the state's obligations to protect or naturalize its citizens' rights against any attempts to denaturalize them. The condition primarily safeguards citizens' rights, including liberty, freedom, and brotherhood (Benhabib 2004). The sincere desire to protect the human rights of minorities and disadvantaged groups is challenging, given the highly hierarchical sociopolitical structure of Asian nation states. Even when rights and freedoms are acknowledged and enshrined in a country's legal system, certain laws grant impunity to powerful decision-makers acting in the name of self-justified peace and order or engaging in extralegal activities. A valuable weapon for geopolitical maneuvering and a justification for governments embroiled in a war to impose severe laws against their populace is the state-led rhetoric that endures regarding what constitutes a danger to national security and interest. Despite appearing to protect people, these laws further limit rights and provide a green light to those who break human rights laws. The idea of human rights also alludes to a distinct spatiality in Asia. "Asian values" are immensely fractured and dominated when it comes to different social norms, ethical values, beliefs, and mentalities, as state sovereignty is paramount in building up human rights violations strategically. As Weissman (2004) finds, there is a "misuse" of the human rights language and this misuse contributes to the "tendency of colonial powers to discredit value systems of other cultures as a means of justifying colonial intervention" (Weissman 2004, 264). Asian human rights narratives show a change from ontological vulnerability, which marks the embodiment of the human person, to its destruction in a warped version of the human form. They also emphasize the embedded openness of the human being as opposed to merely its ostensibly inherent vulnerability. Coupled with this openness is the ontological multiplicities in Asian societies and cultures making universalization of thinking paradigms not only difficult but inherently impossible and untenable.

The Association of Southeast Asian Nations (ASEAN) Inert-Governmental Commission on Human Rights and the ASEAN Declaration of Human Rights (ADHR) were established by ASEAN to safeguard and promote human rights in Southeast Asia. Many ASEAN nations do not adhere to the ADHR even though they all legally accept it (Munro 2011, 1185–1214). However, state-sponsored breaches of Asians' human rights have made their situation worse. The widespread military violations of Asian minority rights, including extrajudicial executions, rapes, torture, house evictions, high taxes, and extortion, have become typical in several Asian nation states. These Asian marginal narratives feature suffering individuals whose identity as susceptible people is shaped by their "wounded attachments" (Brown 1993). These accounts of suffering and "wounded attachments" are typical in peripheral human rights discourse. As Wendy Brown insists:

> [Political identity] installs its pain over its unredeemed history in the foundation of its political claim, in its demand for recognition as identity. In locating a site of the blame for its powerlessness over its past, as a part of injury, a past as a hurt will, and finding a "reason" for the "unendurable pain" of social powerlessness in the present, it converts this reasoning into an ethicizing politics, a politics of recrimination that seeks to avenge the hurt even while it reaffirms it, discursively codifies it. Politicized identity thus enunciates itself and makes claims for itself only by entrenching, dramatizing, and inscribing its pain in politics. It can hold out no future – for itself or others – that triumphs over this pain. (Brown 1993, 406)

The vulnerability in which the narratives of pain and politics exist in the face of state power confirm the Butlerian theses propounded in *Vulnerability in Resistance* (2016). Butler writes:

> If . . . vulnerability emerges as part of social relations, even as a feature of social relations, then we make (a) a general claim according to which vulnerability ought to be understood as relational and social and (b) a very specific claim according to which it always appears in the context of specific social and historical relations that call to be analyzed concretely. (Butler 2016, 4)

Butler also argues that vulnerability and invulnerability are politically constructed and unevenly distributed due to differential power operations and that understanding these processes is crucial (2016, 5). Butler contends elsewhere in the same volume that understanding physiological fragility outside of this concept of social and material relations is impossible and that the body cannot be isolated from the environment and the systems that support it (Butler 2016, 16). From this, people will react morally to those left defenseless. Their approach involves creating "vulnerable subjects" (Fineman 2008, 11) who are victims but do not always associate vulnerability with victimization. In certain instances, they even provide resilient and resistant pictures. Vulnerability and marginality, in this sense, might be described as "a state of constant possibility of harm." Political theorists and philosophers have suggested that it is an innate condition of all humans and life forms. Therefore, the law was interpreted as a symptom of the state's fragility even though it was occasionally thought of as a "state's emissary" (Baxi 2008: 249).

Because of this notion, the accused could envision a way out of the trial—that the state might be susceptible to its own words. They could upend the prosecution's premise by utilizing the law against the practice. Those who are fleeing oppression because of their nationality, faith, race, or membership of a particular social community are particularly vulnerable when taken as a group. It is imperative to underscore that persons who are at risk owing to their nationality, faith, or ethnicity are likely marginalized groups in the countries from which they are fleeing. This acknowledgment is occasionally misunderstood or does not receive due credit. Put another way, there is just too much evidence of a connection between persecution, human rights breaches, and the mobility of marginalized people. There's little doubt that these shifting patterns of violence have a mass impact on Asia. Among the most vulnerable and marginalized groups in Asian culture are minorities, women, and children, who bear a disproportionate amount of the burden from internal ethnic disputes. There are many examples of this, for example, limited or nonexistent access to healthcare and education disrupts the lives of millions of youngsters in Asia. During and after conflicts, women may be singled out for violence, particularly sexual violence. They may be attacked by armed forces or militia whether they are detained or arrested at border crossings, in refugee camps, at home, or in detention centres. Tens of thousands of children are sexually abused, murdered, or taken as child soldiers each year. As stated in the Children and Conflict Report of 1996:

> Horrific levels of violence and brutality have marked the struggles that claim more civilians than soldiers. Any tactics are employed, from systematic rape to scorched-earth tactics that destroy crops and poison wells, to ethnic cleansing and genocide. With all standards abandoned, human rights violations against children and women occur in unprecedented numbers. Increasingly, children have become the targets and even the perpetrators of violence and atrocities. (United Nations Children and Conflict Report 1996)

Migrant laborers in Asia are another group that is particularly vulnerable to violations of human rights, both locally and globally. Because of their susceptibility, migrant workers may encounter:

> assaults and killings by government security forces and private individuals, extensive use of torture and ill-treatment in detention, sexual abuse, widespread labor rights abuses, and pervasive extortion. Many employers still confiscate migrant workers' passports and work permits. Meanwhile, those filing grievances have often faced retaliation from police, officials, and employers. (Human Rights Watch 2017)

The degree to which immigrants, especially those from minority groups, are subjected to discrimination, exclusion, and denial of their fundamental rights can have an impact on practically every element of these marginal lives.

2.4 Human Rights and the Democracy-To-Arrive

The prevailing paradigm in managing human rights within the Asian context, rather than epitomizing a region-specific ethos, reflects an overarching adherence to a statist approach entrenched within the ostensibly frail framework of international law. This systemic predilection towards state-centricity permeates the global milieu, engendering a deleterious stasis in the trajectory towards substantive human rights advancements. The primacy of the sovereign entity of the state as the sole protector of individual rights provides rabid possibilities of the corruption of the ideal as well. A discernible lacuna arises wherein endeavors focalized upon specific local milieus within sovereign entities emerge as veritable crucibles for potential transformative agency, eclipsing the efficacy of broader initiatives tethered to global or regional legal frameworks, even when confronted with a preponderance of formal legal institutions within the ambit of a particular state (DeLaet 2019, 42). Central to any prospective paradigmatic shift is the imperativeness of states assuming a proactive mantle, espousing a conscientious embrace of United Nations (UN) procedures, and concertedly engaging in collaborative endeavors to rectify and redress transgressions against human rights. Establishing or fortifying governmental institutions wielding the mandate to monitor the national landscape becomes exigent, affording a more accessible and productive recourse for easing the plight of vulnerable individuals and marginalized groups. This calls for a nuanced calibration of the domestic apparatus, transcending the mere admiration of formal legal structures and manifesting as a multifaceted commitment to the procedural modalities espoused by the UN.

In the broader panorama, the lamentable inertia characterizing the attention accorded to human rights within Asian nation states remains disconcerting, necessitating a recalibration of priorities. As bulwarks of collective governance, regional entities assume a pivotal role in shoring up their capacities to safeguard human rights. The imperative resides in a concerted and sustained augmentation of regional organizations, endowing them with the requisite potency to confront and rectify the systemic apathy towards human rights issues. In doing so, the latent potential for a substantive paradigm shift materializes, wherein the collective resolve to champion human rights crystallizes into a palpable force for transformative change.

Four sections make up this book. In "Part I: Human Rights Narratives, Literary Activism, and Nationhood in Asia," there are five significant essays. First, Kaifi Azmi's socialist concerns for the ordinary man are explored from the perspective of their human rights in "Voices of Resistance: Kaifi Azmi's Exploration of Reason, War, and Revolution" by Mohammad Asim Siddiqui. Kaifi Azmi has described how he was raised in an environment free from the pernicious effects of communalism, how the seeds of disobedience were sown in his early years, and how he earned his patriotic mindset. The issues that Kaifi Azmi chose for his poems make sense when one considers the Marxist idea that men make history in situations that are not their own. He is frequently inspired to write on topics that touch on the human rights of common people. The poetry of Kaifi Azmi also demonstrates a keen understanding of history, frequently understood in terms of civilization. His poetry often discusses many historical eras and facets of small- and large-scale historical events. Nisreen Yousef in her essay “Refugee Chronicles: Khaled Hosseini’s *Sea Prayer* and the Struggle for Human Rights,” argues that Hosseini presents wars as the main cause of displacement and abuse of human fundamental rights and also contends that Hosseini gives voice to his female characters in ways that subvert the attempts of the European media to isolate and dehumanize women refugees. Sanchali Sarkar sheds insight on the politics behind labeling women who were the victims of genocide rape as “brave” to systemically ignore the grave crimes that have occurred. Women’s suffering following their “service” as “comfort women” or “war heroines” is highlighted in several documented testimonies in Sarkar’s essay. The fourth essay titled “Sovereign Verse: Jacinta Kerketta’s Literary Activism in Rights and Welfare” by Subhayu Bhattacharjee and Sinor Lama examines the postcolonial state’s benevolent sovereign nature embodied in its constitutional guarantees and safeguards and the intricate process of implementing these guarantees that makes them vulnerable to manipulation, leading to the appropriation of Adivasi rights and demands for the sake of national advancement and other statist purposes. With Kerketta, they offer a literary challenge to the complacent assumptions of politico-legal discourse. “Behind Bars: Systematic Violence and Human Rights in *The Plague Upon Us*” by Sk Sagir Ali dives into the vicious cycle of human rights abuses and the political occupation of the Kashmir valley, entwined with violence, militarization, and brutal insurgency in the state. The study addresses the issue of staged recognition failures while navigating the influence of military strikes, informers, and the army on human rights that are slippery in the valley. In addition, it clarifies how lingering motifs of violations of human rights present a dangerous historical confrontation, highlighting the strained bonds in a violent and conflict-ridden region.

“Part II: Cinematic Echoes: Mnemoculture and the Visual Discourse of Human Rights in Asia” also houses some thought-provoking essays. Farddina Hussain examines the visual accounts of the human stories of Vietnam and Cambodia and their respective political and historical histories. The two main films considered are *Boat People* (Vietnam) and *First They Killed My Father* (Cambodia). While the latter shows how people moved from Vietnam to avoid threats to their lives when Saigon fell, the former is an adaption of a survivor’s memoir that highlights human rights breaches during the Khmer Rouge regime in Cambodia. The survivors provide fresh perspectives on how war infiltrates domestic domains and acts as sites of memory by sharing their accounts of trauma, migration, identity formation, and human rights violations. The next essay, “The Spectral as the Political: Dystopia, Myth, and Horror in Patrick Graham’s *Ghoul*” by Rishiraj Pal, argues how the ghoul serves an emancipatory role in the concept of spectropolitics, which conjures up images of dehumanization and revolution, as well as how the spectral has been used to spark a disruption within the heavily guarded system—the detention/execution center—which transforms into a haunted space where the drama unfolds.

The book’s third section, “Part III: Borderless Struggles: Narratives of Marginality and Social Injustice in Asia,” begins with Indira Chakraborty (Bhattacharya)’s essay, “Borders and Boundaries: Resituating *The Tiger Claw* in the Current Times.” It is vitally important that the processes of transformation that determine a person’s "becoming" a "migrant" or a "citizen" or one's return to their homeland be carefully considered. This is because almost all countries in the world are closing borders to consolidate and strengthen their sovereignty, maintaining strict vigilance on who comes in and goes out, and citing "terrorism" as justification for the strictness. This study discusses these potential exchanges. "Marginalised Lives in Assamese Literature: Saga of Loss and Longing in Assam's Chars" inspects two novels, *Rupabarir Palash* by Syed Abdul Malik and *Kahibunor Malita* by Rudrani Sharma, to examine how the greater Assamese society views this subculture. In both works, the lives of Muslims originally from East Bengal are discussed, and the community is engaged with on several levels. Since neither author is from the area, they present the perspective of the greater Assamese community on these individuals and their fight for a life of dignity. Syamantak Shobhan Basu aims to examine farmer suicides and the persistent issue of agricultural distress in India in his essay "Dead Horses Tell No Tales: Agrarian Revolts, Farmer Suicides and the Right to Cultivate in Neoliberal India." Along with Sainath's records of rural poverty, he also examines economist Jean Dreze's work on India's Public Distribution System (PDS).

"Part IV: Activism, the Limits of Agency and the Pursuit of Social Justice in Asia and the Pacific" deals with four significant essays. "Hunger's Cry: Bijon Bhattacharya's 'Nabanna' and the Bengal Famine of 1943" by Subhajeet Singha analyses and problematizes how a respectable community of hard-working farmers, once docile bodies subject to the empire, have been turned into the "Zoē." "Dalit Negotiations: Yogesh Maitreya's Perspective on University Spaces and Human Rights" by Ambalika Biswas illustrates the connections between violence and discrimination against social categories, such as gender, caste, class, and race. The connection between the two can be found spread through higher education institutions. Passages from Maitreya's short stories illustrate how Dalit students' fundamental human rights are violated constantly. A community of inherited temple ritual performers known as devadasis used their performance to demonstrate devotion and support a set of extremely specific rites; P. Muralidhar Sharma's article, on the other hand, tries to uncover patterns of cultural displacement in their lives. The emotional "Anti-Nautch" movement, which began with Evangelical missionaries in the late 1800s and gained momentum in the early 1900s with the backing of nationalists and social reformers, outlawed all female performers and reduced them to mere prostitutes. As new aesthetic standards were being solidified by the middle-class "custodians" of art, their performances started to be perceived as blatant articulations of crass sensuality. By the 1920s, the devadasis were the target of a discourse that saw the "chaste" and "monogamous" Hindu woman as the keeper of cultural values for the country, and their public presence was seen negatively. This discourse framed the devadasi's non-conjugal sexuality as the "other" to the heteronormative respectability represented by the chaste wife. Prominent intellectuals such as Muthulakshmi Reddi, Periyar, Gandhi, and others expressed unease with the devadasis' performance practices and public presence in speeches and publications. The last essay, "Telling, Writing and Translating: Narratives of Reclaiming People's Rights" by Mrinmoy Pramanick, unfurls how writing literature, telling stories, translating literature, and publishing those works are deliberate political projects of promoting humanism and confirming human rights to the communities who have been denied those rights since the beginning of time. In this essay, instead of discussing the idea of universal humanism put forward through literature, the discussion is restricted to the place of a literary practitioner who both teaches and watches the creation of writing. He contends that an academic practitioner participates in the affirmative action initiative to uphold the human rights of people denied by their ongoing involvement with reading and teaching. Thus, the curriculum and pedagogy of literary studies in India are also topics of this study. In addition to a review of recent publishing activities for literature in various regions of India, this paper refers to a few examples from a few case studies completed under a few research projects. Finally, this study concludes by suggesting that academic units and organizations should take on greater academic and social responsibility to, if not affirm the rights of many individuals, then at least raise awareness among various societal groups. As a result, this essay demonstrates the value of academic literature studies and the magnificence of literature in general.

2.5 Reconciliation of the Rights Narrative in the Shadows of Neo-Imperialism: Beyond Definitive Grounds

The imperative to reaffirm human rights law extends beyond mere crisis response; it also endeavors to address the pervasive societal sentiment of paranoia. Acknowledging the inherent complexities within any institutional framework, including contemporary human rights law, underscores the necessity to navigate and mitigate inherent problematic elements. Moreover, challenging the entrenched hegemony of Western narratives and the inherent selectivity of justice poses formidable obstacles. The onset of the twenty-first century heralded a wave of optimism characterized by aspirations for liberty, the dismantling of antiquated systems, and the deconstruction of prevailing narratives. However, the seismic events of 9/11 precipitated a paradigm shift, ushering in a global resurgence of neo-imperialist fascism, which poses profound challenges to the foundational principles of freedom and equality. Within the realm of literature, there exists a pressing need to explore human rights issues comprehensively, encompassing their historical antecedents, philosophical underpinnings, practical applications, and attendant challenges. Across Asia, subcontinental conflicts have persisted since the aftermath of World War II and the onset of decolonization, with the Indian subcontinent serving as a focal point of instability necessitating the implementation of stringent measures to address threats and maintain geopolitical equilibrium. The literature emanating from these regions serves as a poignant documentation of the recurrent violations of human rights, stemming from a multitude of factors including colonial legacies, forced migrations, caste-based discrimination, and systemic administrative corruption. Providing a platform for the amplification and critical engagement with these voices is imperative to articulate and address the collective pain experienced, thus facilitating the pursuit of remedial measures. By crafting narratives grounded in ethics and embracing alternative perspectives, this endeavor aspires to traverse the arduous path towards closure, forgiveness, and reconciliation. It aspires to celebrate the intrinsic diversity within unity by critically interrogating discourses of harmony and peace, which are often marginalized in an increasingly fascistic global milieu.

References

Anker ES (2012) Fictions of dignity: embodying human rights in world literature. Cornell University Press

Anker ES (2015) Teaching the legal imperialism debate over human rights. In: Moore AS, Elizabeth SG (eds) Teaching human rights in literary and cultural studies, vol 38. The Modern Language Association of America

Baxi P (2014) Public secrets of law: rape trials in India. Oxford University Press

Baxi U (2008) The future of human rights. Oxford University Press

Benhabib S (2004) The rights of others: aliens, residents, and citizens. Cambridge University Press

Brown W (1993) Wounded attachments. Polit Theory 21(3):390–410

Bracke S (2016) Bouncing back: vulnerability and resistance in times of resistance. In: Judith B et al (eds) Vulnerability in resistance. Duke University Press, pp 52–75

Cmiel K (2004) The recent history of human rights. Am Hist Rev 109(1):117–135

DeLaet DL (2019) An emerging asian human rights regime as a tool for protecting the vulnerable in Asia? Lessons from the UN human rights system and other regional human rights regimes. In: de Varennes F, Gardiner CM (eds) The Routledge handbook of human rights in Asia. Routledge, pp 30–43

Fineman MA (2008) The vulnerable subject: anchoring equality in the human condition. Yale J Law Fem 20(1):1–23

Goldberg ES, Alexandra SM (2012) (eds) Theoretical perspectives on human rights and literature. Routledge

Human Rights Watch (2017) "Thailand: migrant worker law triggers regional exodus: revise new decree to end disproportionate penalties, protect rights." Human Rights Watch, www.hrw.org/news/2017/07/07/thailand-migrant-worker-law-triggers-regional-exodus.

Hunt L (2007) Inventing human rights. W. W. Norton

Langlois AJ (2005) The narrative metaphysics of human rights. Int J Hum Rights 9(3):369–387

Mohamed S et al (2020) Decolonial AI: decolonial theory as sociotechnical foresight in artificial intelligence. Philos Technol 33(4):659–684

Munro J (2011) The relationship between the origins and regime design of the ASEAN Intergovernmental Commission on Human Rights (AICHR). Int J Hum Rights 15(8):1185–1214

O'Gorman D (2015) Fictions of the war on terror: difference and the transnational 9/11 novel. Palgrave Macmillan

Parikh C (2017) Writing human rights: the political imaginaries of writers of color. University of Minnesota Press

Souaiaia AE (2021) Human rights in Islamic societies: Muslims and the Western conception of rights. Routledge

Slaughter JR (2007) Human rights Inc: the world novel, narrative form and international law. Fordham University Press

Talbott WJ (2007) Which human rights should be universal? Oxford University Press

United Nations (1996) Impact of Armed Conflict on Children, Report of the Expert of the Secretary General, Graça Machel, submitted pursuant to General Assembly Resolution 48/157. United Nations, 1996. www.unicef.org/graca/a51-306_en.pdf

Weissman D (2004) The Human rights dilemma: rethinking the humanitarian project. Columbia Hum Rights Law Rev 35(259):259–336

Part I
Human Rights Narratives, Literary Activism, and Nationhood in Asia

Chapter 3
Voices of Resistance: Kaifi Azmi's Exploration of Reason, War, and Revolution

Mohammad Asim Siddiqui

Literature, in the traditional use of the word meaning poetry, drama, fiction, and human rights, an important subject in political science, law and international relations, appear to belong to two different domains where any kind of link between them would be considered far-fetched. On closer scrutiny of the contents of the two subjects it can be seen that they are two different vehicles to convey some common human concerns. They are two different kinds of discourses which voice some common human themes. As literature departments in different universities around the world have focused more on interdisciplinarity in the past few decades, some specific courses on the relationship between literature and human rights have been introduced. These courses inevitably include works which articulate very strong social and political concerns of people subjected to different forms of injustice and exploitation. They focus on literature's engagement with political issues and theoretical debates about the functioning of power and its implications for human rights. Formal qualities of literature are not the primary concern of most of these courses. Thus more than modernist and experimental classics like *Ulysses* or *Jacob's Room* it is works like *Uncle Tom's Cabin*, *1984*, *Animal Farm* and *Untouchable*, strongly rooted in social and political concerns of the authors, which become relevant in this discussion. A special case can be made for the inclusion of a work like *Poems from Guantanamo* in these courses even though these poems may not score very highly for their formal and artistic excellence.[1]

It is a truism to say that all forms of literature relate to issues faced by humankind. Their engagement with human issues may vary, but the potential of literature to respond to issues of human suffering, injustice, inequality and violence cannot be disputed. However, the success of a literary form also depends on its ability to sufficiently disguise its 'message' to prevent it from becoming a diatribe, a sermon or propaganda, which is not necessarily a formalist argument. And of all literary forms,

M. A. Siddiqui (✉)
Department of English, Aligarh Muslim University, Aligarh, India
e-mail: siddiquiasim.amu@gmail.com

S. S. Ali and A. Basak (eds.), *Marginal Narratives and the Question of Human Rights in Asian Pacific Literature*, https://doi.org/10.1007/978-981-97-4544-9_3

poetry deals with beliefs, ideas and social and political ideologies in the most subtle manner, conveying its power through metaphors, tone, rhythm and various other poetic devices.

The literary school called Progressive Writers' Movement which has had a major influence on Indian literatures in the twentieth century believed in the purposive nature of literature. It had a beginning in Urdu literature and had in its fold a number of progressive Urdu poets like Makhdoom, Majaz, Sahir, Faiz, Majrooh and Kaifi Azmi. Rakhshanda Jalil explains how "the Marxist slogan of 'the Workers of the World Unite' was commandeered by the progressives as a weapon of direct attack on the imperialist design of exploitation at home and slavery abroad. With time, certain other preoccupations began to come to the forefront—inequality among the sexes, social injustices, oppression by the powerful, and the latent capacity of the ordinary people to be the agents of change and renewal (Jalil xx)." The poetry of the progressive poets has responded to all national and international issues faced by people in their times. Theirs is a poetry which raised its voice against an unjust system, conventional morality, gender inequality, oppression, colonialism, and fascism. In other words, progressive poetry took up many issues which are the concern of many human rights activists in different parts of the world. Jean Paul Sartre has talked about the value of literature which engages with issues, responds to them and does not shy away from taking a position. His concept of 'literature engagee', as David Caute explains in his introduction to *What is Literature*, suggests that "the writer–any writer–is inevitably committed because he cannot soar above history....Willy nilly he is involved in his own time; impartiality is impossible....Literature should not be a sedative but an irritant, a catalyst provoking men to change the world in which they live and in so doing to change themselves (x–xi)." Sartre had both his agreement and serious differences with communists, but his concept of literature—though his frame of reference was mostly prose in this book—is very close to the concept of poetry practiced by progressive poets who were inspired by Marxist ideology. Thus poetry in the hands of Sahir Ludhianvi is never a sedative but a catalyst to change the state of affairs. He takes a position against war in his long nazm "parchaiyaan", (translated as "Shadows Speak" by Khwaja Ahmad Abbas) which has caused inflation, hunger, famine, poverty, suffering and death on an extensive scale:

> O'er the bright face of Life
> Flickered the shadow of Death
> The devils danced in every village, The jungle came to town. From the 'civilised' western lands
> Came the swaggering battalions in khaki
> Arrogant, boastful tyrants,
> Drunk with blood(Abbas)

Sahir's famous anti-war poem about the 1965 India-Pakistan war "Ai Shareef Insano, Jang Talti Rahe to Behtar hai"(Oh Good people it is better if war does not take place) is often cited in most discussions of the futility and brutality of war. Majaz, another prominent progressive poet devoted to the idea of freedom, prefers that his beloved makes a flag of the cloth that contributes to her beauty: "The veil on your forehead looks very pretty,

> It would be better If you made a flag out of it."
> Faiz Ahmad Faiz fuses romantic love with revolution and concerns for the common man in a number of his nazms.

Andrew Clapham writes that "Human rights movement is about people standing up to injustice and showing solidarity in the face of oppression (Clapham, Foreword)." All progressive poets stood up against injustice and showed solidarity in the face of oppression, going even to jail for their ideals.[2] In fact, it was because of their solidarity and commitment to the lot of the common people that a lot of progressive poetry appears similar in its tone, temper and subject matter. A charge against progressive poetry is its lack of distinctive individual voice where a poem written by one progressive poet could well have been written by another.

Like many of his fellow progressive Urdu poets and closer to the concerns of the advocates of human rights, Kaifi Azmi's poetry is also the poetry of commitment where he celebrates common people's solidarity against oppression, raising his voice against inequality and denial of rights to the common man. There are four important dimensions of Kaifi Azmi's work which touch human rights issues in different ways: his commitment to socialist ideology, his contribution as a lyricist and story and dialogue writer in Hindi films, his large corpus of poetry in *Jhankar* (1944), *Akhiri Shab* (1947), *Awara Sajde* (1974) and *Iblis Ki Majlis-e Shoora* and his impressive appearance as an actor in Saeed Mirza's film *Naseem* (1995). All these aspects of his work are interrelated and one cannot neatly separate his art revealed in film songs from the one in his three collections of poems. Surely the demands of the film medium forced him to mostly write romantic songs but he did distinguish himself in many songs like "Meri Avaz Suno", a heart-felt lament on Jawaharlal Nehru's death and his commitment to causes and people, and "Kar Chale Hum Fida", a patriotic song sung routinely on India's Independence Day. In fact, Kaifi Azmi is part of an illustrious galaxy of literary figures along with Sahir Ludhianvi, Majrooh Sultanpuri, Kamal Amrohi and many others who brought a rich literary culture to Hindi films. His lone appearance as an actor in *Naseem* also reflects his socialist vision, his stance against communalism and his sense of disillusionment in an India which sadly changed for him in the last phase of his life.

In Marxist view of literature content of a text holds greater significance than form, despite Marx's disavowal for the expression of any ostensible ideology in a literary work. Marx's praise for French writer Balzac suggests that he could fully appreciate the work of a writer who was sympathetic to bourgeois beliefs. He was of the view that a literary work must have its imaginative quality, its own logic and momentum and it should not appear a propaganda. On the other hand, Lenin's view of literature found room only for that literature which served the interests of the Party. In poets committed to Marxist ideology there would always be a struggle to blend form with content. On the other hand, a non-Marxist critic, especially the one fixated on formalist aspects of a work, would pay least attention to ideology but to how the poet has command of his medium.

As a poet well-read in the classical traditions of Urdu poetry, Kaifi Azmi could not underestimate the importance of form.[3] However, poetry is never an indulgent activity for him. It is too serious an art not to have a purpose and target for Kaifi Azmi. In his Foreword to Kaifi's first collection of poems titled *Jhankar*, Sajjad Zaheer, a pioneer of progressive movement in Urdu, praised Kaifi's love for communism, Soviet Union, Revolution and referred to his praise of Stalin (Zaheer 27–31)" Sajjad Zaheer distinguished the progressive aspect of Kaifi's poetry from the work of certain writers in his times who presented nudity, sex and obscenity in the name of progressive thought.[4] Sajjad Zaheer's concern appears to distinguish Kaifi's true progressivism from a mere indulgence in progress of some writers. Sajjad Zaheer's praise of Kaifi Azmi at Kaifi's young age of twenty -six and his view that with age his poetry would further mature reminds us of Victorian English critic Matthew Arnold's praise of John Keats for his promise rather than performance. Kaifi's art certainly matured but his socialist concerns remained consistent throughout his poetic career. If Sajjad Zaheer finds his expression "simple and direct", years later Faiz Ahmad Faiz would praise Kaifi Azmi for his crispness of tone, his choice of right words, his frankness and his shunning of all artificiality in his expression (Faiz 258).[5]

Marx has also said that "Men make their own history but not of their own free will; not under circumstances they themselves have chosen but under the given and inherited circumstances with which they are directly confronted (Waugh 143)". In his write-up "Me and My Poetry", Kaifi Azmi writes how the seeds of rebellion were planted early in his childhood, how he inherited his love of his country and how he was brought up in an atmosphere free from the poison of communalism. Kaifi's pride in his grandfather's resistance against the cultivation of indigo, his own participation in Swadeshi movement, his role in the organization of a protest against a racist British collector by making black flags, his fascination for Gandhi and Nehru and his desire to go to jail for a revolutionary cause were all important formative influences on his work (Azmi 7–22).

The Marxist insight about men making their history under circumstances not chosen by them elucidates Kaif Azmi's selection of subjects in his poetry. Inspired by his context, any subject touching the lives of ordinary individuals motivates him to write. In all his collections of poems he has responded to important national and international events that he followed keenly. Marx believed that the spiritual creation of a nation is the common property of the international community, a part of the common heritage of mankind. In a way Marx lent his support to the concept of world literature. Kaifi's concerns for the common man, informed by his Marxist ideology, at once bring him closer to an international community of writers. Kaifi Azmi's poetry also shows a very strong awareness of history, often viewed in civilizational terms. Many of his poems refer to different periods in world history. His distinction lies in presenting both little and big history, the big history of war and revolution and the small history of how big events affect the common people.

Awara Sajde was written at a time when India was witnessing great changes. The nation had become independent but the common man in the country was faced with social and economic issues. The country still had to realize its dream of a socialist society. As Kaifi has said in his essay "Me and My Poetry": "I was born in colonial India, grew old in independent India and will die in socialist India (Azmi 7)." His commitment to a socialist society gave him hope and shaped his optimistic outlook on life. The book drew sharp criticism, even calls for a ban, but it also won Kaifi fulsome praise and the prestigious Sahitya Akademi Award which he valued more than his any other award. "Telangana", an important poem in this collection, is Kaifi's response to Telangana Rebellion of peasants against the feudal system in the princy state of Hyderabad in the mid forties. The rebellion, led by communists, held an appeal for Kaifi because of its potential to overthrow insensitive and authoritarian rulers. Glorifying the revolutionary spirit of the common people, the poem suggests that it was a mass movement which united men and women of all age groups against the authority.

Three specific references in the poem hint at the use of the context in the poem: the title Telangana and references to Russia and China. However, the poem can stand on its own without its context, generating new meanings in different times because the fight of the common man against exploitation has not ended. The poem's meaning resonates with people in many other places, in India and elsewhere, where they are fighting oppression. American hermeneutist E. D. Hirsch Jr. made a distinction between the meaning and significance of a literary work where meaning is something what is there in the author's mind whereas the significance of a work refers to its later consumption(Eagleton 58). "Telangana" holds significance for any reader who is interested in the poetry of revolutionary fervor. Much as a formalistic reading is disapproved by Marxist theory, the poem can be read as a people's movement against authority anywhere in the world simply on the basis of its use of language. Even without its title the "Telangana" conveys its message, its revolutionary fervor imparting the poem a strong rhythm and momentum:

> Warn the dwellers of the palaces of the rulers
> To save those who sit on the throne if they can
> Arms that cannot even afford sleeves
> Overrun the earth in their rage(Ali 44)

The common man who participates in specific rebellions like Telangana also becomes Kaifi's universal common man in a number of poems. This common man has seen exploitation and injustice but he has never lost hope and optimism. His poem titled 'Makan' exhorts the common man to remain hopeful in the midst of his problems. The hot winds in the poem make it difficult for the common man to sleep outside and he probably needs a house. The speaker is sure that a window will open for this common man who has changed the shape of the world by his hard work and resilience. "Makan" can also be read anywhere as conveying the nature of an unequal society where a common man needs hope to survive:

> Tonight the wind is too hot
> Tonight we will be sleepless on the footpath

All rise, I will rise too, you also rise
Some window will open in this wall(Rafiq 24)

The common man with his history of injustice and exploitation is also the subject of "Ibne Marium"(Son of Mary), structurally a compact poem. The speaker in this poem does not reject different views about Christ, but he is certain in his mind that he loves Christ for his honesty and truthfulness which is sharply contrasted with a world full of lies and violence. The speaker presents the world of smugglers in a port city, similar to Bombay of the 1960s and 1970s, but ironically this is the only world where some principles are followed honestly. "Choro ki hi to usool hote hain(Only thieves have some principles)", says Michael Disouza, a thief played by Pran in the 1974 hit film *Majboor*. The image of the crime world is followed by the image of powerless, faceless and badly exploited masses of the city:

Look at me I am that very person
Whom the world under whiplashes
Bought and sold

Look at me I am that very person
When I created some machines
Then the owners of those machines
Thoughtlessly flung me into them
As if I were nothing but fuel(Rafiq 35)

Christ's sheep are transformed into ordinary workers and the speaker also becomes part of a faceless crowd. This faceless common man was equally exploited and oppressed during the feudal and industrial periods. In a remarkable turn of irony, much like in Faiz's poems, the poem develops a concrete political context in its climax by bringing in the Vietnam issue. Invoking Christ and the Bible in an ironic manner, the speaker exhorts Christ to crucify himself once again for his followers who have turned great oppressors in Vietnam:

Go to those jungles of Vietnam
It's crucified town and wounded villages
Who the readers of the Bible
Have trampled and blown out
Who knows how long they have called to you?(Rafiq 35)

The common man is also the subject of his poem titled "Bangladesh", where seen as a mass he cannot be defeated by any power. Having taken a stand against geographical boundaries, Kaifi's common man only has history but no geography in this poem.

All modern legal systems which emphasize human rights are based on reason, rationality and logical thinking. Kaifi Azmi celebrates reason in a number of his poems. True to his Marxist ideology, he realized that reason could fight dogma and obscurantism. His poem titled "Nehru", in which Nehru stands for reason, starts with some predictable and hackneyed similies like 'a fountain in desert' and 'lamp post in sea'. However, what turns the entire poem around is a very original simile 'like a thought in superstition'. This thought, this power to use one's mind rather than received ideas, has always landed the thinking minds in trouble. The poem makes oblique reference to Socrates and the Christ who died because they cared to think differently. The best thing about reason is that though it has faced stiff opposition down the ages, it keeps growing.

Even his broken heart finds its consolation in reason. The poem titled "Awara Sajde" articulates his pain and anguish on the division in the Communist Party in 1964 when the two factions of the Communist Party in India separated from each other. With this development Kaifi's dream appeared shattered and he did not know where to turn as the Party was everything for him. A very existentialist fear grips him and the speaker in the poem realizes that his own self is his guide. Discovering himself to be an iconoclast, his reason rejects all gods, including the secular god represented by the Party.

It is the distinction of Kaifi's poetry that many of his poems, though written in response to an immediate context, acquire a different context in our times. His poem "Pir Tasme Pa"(Old Man with Feet Bound) is the poet's response to man's landing on the moon. But it is not the landing as such but the irrational response to this momentous event that Kaifi the rationalist finds ludicrous. The landing on moon generated a sense of wonder in man's capacity to reach new heights, celebrating the myth of progress and the power of reason. However, there were many accounts of damning this important event, much like the irrational account of reading all modern signs of progress in the past. In fact, Kaifi's poem joins the debate about Sangh Parivar's reading of the history of science. Appearing a sceptic par excellence in this poem, his materialist view of history, which does not accept divine accounts of wonders, is also evident in this poem.

An important intervention in the discussion of human rights is made by feminist scholars who have addressed the issue of structural inequality of sexes and the denial of rights to women. Violence against women in different societies, despite the provisions made by various legal systems, have not helped the fight of gender justice. Thus despite provisions for gender justice in the Preamble, Articles 14,15,16,21 and the Directive Principles, India is far from realizing the dream of gender equality for its vast millions. Kaifi's poetry shows an awareness of the poor plight of women in society. He disagreed with the view of many poets of his time who thought that the freedom of the country was the prime need and efforts to ameliorate the condition of women could wait. For him equality of sexes and gender justice was the primary concern, as important as the independence of the nation. In his famous poem "Aurat"(Woman) he advocates equal status of women in all spheres of life. The refrain in the poem "you have to walk with me" is repeated a number of times to suggest the sincerity of the poet's intention. If men participate in war or the struggle for freedom and face difficult times, the woman cannot be left behind. "you too have to burn in the fire along with me". If times are changing then "you must flow with its free current". The poet has a painful awareness about the exploitation and humiliation suffered by women down the ages. She has usually been defined in terms of her romantic and sexual identity. For him she is not just "an interesting story" but "reality too", having "an existence too not just youthfulness." But he is also aware of the power that a woman holds within herself. It is this power in her which can change her position in society:

> History has not known your value till now
> You hold not only tears but embers too(Rafiq 100)

Different forces in society have conspired to hold women in chains. They include "prison of antiquity", "statue of traditions", "the prison of love" "confusions of morality", or the focus of society on her youthfulness. Kaifi's view of this empowered woman not only grants her power but also does not deny her intellectual gifts. She possesses both beauty and intelligence, subsuming within her the best philosophical traditions:

> You are Aristotle and Plato, you are Venus and the Pleiades
> You uphold the firmament and foreheads at your feet(Rafiq 101)

Starting with images of loneliness and desolation, "Beva ki Khudkashi"(Widow's Suicide), a long nazm of seventy lines, addresses the specific issues of the life of a widow in an essentially patriarchal set-up. Images of "dark night", "silent atmosphere" "disappearing stars", "stale garlands", "crumpled flowers", "suppressed desires", "desolate neighborhood", "silent lanes and pathways" and "dissonance between beauty and love" invoke a world which prepares the reader for the wretched life of a widow which worries the poet in the poem. These images are an external manifestation of the inner turmoil in the mind of the widow who faces problems of all kinds at different levels. Her beautiful face marred by sadness, the young widow keeps changing positions in bed in a state of restlessness. Her desires have died; her complaints remain unexpressed; but she is not old enough to think about death. The empty bed makes her feel wretched. The sound of her sleeping daughters' bangles makes her even more miserable. She sighs and cries alternately, knowing no peace of mind. Her wrist without bangles makes her aware of her misery.

What is remarkable about her lot is that her misery has almost deleted the memory of her husband's death, the cause of her misery, as it has completely changed her status in society. It is miseries and problems given by her present set-up which occupy her all the time. She remembers the ill treatment given to her by her sister-in-law and mother-in-law. Even her own mother and sisters have not always been kind to her. With no one to support her and to sympathize with her, the widow has thoughts of suicide. The vision of a peaceful grave appears more appealing than the miseries that she faces:

> Noone will see you with a view to humiliate
> whether you want to laugh or cry no one will stop you

She has a vision of life after death which will be just. Filled with such thoughts the widow drinks the poison from a bottle. In the last two lines Kaifi salutes the widow but blames the oppressive customs of Indian society for her death. Feminist criticism has shown how the psychological problems of women in literature are political problems created by a patriarchal structure. Kaifi's widow appears to be a Muslim woman as suggested by her thoughts of a peaceful grave, and even though Islam treats its widows fairly, the customs in Indian society have eliminated any distinction of religion in its treatment of widows.

Like other Marxist poets of his generation Kaifi was greatly inspired by the Russian revolution, holding the red flag in great pride. Soviet leader Stalin, who represents hope for Kaifi, figures in a number of his poems. In equal measure he was opposed to the ideology of fascism which threatened the peace of the world and credited Stalin for defeating fascism in many of his poems. In "Surkh Jannat"(Red Heaven), which was written on the occasion of the twenty- fifth anniversary of Russian Revolution, he is pained to see "this Russia which is being destroyed by demons", making an indirect reference to Hitler's army which was at war against Russia. Kaifi reminds everyone that Russia, a land of humanism, love and awakening, was the place of revolution in the first place before any other country. Furthermore.

> This very land has known the value of farmers
> This very garden has the rule of labour
> This is the capital of not the emperor but of human being

In "Aitraaf"(Admission) he explains why the Nazi agents could not succeed in Russia. He praises the patriotism of the people of Russia, their love of education and their love of their system. Praising Lenin for awakening them, and Stalin for putting his ideas in their hearts, the Russians love their country so much that they cannot be bought or influenced by the sinister forces represented by Nazism.

In another poem "Rusi Aurat ka Naara"(Russian Woman's Slogan), Kaifi speaks of a Russian woman's determination to save her country from its enemies. Making a reference to the threat coming from the Nazis, Kaifi's Russian woman is a picture of empowerment:

> One who was ignorant is awake now
> One who was a lullaby is a battle cry now
> one who was a song is a strum now
> one who was a needle is a sword now
> This empowered Russian woman:
> will sprinkle the red in the atmosphere
> will save the motherland squarely

In yet another poem titled "Stalin ka Farman: Surkh Faujo ke Naam"(Stalin's Order to the Red Army), Kaifi pays a tribute to Stalin's leadership qualities especially in motivating his Red Army to fight the Nazis. The refrain in the poem "Yes continue fighting, continue fighting, continue fighting", repeated five times in the poem, shows Stalin's determination and his iconic status for the poet. The red army is hailed in a celebratory tone:

> You are the character of a new world, a new civilization
> …….You are the chief of the army of laborers

Yet another poem simply titled "Stalin" is an unabashed tribute to his leader for giving a blow to oppression, especially represented by Nazis:

Praise Comrade Stalin
You shook the heart of oppression

As is obvious from his poems about Stalin and his Red Army, Kaifi has written a number of poems highlighting the horrors of the second world war, especially the threat to humankind from the fascist ideology of Hitler. It is interesting to note that Kaifi started writing his poems against fascist ideology at almost the same time when human rights were being invoked. H.G.Wells discussed the issue of rights and the aims of war very spiritedly around this time. His widely read, distributed and translated book *The Rights of Man* (1940), which included his famous World Declaration of the Rights of Man, highlighted different rights of man. Andrew Clapham sums up the rights in the ten paragraphs of the Declaration: "discrimination; natural resources; health; education; paid employment; the right to buy and sell personal property; the right to move around the world freely; no imprisonment longer than six days without charge, and then no more than three months before a public trial; access to public records concerning individuals; and a prohibition on mutilation, sterialization, torture, and any bodily punishment (30)." Clapham rightly says that "the horrors of the second world war provided this impetus for the modern human rights movement (31)."

Like many philosophers and thinkers whose ideas inspired the discussion of human rights movement, Kaifi's poems about the horrors of the second world war participate in the discourse on human rights of common people. His poem "Ittihadion ke Naam" (For Allied Powers) also offers a trenchant criticism of Nazi ideology and praises Russia "for breaking the back of Nazi plunderers". Similarly "Jagaao"(Awaken), which is an address to the youth of India, talks about 'the dagger of fascism', and the destruction that it has caused in the world. It also sees fascism as another form of monarchy and in the defeat of fascism lies the departure of monarchy. Adopting a very angry tone the poet exhorts the youth to defeat German Nazi leader Hitler and General of the Imperial Japanese Army Hideki Tojo:

If Tojo comes here, behead him
If Hitler advances, turn him into dust
Those traitors in the house, burn them alive

Kaifi's hatred of fascist ideology was so total that he was not ready to approve of the approach of Subhas Chandra Bose, who wanted to liberate India from the British rule with help from Nazi Germany and Imperial Japan. His poem "Burma ka Chawal"(Burmese Rice) which is written in the form of a response of the famine-stricken Bengal to Bose's announcement from Singapore radio to send rice for Bengal, takes a position of not having any truck with fascism. In a hard-hitting rejection of Bose's offer the poet says:

In your poison-infected rice there is the smell of blood
Congratulations to you but we cannot see them

We love each and every part of India
You cannot unfurl the flag of fascism here

Kaifi's most hard-hitting attack against fascism is expressed in his poem "Istaqlaal"(Firmness) which is written in response to "a respectable senior", probably Josh Malihabadi, who "praised the Nazi demons for their firmness and manliness". In fact, there were many people who subscribed to this view for different reasons. Kaifi's trenchant criticism of fascism in the poem appears to invoke the right to food, water and education. Nazi's destruction of gardens and green fields is a gross violation of ordinary people's right to food. Even the famine in Bengal which moved Bose to make an offer of Burmese rice to the famine-stricken people, was the result of the poor planning of the British government. Food security, proper distribution of food, and proper planning for any shortages of food is the responsibility of the government and the failure of the British government to do so was violative of people's right to food. He also takes Nazis to task for violating people's right to education. Nazi's hatred of scholars, demolition of universities, and setting fire to libraries is a blow to people's right of education.

He holds the Nazis responsible for initiating the war and spreading it everywhere in every walk of life be it a market, a neighborhood, hotel, station, lanes, theatres, colleges, training centres, closets, homes, fields, factories, shops or hospitals. He considers nazis hypocritical of the meanest order who first mislead people with a message of peace and then conspire against them. Nazis are guilty of committing crimes against humanity which are mentioned in article 7 of the statute of the International Criminal Court. For them

There is no love of humanity or their time
Loot is good, oppression better, murder is justified, killing is halal

They destroy gardens and green fields, loot the property of laborers, rape women, kick the heads of children to death.

Natural hatred of scholars, enmity with artists
Demolishing the universities, setting fire to libraries
Their brutality cannot be termed bravery because
Jackals, cheetahs, demons, thieves, dacoits, highwaymen
They show their bravery to unarmed people

After showing the brutal character of the Nazis, Kaifi praises the Red Army of Stalin for confronting the danger of fascism. It is Stalin who has the firmness and manliness which is wrongly attributed to Nazis by his respectable senior.

Kaifi's poetry also touches on some important international issues where the question of the violation of human rights was involved. His poem "The Present War and the Progressive Elements" takes a very clear position on the Second World War against the Nazis. Beginning with presenting images of death and destruction, "These corpses and these fields God save us/Weeping and crying people God save us", Kaifi's speaker speaks for all progressive people who oppose the forces of destruction in the war. Adopting a very urgent tone akin to a proclamation, the speaker announces that "we are entering the war". The speaker is aghast to realize that reactionary forces have crossed all limits, caused so much bloodshed, created a mayhem. It is now or never for the progressives who must attack the reactionaries and control the missiles, armies, tunnels, tanks and canons of the Nazis. The Nazis' cruelty- burning of populations and bloodshed- has to be countered by the progressive forces. Kaifi's speaker is hopeful of his side's victory because on his side are hearts of workers and labourers of the world. The reference to the power of Allied Forces- Russian pluck, Chinese bravery, Indian warriors, some faithful Englishmen, some Americans- who will counter the Nazis makes it very clear that for the progressive speaker this is a necessary and just war. He is proud of his red flag which will conquer and end violence in the world.

His poem "Bangladesh" takes a stance against the excesses in Bangladesh by the Pakistani army without mentioning the name of Pakistan. The poem refers to the tanks acquired by Pakistan in aid and mentions the raining of napalm bombs by the Pakistani army on the people of Bangladesh. He considers the war of Bangladesh's liberation an idea which is close to the heart of all 70 million people of Bangladesh. Kaifi turns the battle of the two ideas-dream of liberation of 70 million people and their voice of resistance against the excesses done by the Pak army- into a history of conflict between the forces of oppression and the forces of resistance. All through history there has been a conflict between these two forces in different places. More than the geography it is the history of oppression and resistance against it that interests Kaifi. For him Bangladesh is not simply a country, wall or border that can be destroyed, demolished and erased. It rather is an ideal for millions of people and its roots can be seen in the ideals of many people in history who have stood against oppression in different places of the world. The voice of resistance appears again and again in individual and collective hearts and cannot be suppressed.

Notes

1. *Poems From Guantanamo: The Detainees Speak,* Edited by Marc Falkoff. University of Iowa Press, 2007. The poems in this book present the innermost feelings and emotions of the detainees held in the US detention centre at Guantanamo Bay, Cuba. The editor, with help from lawyers, got the clearance from the military and the Pentagon "Privilege Review Team" to publish them. The poems reveal the brutal interrogation techniques that the detainees were subjected to and offer a criticism of the violations of the human rights of prisoners, many of them were detained even without facing a trial.
2. Thus Ali Sardar Jafri was expelled from Aligarh Muslim University during his student days for 'political reasons' and was arrested for writing anti-war poems in 1940-01 and second time in 1949 for organizing progressive writers conference as PWA was banned by the government at this time. Faiz and Sajjad Zaheer spent four years in prison from 1951 to 1955. Majrooh Sultanpuri also spent some time in hiding to evade arrest. Makhdoom was jailed twice in the 1941 and 1944 for raising his voice against authorities.
3. Sajjad Zaheer's target was Saadat Hasan Manto who was shunned by the progressives.
4. All translations of Urdu prose works and poetry in the paper not stated in the text, are mine.

5. This rebellion also inspired Krishan Chander, another progressive writer, to write "Jab Khet Jage"(When the Filelds Awakened).

References

Abbas KA (2020) "Shadows Speak/Parchhaiyan". In: The Year of Sahir:2021 Diary. Presented by Nasreen Munni Kabir. Hyphen Films, Chennai

Alvi HM (2019) In: Kaifi A (ed): Poems|Nazms. Edited and Co-translated by Sudeep Sen. Bloomsbury, New Delhi

Azmi, K (2012) "Main aur Meri Shayari/Me and My Poetry". In: Kaifi A (ed) (2003) Kaifiaat: Kulliyat-e- Kaifi Azmi. Educational Book House, Delhi

Caute D (1948) Introduction. Jean-Paul Sartre. What is Literature?. 1948. Translated by Bernard Frechtman. Routledge

Clapham A (2007) Human rights: a very short introduction. Oxford University Press, New York

Eagleton T (1996) Literary Theory: An Introduction. 1983, Maya Blackwell, New Delhi

Faiz AF Foreword. Awara Sajde. Kaifi Azmi. Kaifiaat: Kulliyat-e- Kaifi Azmi

Jalil R (2014) Liking progress, loving change: a literary history of progressive writers' movement. Oxford University Press, New Delhi

Rafiq S, Pilibhiti R (2019) The second exile: an english translation of Kaifi Azmi's Doosra Banbas. Viva Books, New Delhi

Waugh P (2006) Literary theory and criticism. Oxford University Press, New Delhi

Zaheer S Foreword. Jhankaar. Kaifi Azmi. Kaifiaat: Kulliyat-e- Kaifi Azmi

Chapter 4
Refugee Chronicles: Khaled Hosseini's "Sea Prayer" and the Struggle for Human Rights

Nisreen T. Yousef

4.1 Introduction

"Sea Prayer" (2017) is a forty-eight-page illustrated short story. The story is composed in the form of a letter in which Marwan's father reflects on the hazards of the journey they will take into the sea, fleeing the war in Syria and seeking refuge during night. While keeping his sleeping child, the father recalls their life back in the city of Homs, Syria. The story provides portraits of the city before and after the war and displays the turmoil and destruction caused by the war. At the end of the story, the father is helpless but hopeful that the sea will listen to their prayers and that they will arrive at a safe place.

As indicated in the last page of the short story, "Sea Prayer" was inspired by the story of Alan Kurdi, the three-year-old Syrian refugee who drowned in the Mediterranean Sea while his family was trying to reach safety in Europe in September 2015." The book was dedicated to the refugees who died at sea while trying to escape the atrocities of the war. In an interview entitled: "Khaled Hosseini Says Refugees Are Essential to America", Hosseini states that he was moved by the photo of Kurdi washed ashore ("Sea Prayer"). He declares that he wrote the story to keep Kurdi's memory and to pay tribute to him as well as other refugees around the globe ("Sea Prayer"). As indicated by the Khaled Hosseini Foundation: "Author proceeds from the sale of "Sea Prayer" will go to the UNHCR, the UN Refugee Agency, and The Khaled Hosseini Foundation to help fund life-saving support and build better futures for refugees around the world. This statement shows Hosseini's deep concern with supporting refugees not only by depicting their experiences in his literary works but also by providing financial aid for them.

In an interview conducted by Carvell Wallace and entitled "How Khaled Hosseini finds hope in telling refugees' stories", Hosseini states that the main objective of his

N. T. Yousef (✉)
Middle East University, Amman, Jordan
e-mail: ntyousef@meu.edu.jo

S. S. Ali and A. Basak (eds.), *Marginal Narratives and the Question of Human Rights in Asian Pacific Literature*, https://doi.org/10.1007/978-981-97-4544-9_4

writings is “to prickle the consciousness of the Western world.” As he indicates in this interview, he himself went through the experience of being a refugee. When Russia invaded his country Afghanistan in 1979, he was fifteen years old. His father was a diplomat in Paris. Hosseini’s family had to seek asylum in the United States. Before he commenced writing his novel *And the Mountain Echoes* (2013), he joined the UNHCR. This experience influenced his perceptions of war and refuge. As Hosseini states: “Displacement, refugees, these things are still very much with me … I think I live now, not preoccupied, but engaged in my mind with bigger issues than I was when I was writing *The Kite Runner*.” Hosseini’s short story, this chapter argues, depicts the horrendous outcomes of armed forces and the ensuing violation of refugees’ human rights. He tries through “Sea Prayer” to raise awareness about the infringement of human fundamental rights that results from wars and calls European politicians as well as European public to provide humanitarian support for refugees.

Although Hosseini’s ‘Sea Prayer’ has been approached by some critics, it is still in need of further scholarly examination and in-depth analysis. In this regard, Sreekutty provides a descriptive account of the story. The author describes the city of Homs before war in positive lights and then shows the sudden shift in the city after the clashes take place (97–98). Sreekutty shows how the journey to the European shores is a dangerous one and despite its harshness, Marwan’s father still has a glimmer of hope of arriving safe. Plunkett (2018) argues that Hosseini’s illustrated story is meant to present the suffering of the refugees through narrating personal experiences. For her, dealing with refugees in statistics is humiliating; story telling keeps human dignity and provides better understanding of this experience as it can illuminate some misconceptions about or misunderstanding of it.

This chapter expands on the above critical works by exploring Hosseini’s endeavours to defy the European media’s inhumane representations of refugees. In addition, it examines his attempts to depict the violation of the human rights of refugees, which is a direct result of war. The chapter argues that through providing literary depictions of such issues, Hosseini questions Europe’s moral obligation towards protecting the human rights of refugees and calls for ending war as it is a main cause of abusing such rights. Thus, the chapter develops existing examination of Hosseini’s short story regarding the so called “Refugee Crisis” in 2015 following the war in Syria. In this short story, which embodies a departure in the author’s style of writing, Hosseini avoids drawing solely on narratives; rather, he presents his refugee characters as identified human beings who have clear features and who speak for themselves.

4.2 Discussion

The year 2015 witnessed an increase in the number of refugees and migrants fleeing war and poverty in the Middle East and seeking asylum in Europe. A vast number of these refugees were escaping the war in Syria. This action of people’s movements from threatening places to more secure lands was referred to by the European media as “Refugee Crisis”, a crisis that provoked a response from European politicians as well the public. The European media played a significant role in presenting the flow of people to Europe as a "crisis"; it portrayed them as outsiders who pose a threat to Europe. Most often, refugees were spoken for; they were rarely invited to speak about their own stories of suffering. Refugees appeared in the European media as passive and silent actors who are spoken about. The European public relied heavily on the mainstream media in being informed about the refugees for two reasons: the speed of delivering news as well as the unfamiliarity of the newcomers to the European publics. The European media provoked hostility and hatred towards refugees and little attention was directed towards their suffering and plight (Georgiou and Zaborowsk 4). In terms of political discourse, Barkin indicates that German Chancellor Angela Merkel described the refugee issue in 2015 as the biggest challenge for Europe, a dilemma that surpassed Greece crisis. It can be concluded form the accounts above that the European political discourse and media played a crucial role in presenting refugees as a menace to Europe and thereby creating feelings of distress towards them. This can be seen as a kind of human rights violation as it abuses human dignity.

On September 2, 2015, the whole world was moved by the picture of Alan Kurdi, a Syrian little boy who drowned on the Turkish shore while his family was trying to flee the atrocities of the war in Syrian in order to find a safer place in Europe. The picture, which was captured by a Turkish journalist, not only moved the publics in Europe but also provoked a response from politicians. According to Narula, following the image of the three-year old child, Kurdi, the British Prime Minister David Cameron announced that more numbers of refugees to be accepted into the UK. Moreover, Angela Merkel and France's Francois Hollande were discussing an agreement to enhance the number of refugees to Europe. On this occasion, Merkel's approached was seen as the warmest welcome of refugees in Germany and accordingly she was praised for it. Thus, Kurdi's photo on the shores left a vast psychological effect on the European public as well as politicians (Narula).

Nevertheless, in in-depth research on the psychological and emotional impact of the photography on humans, Slovic et al., argues a single photo of Alan left a greater influence on the European public and politicians than that of many statistical reports about hundreds of thousands of losses. The researchers argue that statistics on mass human disasters do not succeed in attracting enough attention to take action. They maintain that Alan's picture was able to catch public and political attention, catalyzing a change in political and public stances towards refugees as the picture was for an identified human being. According to the researchers, the iconic photo of the drowned child was viewed by more than 20 million people on social media. However, Adler-Nissen et al., contend that the impact of Kurdi's picture was temporary. Although the photo played a role in shifting European policies towards refugees, a year later the photo and its implications contributed towards signing a controversial agreement between Turkey and Greece in 2016 according to which the migration route from Greece to Turkey was closed. Such argument indicates that the effect of Kurdi's photo did not stay for a long time. Instead, it led to more anti-refugee policies in Europe.

Taking the previous accounts into consideration, I argue that Hosseini's use of images in his illustrated story "Sea Prayer" is deployed to serve a humanitarian objective. Through his short story "Sea Prayer", Hosseini tries to challenge the European media's dehumanizing images of refugees by presenting them as masses that pose a threat to European values of civilization and progress, which ultimately violates their dignity as humans. In this respect, it becomes crucial to reflect on images of refugees in the European media. Esses et al., argue that the media had a significant role in shaping discourse and policies regarding immigrants and refugees (520). They maintain that the media represented immigrants and refugees as a menace to the host society which ultimately dehumanizes them (531). Thus, it is clear that the European media contributed towards creating anti-immigration policies and provoking the public against refugees. Nevertheless, Hosseini shows deep concern about showing that displacement is a consequence of war that people involuntarily deal with. As we notice in the story, Marwan, his father, his mother, the people in the neighborhood and the refugees appear as identified human beings. Hosseini endeavours through his story to defy the European media' attempts to dehumanize refugees by presenting them as threatening herds mentioned in statistics. Moreover, the story is told from the perspective of the father. Instead of being spoken for, Hosseini's refugee characters have the dominant voice in the story. He grants his refugee characters voices through which they provide their own narratives and express their personal suffering. On this subject, Gallien argues that authors' efforts of presenting refugees' experience expose what the media endeavours to keep invisible (722). Hence, such writings allow refugees to renarrate their experiences from their own perspectives in ways that undermine the European media's efforts to dehumanize refugees and to abuse their dignity as well as their right of being presented respectfully.

Moreover, in "Sea Prayer", there is much focus on presenting women. The majority of illustrations include female characters. Women in the story appear as functional characters who are capable of running life's activities and to speak up their minds; the illustrations in the story show women conducting everyday activities at the marker and taking care of children (Hosseini "Sea Prayer" 14, 16, 17). The reader can see Marwan, accompanied by his mother, walking through the green fields safe and happy (Hosseini, "Sea Prayer" 17). In addition, Marwan's grandmother runs basic duties at the farm such as taking care of the goats and providing them with food (Hosseini, "Sea Prayer" 8). Hence, the story depicts female characters as an essential and integral part of life in the city of Homs before the war breaks out. Before commencing their journey towards safety, Marwan's mother expresses the agonies they face in their countries in the aftermath of the war. The father, who is also the narrator, says: "But I hear your mother's voice, over the tide, and she whispers in my ear. "Oh, but if they saw my darling. Even half of what you have. If only they saw. They would say kinder things, surely" (Hosseini, "Sea Prayer" 34). The mother's statement, which represents the female refugees' perspective, is heard. Instead of being muted, she is given the chance to express her own feelings and viewpoint. Nevertheless, Georgiou and Zaborowsk (3) argue that the voices of female refugees were 'hardly ever heard' in the European media. Thus, while the

European media attempts to marginalize female refugees, Hosseini gives much attention to female refugees and their agonies as the story places the suffering of women at its centre. Moreover, Hosseini undermines the European media's efforts to present refugee women as passive objects that are spoken for in ways that violate their human dignity.

Hosseini endeavours in "Sea Prayer" to present war as a destructive force that results in displacement and consequently in the violation of human rights. In this regard, it becomes crucial to reflect on the history of the war in Syria which Hosseini depict in his short story. The war in Syria which started in 2011 as anti-government protests before turning into a civil war resulted in a massive damage. According to a report entitled "Syrian Cities Damage Atlas—Eight Year Anniversary of the Syrian Civil War: Thematic assessment of satellite identified damage", (2019) the war in Syria left a vast devastation in the country. A satellite-detected damage was run by UNITAR-UNOSAT (United Nations Institute for Training and Research—Operational Satellite Applications Programme) to assess the amount of damage in Syria. This kind of analysis provides a comprehensive overview of the destruction inflicted on the country. According to the report, facilities including schools, hospitals, and homes were destroyed or damaged. As the report indicates, 53% of urban areas were impacted by bombing attacks. In addition, the report states that "11.7 million people in Syria are reportedly in need of humanitarian assistance". To give specific examples, in Deir-ez-Zor, most of the medical facilities were damaged and accordingly, the medical staff was displaced to other places. The routes to other alternative places where people can receive medical attention were also destroyed, which hindered people's search for the medical services needed. In this regard, Overton and Dathan indicate that "In Aleppo alone, at least 15 million tons of rubble were created by this violence by 2017. Such accounts show the vast ruin caused by war, impacting both humans and land. According to, Nowak (v–vi), on the sixtieth anniversary of the Universal Declaration of Human Rights, an agenda entitled "Protecting Dignity" was presented by the Swiss Foreign Minister. In this agenda, armed forces, war crimes, and weapons of mass destruction were identified as serious human rights violations that attack human dignity. Accordingly, it can be argued that wars and its consequences are represented as a major cause of abusing human rights.

As the reader can notice in the short story, the dwellers of the city of Homs at the beginning of the story appear as people who live peacefully. The city is presented and illustrated as a peaceful arena (Hosseini, "Sea Prayer" 14). Through images followed by commentaries, Hosseini shows the radical shift in the city of Homs before and after the war. For instance, the reader can see a woman, walking on the streets of Homs, safe and secure. The illustration reflects the nonviolent atmosphere in the city. Describing their cheerful and stable life in the city the father says to Marwan: 'We woke in the morning to the stirring of olive trees in the breeze, to the bleating of your grandmother's goat. The clanking of her cooking pots, the air cool and the sun a pale rim of persimmon to the east' (Hosseini, "Sea Prayer" 8). The father's narratives as well as the colourful pictures signify that the city used to be peaceful, quiet, and beautiful before the start of war. In addition, the city appears as a multi-faith one in which both Muslims and Christians are allowed to practice their religious rituals

(Hosseini, "Sea Prayer" 15). The illustration is colorful; it indicates that the dwellers of the city happily and peaceably coexist. p

However, one can notice a clear shift in the illustrations (Hosseini, "Sea Prayer" 20); the pictures are drawn in dark colours, announcing the breakout of the war in Syria starting with the protests followed by the siege. The narrator describes the consequence of the clashes by saying: "The skies spitting bombs. Starvation. Burials" (Hosseini, "Sea Prayer" 22). Comparing the conditions of the city before and after the war, the father says: "But that life, that time, seems like a dream now, even to me, like some long-dissolved rumour (Hosseini, "Sea Prayer" 19). In addition to what the narrator informs the reader about the impact of war on the city, dark images are used to indicate the destruction of war and the sorrow in which the city is plighted. The whole city which is depicted and illustrated in earlier pages as a stable and non-violent one is in total devastation in following pages (Hosseini, "Sea Prayer" 24). As indicated through images, the situation in the city becomes worse and the place is ruined further. Consequently, the dwellers of the city are deprived of their fundamental rights of living a decent life.

In Homs, which is transferred into a conflict zone, the dwellers of the city commence their journey towards safety (Hosseini, "Sea Prayer" 30–31). As the mother indicates: 'Oh, but if they saw my darling. Even half of what you have. If only they saw. They would say kinder things, surely' (Hosseini, "Sea Prayer" 34). The mother's statement reflects the deep sorrow refugees witness in their countries due to the outbreak of war. She sounds traumatised by the experience of war and its consequences. Her words suggest that becoming a refugee is not a choice but rather a horrific experience one involuntarily gets exposed to.

Thus, the images along with the commentaries in the story indicate that refugees resort to fleeing the country and searching for asylum as this is the only option they have. In this respect, the father says: "Afghans and Somalis and Iraqis and Eritreans and Syrians. All of us impatient for sunrise, all of us in dread of it. All of us in search of home" (Hosseini 2018a, b: 33). As the story shows, refugees from different countries find themselves obliged to face the same destiny of leaving their homelands due to the horrendous conditions surrounding them. Hosseini portrays refugees as people who miserably escape their countries at which they used to lead happy and stable life. He tries to establish the notion of seeking asylum as a grim experience that one goes through involuntarily. This takes us to Said's experience of exile. Reflecting on his personal experience of displacement Said (2000) writes, "Exile is extremely compelling to think about but terrible to experience" (173). By providing such literary depictions of the experience of becoming a refugee, Hosseini stresses the humanitarian dimension of the problem and constructs it as a humanitarian and ecological issue rather than a threat to Europe's economies, cultures, and social norms, as constructed by the European media.

Hosseini portrays the massive destruction of the city and the ensuing displacement as a miserable experience through which humans' fundamental rights are violated. Haenens and Joris (2019) argue that although refugees were facing hard and horrible conditions, many European countries were hesitant to allow these refugees in and to provide them with their essential needs including shelter, residence, educations and job opportunities (8). Abbasi et al., "Europe's refugee crisis is the greatest test of humanity faced by the world's rich countries this century" (1). They indicate that this crisis is not new and was not difficult to expect (Abbasi et 1). The authors maintain that the photo of Kurdi "exposed" Europe's morality. According to them, Human Rights are currently a defining feature of Europe and therefore, "giving asylum to refugees, regardless of culture and religion, is a minimum standard expected of a civilized society." (Abbasi et al. 2015: 1). According to Article 14 of the Universal Deceleration of Human Rights: "Everyone has the right to seek and to enjoy in other countries asylum from persecution." Thus, Hosseini, I contend, is critical of Europe's stance on refugees and urges the European politicians as well as the public to protect refugees' right of asylum.

In light of this argument, I contend that Hosseini directs sharp criticism to Europe's stance of refugees and questions Europe's alleged moral obligation towards asylum seekers and human rights. In an interview, Hosseini sates that through "Sea Prayer", he tries to address some misconceptions about refugees. He argues that refugees have been seen as people who try to steal Western jobs. For him, being a refugee is not a choice that one makes likely; no one likes to put his life in jeopardy (Hosseini, "Sea Prayer" 2017). Hosseini's portrayal of the experience of seeking asylum goes against the European media's as well as political discourse's efforts of emphasizing the negative influence of refugees on economic and social life in Europe. Taking Hosseini's statement in the interview as well as my own analysis of the story, I contend that Hosseini tries to defend the human rights of refugees by defying the European media's efforts to dehumanize them. Moreover, the author shows great concern in urging the European people and politicians to act upon their moral obligation of protecting the human rights of displaced people. In "Sea Prayer", the father indicates: "I have heard it said we are the uninvited. We are the unwelcome. We should take our misfortune elsewhere." (Hosseini 33) The father's commentary is meant to reflect on the European stance on refugees. In response to the arrival of refugees to Europe in September 2015, The European Union proposed a set of plans to strengthen external borders (European Council 2016). As we can see in the short story, the sea, which is presented as the refugees' only escape from the atrocities of war, is illustrated as violent, dark, uncertain and unwelcoming place (Hosseini, "Sea Prayer" 32, 33, 36). The father confesses his fears of the sea, "Because all I can think tonight is how deep the sea, and how vast, how indifferent" (Hosseini, "Sea Prayer" 38). Such statement by the father reflects the uncertainty of the journey.

Hence, it can be concluded that Hosseini produces negative images of war in the story and constructs it as a humanitarian and ecological disaster that leads to the abuse of human rights. As the story suggests, war leaves horrendous impact on people, infrastructure and the environment. In light of the data provided in the reports mentioned above and my argument about Hosseini's depictions of war, I contend that Hosseini tries through his literary work 'Sea Prayer' to condemn the notion of war and to present it as a destructive force that leads to the violation of human rights.

Further to my argument above, Hosseini as a postcolonial author shows great concern with depicting the horrible consequences of military clashes on women and children. The story revolves around Marwan, his childhood, his life before and in the aftermath of the war and his family's search for safety. It traces the shift in his life from a merry child to a helpless refugee. As argued earlier, Marwan's life has been plighted by the experience of war and displacement. Moreover, Hosseini endeavours to portray the negative consequences of war on women. On the night of departure, the father addresses Marwan saying, "Your mother is here tonight, Marwan, with us, on this cold and moonlit beach, among the crying babies and the women worrying in tongues we don't speak" (Hosseini, "Sea Prayer" 33). The father's statement indicates that both women and children have to experience the turmoil of displacement after witnessing the harsh circumstances of war in their country. Reflecting on the suffering of women during war, the father says: 'You have learned that mothers and sisters and classmates can be found in narrow gaps between concrete bricks and exposed beams, little patches of sunlit skin shining in the dark (Hosseini, "Sea Prayer" 28). Hence, Hosseini tries to present both women and children as victims of the war.

In this respect, it becomes essential to discuss the effect of Syria's war on both women and children. For Al-Hawat, women faced "extremely adverse conditions." For him, the media overlooked the suffering of women though war changes the very details of women's life. He indicates that Syria's war increased violence practiced against women, disrupted women's access to health services, and imposed economic burden on them. As stated by a UNICEF report, "every Syrian child has been impacted by the violence, displacement, severed family ties and lack of access to vital services caused by massive physical devastation." Accordingly, it is clear that the war in Syria helped women and children in nothing but creating challenging circumstances that forced them to escape their homeland. Thus, it can be argued that the Hosseini, by means of literary depictions, attempts to show an anti-war stance and to call for establishing peace as military action is a main cause of humanitarian crises.

4.3 Conclusion

As I have argued in this chapter, Hosseini shows a profound interest in the human rights of refugees in his illustrated short story "Sea Prayer". Hosseini tries to defy the European media's attempts to dehumanize refugees in ways that violate their human rights. The author presents his refugee characters as identified human beings who speak for themselves and narrate their own stories of being refugees. In response to the European's media's effort to draw images of refugee women as passive objects in ways that harms their dignity, Hosseini depicts his female refugee characters as functional characters who have central roles to play in running daily activities and in reflecting on the experience of displacement. In addition, through "Sea Prayer", Hosseini tries to raise public awareness to the amount of human rights violation that can be caused by armed forces. The author presents grim images of war and presents it as a destructive force that leads to the violation of human rights. Hosseini stresses in his story the horrendous impact of military action on both children and women. By means of such images, Hosseini questions Europe's moral obligation of protecting refugees' human rights and calls for ending war.

References

Abbasi K, Kiran P, Fiona G (2015) Europe's refugee crisis: an urgent call for moral leadership. The BMJ. https://doi.org/10.1136/bmj.h4833

Adler-Nissen R, Katrine EA, Lene H (2020) Images, emotions, and international politics: the death of Alan Kurdi. Rev Int Stud 46(1):75–95

Al-Hawat S (2016) The Impact of War on Women in Syria. weareiguacu, 24 June 2016. https://medium.com/@weareiguacu/the-impact-of-war-on-women-in-syria-82f3f23bbc79#:~:text=In%20conflict%2C%20women%20have%20limited,support%20efforts%20to%20protect%20them. Accessed 20 Aug 2020

Barkin N (2015) Refugee crisis is suddenly Merkel's biggest challenge. The Japan Times, 1 Sep 2015. https://www.japantimes.co.jp/opinion/2015/09/01/commentary/world-commentary/refugee-crisis-suddenly-merkels-biggest-challenge. Accessed 20 Aug 2022

European Council (2019) Strengthening the EU's external borders. Consilium, 11 Apr 2019. https://www.consilium.europa.eu/en/policies/strengthening-external-borders/. Accessed 24 Aug 2020

Gallien C (2018) Refugee literature: what postcolonial theory has to say. J Postcolon Writing 54(6):721–726. https://doi.org/10.1080/17449855.2018.1555206

Georgiou M, Rafal Z (2019) Media coverage of the "Refugee Crisis": a cross-European perspective. Council of Europe, 2019. https://rm.coe.int/1680706b00. Accessed 20 Oct 2020

Hosseini K (2017) How Khaled Hosseini finds hope in telling refugees' stories. Interview by Carvell Wallace. The Guardian, 2 Sept 2017. https://www.theguardian.com/books/2017/sep/02/how-khaled-hosseini-finds-hope-in-telling-refugees-stories

Hosseini K (2018a) Sea prayer. Penguin, London, p 2018

Hosseini K (2018b) Khaled Hosseini says refugees are essential to America. In: Interview by Seth Meyer. Late Night. YouTube, 18 Sept 2018

Manfred N (2010) Foreword. In: Kaufmann P et al, (eds)Humiliation, degradation, dehumanization: human dignity violated, vol 24, Springer Science & Business Media, pp v–vi

Narula SK (2015) After a drowned Syrian boy's photo goes viral, the UK softens its stance on refugees. In: QUARTZ, 4 Sept 2015. Accessed 16 Aug 2020. https://qz.com/495593/after-a-drowned-syrian-boys-photo-goes-viral-the-uk-softens-its-stance-on-refugees/

Obama B (2013) Remarks by the President in Address to the Nation on Syria. In: The White House, September 2013. https://obamawhitehouse.archives.gov/the-press-office/2013/09/10/remarks-president-address-nation-syria. Accessed 23 Sept 2020

Overton I, Dathan J (2019) Syria in 2020: the deadly legacy of explosive violence and its impact on infrastructure and health. In: Forum on the Arms Trade. 17 December 2019. https://reliefweb.int/report/syrian-arab-republic/syria-2020-deadly-legacy-explosive-violence-and-its-impact. Accessed 7 Sept 2020

Plunkett A (2018) Strife review—Khaled Hosseini, Sea Prayer: refugees, storytelling and the importance of human dignity. In: STRIFE, 3 October, 2018. https://www.strifeblog.org/2018/10/03/strife-review-khaled-hosseini-sea-prayer-refugees-storytelling-and-the-importance-of-human-dignity/. Accessed17 Sept 2020

Said EW (2000) Reflections on exile and other essays. Harvard University Press, Massachusetts

"Sea Prayer" (2017) The Khaled Hosseini Foundation. https://www.unhcr.org/sea-prayer.html. Accessed 17 Aug 2020

Sreekutty S (2019) Contemplation of refugee trauma as an outcome of ethnic cleansing; an analysis of irregulars, Sea Prayer and Upavahana. J Rajasthan Assoc Stud English 15:95–99

"Syrian Cities Damage Atlas- Eight Year Anniversary of the Syrian Civil War: Thematic Assessment of Satellite Identified Damage. (2019) Relief Web, 16 March, 2019.https://reliefweb.int/report/syrian-arab-republic/syrian-cities-damage-atlas-eight-year-anniversary-syrian-civil-war. Accessed 14 Dec 2020

Universal Declaration of Human Rights (1948) UN General Assembly. 2:14–25

Chapter 5
Wartime Rape: The Figures of the 'Birangana' and the 'Comfort Woman'

Sanchali Sarkar

The essay draws in references from Nilima Ibrahim's *Ami Virangana Bolchhi* (1996) (along with various other literature on *Biranganas*) and Yuki Tanaka's *Hidden Horrors: Japanese War Crimes in World War II* (2017) and other testimonies, to highlight the politics behind homogenizing women who were victims of genocidal rape during war, as "brave" in an attempt to systemically overlook the atrocities that went on. Violence is a pervasive factor of the human experience. It can be structural, cultural, and physical. In cases where violence is physical or bodily, the body it violates varies in degree. Treating women's bodies as sites of violence is not a notion that is predominantly familiar only within the realms of peacetime but also within the context of war.[1] It is well known that as a war strategy, sexual violence on women has been habitually utilized in war operations to humiliate, control, and induce terror in the enemy. From wars in the distant past to the recent Russia-Ukraine war, incidents of sexualized violence have been rampant. Identifying wartime sexual violence as a human rights violation has been explored extensively by feminist researchers and human rights activists (Chinkin 2001; Palmer 2009; Mookherjee 2015; Tanaka 2017). In the introduction to her edited book titled, *Sexual Violence in Conflict Zones: From the Ancient World to the Era of Human Rights*, Elizabeth D. Heineman writes,

> Wartime sexual violence shares a great deal with sexual violence in civilian settings, from the context of institutionalized male privilege, through consequences such as the denial of

[1] I am aware that men, and members of marginalized communities are victims of wartime sexual violence as well, but this essay focuses on women.

I briefly presented this paper at the "Combating Conflict-Related Sexual Violence - Comparative Insights on International and National Capacities" workshop at the Department of Law, Freie University, Berlin in May 2023.

S. Sarkar (✉)
University of Passau, Passau, Germany
e-mail: sarkar04@ads.uni-passau.de

S. S. Ali and A. Basak (eds.), *Marginal Narratives and the Question of Human Rights in Asian Pacific Literature*, https://doi.org/10.1007/978-981-97-4544-9_5

reproductive autonomy, to situational detail like the public nature of gang rape… (Heineman 20)

Delineating the effects of violence during war, and sexual violence during war are two separate issues. Violence comprises violent behaviours of different kinds which include torture, murder; but *sexual* violence in every case means violation of one's body. And while murder, acts of torture are considered heinous, sexual violence is not to that extent. The act of rape, as one of the many sexually violent acts that occur during times of conflict often go undocumented as "serious crime", since it is considered as a tool like any other weapon, as a military strategy in war. Even though the general consensus is that, rape and war can be disassociated (stemming from the notion that rape is inevitable and serves certain strategic interests during war), in actuality though, the two are intrinsically linked; a point that Inger Skjelsbæk clearly emphasizes on when she highlights the psychological aspect of trauma that the wartime rape survivors endure; and which is precisely an entry point for this essay.

Patriarchal norms, military discipline and complex group dynamics are significant factors that are considered to have contributed to wartime sexual violence. This particular phenomenon is nothing but an extension of the established practices of cultural and political norms that always already stratify gender and commodify women, alongside regulating women through "a conscious process of intimidation by which all men keep all women in a state of fear" (Brownmiller 73). And this further contributes to the already existing "gender socialization of male entitlement over women's bodies [which] perpetuates the cycle of objectification of and violence against women" (Hagen 31).

Sexual violence is a human rights violation that "happens in a place, and involves violent acts, perpetrators, victims, survivors and impacts ranging from health to a broad array of social consequences" and when these happen during war, it is used as "tool or strategy of war that encompasses the pre-conflict, conflict escalation and post-conflict phases." Sexual violence has been a constant form of abuse and also "when [it is] conflict-related, often has no relation to sexual desire, but is instead linked to power, dominance and abuse of authority" (Gaggioli 53) and "the 'sexual' part of sexual violence (and attending notions of desire and pleasure) and its relation to violence rarely appear as sites of sustained critical theoretical engagement" (Baaz, Stern 28). One of the many horrid manifestations of sexual violence is rape and "history has shown, however, that the reality of wartime rape is unexpectedly complicated, and that the pervasiveness of sexual violence varies across and within conflicts" (Babar 41). To put it in psychiatrist Ruth Seifert's words, "rape is not an aggressive expression of sexuality, but a sexual expression of aggression" and is described as lack of consent to any form of sexual activity; but during conflict, rape is perceived as an overarching strategic policy that has been a recurring occurrence throughout history, further exacerbating gender inequalities; and the normalization of wartime rape has added to the widespread acceptance that it is unavoidable. Therefore, what is crucial to note here is that,

> Although a "conflict zone" may be a war zone, many conflict zones consist of situations where the state lacks a monopoly on violence and where, in that absence, various groups try to assert their own dominance through force against agents of the state (Kamp 56)

In most conflict zones the state's "lack [of] monopoly" functions as contributory factors in acts of sexual violence. The United Nations describes rape as a tactic of war and a threat to international security. The United Nations Security Council has been noted saying,

> ...women and girls are particularly targeted by the use of sexual violence, including as a tactic of war to humiliate, dominate, instill fear in, disperse and/or forcibly relocate civilian members of a community or ethnic group.

Though sexual violence in war zones is recognized as a war crime by the United Nations, the organizers of the Summit hosted by Foreign Secretary William Hague and Special Envoy for the UK High Commissioner for Refugees in 2014 say that to initiate change, more work must be done to sensitize individuals and communities, and this also resonates with what Seifert says when she writes, "when sexual violence is perceived as a political issue, when it is publicly discussed and analyzed, will it be possible to establish the causes and contexts and to envisage strategies to overcome this situation", but if wartime rape is still considered a private incident then it will keep failing to get the attention it needs. During the Bangladeshi war, there were reports that read that the reason why women were kidnapped and then raped was because they were catering to the soldiers' sexual desires, and similar was the purpose behind setting up "comfort stations" for the Japanese army. If one looks into history, it would be difficult to discuss any war where the act of rape cannot be traced, "Crusaders raped women as they marched to Constantinople in 1096 and 1204; German troops raped Belgian women in World War 1; Russian troops raped German women and Japanese troops raped Chinese women in World War II; Pakistani soldiers raped Bangladeshi women in 1971; and American soldiers raped Vietnamese women during the Vietnam war" (Inal 13). But no matter how rampant such acts are, these are mostly overlooked as crime. For instance, in 1992 Kashmiri women were denied justice even after it was evident that they were raped by the Indian troops.[2] The United Nations Commission on Human Rights defines war rape as "a deliberate and strategic decision on the part of combatants to intimidate and destroy the enemy as a whole by raping and enslaving women who are identified as members of the opposition group" (Farwell 34). However, the International Humanitarian Law has only recently accepted wartime rape as a serious crime that needs to be addressed. This "acceptance" has been possible after the Yugoslav wars of succession and the Rwandan genocide brought the theme of sexual violence in war onto the international agenda, and in doing so, accounted for the first convictions of rape as a war crime and crime against humanity. Pascale R. Bos writes,

> Since the 1990s in particular, in the wake of mass rapes in the former Yugoslavia and in Rwanda, great strides have been made in having the scale and severity of rape during wartime acknowledged as a unique and separate crime in war, in defining the harm done by

---

[2] Asia Watch, *The Human Rights Crisis in Kashmir*, 106.

wartime rape in terms of gender violence, and in finding ways to prosecute this act as a war crime, as a form of genocide, or as both. (Bos 83)

The transition from ignorance to acceptance has given the victims and anti-rape advocates the access to "the opportunities and tools to counteract widespread denial of rape" and increase the public voice of victims (Farwell 34). Catherine Mackinnon notes how Serbian men raped their neighbours who were muslim women as a "justification" to build a "Greater Serbia" and this act of "public rape" (which also included filming non-Serbian women getting raped) continued "as ritual degradation of Muslim women" (MacKinnon 17). Women's testimonies of war (including their experiences of rape) have not been documented the way it should have been, and this has also been a result of the state and the international community's lack of attention. Adding to that, the other important aspect that needs to be noted when studying wartime rape is the "gaps" that remain in women's testimonies, as Elizabeth Baer points out, "…as scholars read women's memoirs more extensively not only for what they say, but also for what is coded and for elisions, and gaps we have detected much more sexual violence than had been acknowledged" (Fangrad 2013).

The violence on Bangladeshi women by the Pakistani army have been discussed; what remains somewhat overlooked is how since the 1971 Bangladeshi Liberation war, metaphors like "birangana", "brave soldier", "war heroines" have been socially and culturally naturalized without attending to the "context sensitivity" (Moser 2000) of the subject, and thus limiting the scope of the study in a broader scale. Academics and activists have meticulously addressed the plight of these women. This paper refers to the existing literature, shedding light on the problems that the Biranganas faced and is still facing because of being labeled such. A similar instance is the case of Japanese "comfort women" during the 1930/40 s. Such metaphoric terminologies homogenize women's diverse experiences, and valourize the sexual act and the women experiencing such as solely political and strategically required to consider them as significant contributors of their respective nations' fight for liberation.

Bangladesh's founding prime minister, Sheikh Mujibur Rahman coined the term *Birangana,* which means 'war heroine' or 'brave heroine' or 'brave female soldier' for women who were raped during Bangladesh's Liberation War. It was his way of honouring and recognizing women's "sacrifice" and their contributions during Bangladesh's freedom fight. Initially 'Birangana' was meant to designate all women who helped in the freedom struggle, for instance, the freedom fighters, political activists, and rape survivors who were raped by the Pakistani army. But gradually it started getting associated with only women who were raped during the nine-month Liberation War. The 1971 Bangladeshi Liberation War has been well documented, but the birangana women's roles have hardly been talked about, except for a few seminal works that are integral when studying about the 'biranganas'. Close to 20 0000 women were held in rape camps and raped. Mujibar Rahman's intent to designate wartime rape survivors as "birangana" was to respectfully reintegrate them back into mainstream society. In the newly formed nation, the government made it an effort to make the "Biranganas" feel secured. Nayanika Mookherjee writes about the innumerable programmes that were set up in order to take proper measures. Lakoff and Johnson in their 1988 book, *Metaphors We Live By* argue that a 'metaphor' is the core driver of meaning-making in both language and thought. Human beings make meaning at a fundamental level by taking the source domain (an area of experience in which they have solid understanding) and mapping it into a target domain (an area that is new or less understood). Rahman's use of the metaphor of the brave woman/Birangana could be read as a meaning-remaking of the traditional heroic figure of the woman, by reconfiguring the notion within the post-war context of Bangladesh; and how it shaped "the accepted system of concepts and in turn is influenced by it" (Fiumara 1995). Reading political speeches as merely linguistic texts limit the understanding of the content. Such speeches carry covert ideologies which are naturalised in a country's socio-political discourse. Shakila Nur examines the triadic relationship between the discourse of speech/text, covert ideology and context while examining Mujibur Rahman's speech and focusing on his rhetoric skill. But her analysis also marks a departure point for a reading that could be focused around Rahman's need to metaphorize the wartime rape victims. Even though the term was given to officially recognize the raped women's suffering which in the first place was a form of passive sacrifice, or it would not be wrong to say a forced one, the name "Birangana" started getting associated with the word "barangana", which means 'sex worker'. The phonetic proximity of the two terms is all too obvious to go unnoticed. While the nation categorically designated the women a stately "honour", the ground reality of carrying the responsibility of such an "honour" was often ridiculed since most of the people failed to recognize the link between war-time rape and honour. Perhaps, the point of contention was, on one hand the inability to accept women as indispensible during war (albeit and even if as commodities) which is supposed to be a hegemonically masculine territory at its core; and on the other hand, refusal to accept raped women of war as "honourable". Such receptions were not mere outcomes of the war but a continuation and reflection of how women were/are perceived even during peacetime in society. When looking at narratives of conflicts from a gendered perspective, gender emerges as a power dynamic: men are treated as valiant fighters and women as victims. The innumerable women who were raped during the Liberation war were indeed victims as they were forced to function as objects of rape, one of the commonest and strategic wartime machineries. Women and girls from the ages of eight to seventy five were sexually assaulted, then murdered or kidnapped from their families, public places by the military for sexual slavery to officers and soldiers for the duration of the war. These are women whose bodies were sexually violated as part of a standardised operating system during conflict, bodies that eventually became the conquered subject through which national boundaries were marked; and to use the metaphor of 'birangana' could be seen as subtly manipulating people. Yet, their sacrifice had a scornful reception beyond Mujibur Rahman's speech. Therefore, it is essential to address the ramifications behind the term Birangana and birangana's plight since.

However, after Rahman's assassination in 1975 there was a change that came about among Bangladeshis as to how to "accept" the "Biranganas", since it became crucial to look at "how these narratives and their historicity came out and lived out depended on a plethora of power dynamics, current events, and political priorities"

(Jahan 2021). In Ibrahim's *Ami Virangana Bolchi* (translated as *A War Heroine: I Speak* by Fayeza S. Hasanat) that traces the untold stories of the women, Meherjan is noted saying,

> I am very much aware and deeply believe that I am a war heroine. My country has given me that acknowledgement, my father and mother have embraced me with open arms, but I could not go back to them because of the terror and violence of my own society. I have understood the essence – that above everything I am a female. I have seen the lusty, cannibalistic nature of man, tolerated his rape and torture for eight long months. Every moment I thought I am a woman but not less! Born as a female, we are given the power to create life and to feed the newborn our milk. That is why I am also the mother of a child. I did not get the affection of a husband, a happy family, but I still stand tall on my two feet with self-respect. (Hasanat 51)

What started out as an empowering stance in support of the Biranganas on part of Mujibur Rahman's government, ended up getting restricted eventually without any follow-up whatsoever. As years passed the Biranganas were forced to bribe in order to get housing. The State Recognition and Rights of Birangana Freedom Fighters: Government Challenges and Way Out project outlines how flawed the bureaucratic system is when it comes to providing government support to the Biranganas. In 2014, women rights activists along with many Birangana women have called for the Birangana to be declared "Muktijoddha" or Freedom Fighters. The reason behind this is, that way the biranganas would benefit both in terms of money and honour. But, since 2015, the government has been unable to list the number of Birnaganas/ Muktijoddhas. During an interview, one of the Biranganas have said, "they said I have to spend money to avail the government's housing facility. They also asked for Tk 1 Lakh (€850 approximately). Otherwise, there is no house for me" (TBS report 2022).

Yasmin Saikia in her 2012 article writes about various Biranganas and how they have lived and made to live their lives. One of them says,

> Who do we blame - the men who committed the violence, or the leaders who legitimized violence as a national duty?

Recently, Toru Hashimoto, Osaka's Mayor remarked that comfort stations or "military brothels" served a needed role in giving relaxation to distressed soldiers:

> *When soldiers are risking their lives by running through storms of bullets, and you want to give these emotionally charged soldiers a rest somewhere, it's clear that you need a comfort women system.*

He added that it was "necessary at the time to maintain discipline in the army" and that the brothels served as a healthy outlet for soldiers in controlling sexual energy. Azra Rashid in her 2014 article delineates the points about eradicating gender neutrality in Genocide studies and refers to Joan Ringelheim's take on gender based violence during the Holocaust. The numerous accounts of gender-based violence during the Holocaust that are now being made visible, foreground the discrepancies that women faced and the gender dynamics the existed before the Holocaust. This is a point that resonates within the context of Bangladesh and Japan as well. The society laid the most importance to a woman’s body and if that gets “tainted” she is left with nothing but dishonour. Metaphorising their “national duty” further stigmatized them. The dominant post-Holocaust narrative also keeps women’s voices marginalized;

> Gender-specific experiences are overlooked [...] stories told seem to erase or obscure women. In the instance of erasure, the fact that the main person in the story is a woman seems irrelevant to the teller. Women’s lives are neutralized into a so-called “human perspective,” which, on examination [,] turns out to be a masculine one. Women are obscured (or mystified) when their perceptions, understanding, or actions are ignored in stories that are clearly about them (for example: rape, forced abortion, prostitution). It is as if stories about women were being used to tell about the men involved. Women are there, but they are in the background. Consequently, we are blinded to the fuller context—why something is happening and to whom. Just as those who write about the Holocaust from a “universal perspective of evil” ignore Jews, those who write from a “universal perspective of man” ignore women. (Ringelheim 1985)

Hashimoto’s statement clearly overlooks the trauma and the plight that comfort women still carry with them after all these years.

Brownmiller asserts that in patriarchal societies one of the mediums through which men exercises their power, “their cannibalistic nature” is sexual violence. For instance, Nitan Pai traces various incidents of hit-and-run rapes that took place during the liberation war, where male family members were physically forced to see their female family members getting raped by soldiers. These acts are not typical of just Bangladesh but also Congo’s War, during which

> ...they take a woman to rape her, they’ll line up the family, they’ll line up other members of the communities to actually witness that. . . . They make them watch. And so, what that means for that particular woman when it’s all over, is that total shame, personally, to have been witnessed by so many people as she’s being violated (Wadende 74).

The desire for power and dominance is integral to hegemonically masculine men, whose purpose is to inflict control over others foregrounding the conventional triadic structure of men, war and violence working its way through the narratives of power; and solidifying a “nuanced picture of how hegemonic masculinity is inseparable from power in its many forms: physical power, including power to attack and protect, sexual power, economic power, political power, intellectual power, and moral power” (Ruzicic 2003) as opposed to what McPhail observes regarding the twentieth century discourse around the act of rape being sexual and that it has nothing to do with violence. The other factor to note within the framework of war is that, “perpetrating violence upon enemy combatants or civilians assists in dehumanising an enemy. Violence assists in ensuring an enemy knows that the perpetrator is the one with the power, the victim is, therefore, the perpetrator’s subordinate” (Campbell 2018) and is a way to break the spirit of the enemies and dilute ethnic populations. Rape, be it during wartime or peacetime, is integrally placed within thin network of power and control.

In December 1937 Nanking, the capital city of Nationalist China fell to the Japanese. Iris Chang in her book *The Rape of Nanking: The Forgotten Holocaust of World War II,* the only narrative non-fiction English book on the massacre, writes about the “public rampage” that was carried out in Nanking even after international interventions, and that it went on for seven whole weeks. To prevent sexual violence and atrocities after the 1937 Nanking Massacre that witnessed 20,000–80,000 women being raped by Japanese troops, Emperor Hirohito in a bid to "save" Japan's image, instructed people to set up *ianjo* or "comfort stations"—officially sanctioned brothels. Women were systematically recruited as "comfort women" to satisfy the sexual appetites of the Japanese troops. The majority of the women were from South Korea, but there were also women from China, Indonesia, Myanmar, the Philippines, Singapore, Taiwan, and Vietnam.

The term "comfort woman" is derived from the Japanese word *ianfu*, combining the Chinese characters meaning "comfort or solace" (*i-an*) with woman (*fu*). It "refers to the legalized system of sexual slavery created and controlled by the Imperial Japanese government between 1932 and 1945", which basically meant that women were forced into prostitution by the state officials. In order to find a solution to the reported rapes by Japanese troops, Japanese Lieutenant-General Okamura Yasuji asked for comfort women to be sent for his soldiers in Shanghai, China. "At a typical comfort station, a soldier paid a fee, obtained a ticket and a condom, and was admitted to a woman's space, which might have been partitioned with sheets" writes Carolyn Berndt. While the men were strictly instructed to use condoms, many men refused to use protection. There is perhaps no need to elaborate on the uselessness of keeping a moral high ground about sex work even though this has divided schools of Feminists all over the world. Sex work must be considered labour just like any other labour, albeit with proper understanding of the circumstances. But when sex work is enforced, for instance, in the case of these "comfort women" it demands introspection which Yuki Tanaka meticulously does in his book. Tanaka also mentions the complicity of the government to keep the endeavour hidden from the international community. Hicks in his book writes about the horror of not just the ideation and execution of such a comfort system but the fact that they got away with their crimes "highlights how the exploitation of women for profit from sexual service continues today" (Hicks 1997).

In a photo story by Julie McCarthy and Cheryl Diaz Mayer, they interview one of the comfort women. She narrates her experience and the trauma of the time—"rape is still rape whether it was done for days, for months or for years. The effect is the same. It destroyed our bodies, our sense of self. We lived in shame for years". The whole plan of setting up comfort stations is recorded to have been the largest case of government-sponsored human trafficking and sexual slavery in modern history. One of the accounts of the plights of the comfort women reads,

> A Korean woman or girl who responded to an ad to work in an office, as a nurse, a restaurant server, or even an entertainer rarely had any idea of what awaited her when she arrived at a military camp in the Pacific War Theater. Upon arrival, these women and girls were introduced to a routine where they were coerced into having multiple sexual encounters daily, even several each hour in some cases. [...] Military doctors and medical workers frequently raped the women during these examinations. The comfort women felt threatened and were forced to perform sexually on a daily basis, even during their menstrual cycle. Their military "johns" could punish them if they left a session unsatisfied. When women resisted having sex, they could be sharply disciplined through various means, including severe beatings. (Hicks 133)

In the case of the wartime rape survivors in Bangladesh and Japan, the terms "birangana" and "comfort women" obscure the gravity of such a crime and homogenize women's diverse experiences, valourize the sexual act and the women enduring it as purely political and strategically required. While the intention behind Rahman labeling Bangladeshi wartime rape survivors "Birangana", and the Japanese officials labeling the about-to-get-raped women *ianfo* remain very different, yet both parties still fall prey to essentializing women, rendering them as individuals who only embody the experience of rape. Romel Bagares has remarked that the term 'comfort women' "hides the untold abuse the victims suffered under the Japanese Imperial Army and denies the victims the dignity they deserve". In her article "Rape as Genocide: 'Born Together' On Children Born of Rape in 1971 War", Shoma A. Chatterji reviews Shabnam Firdousi's moving documentary called *Born Together*. The documentary narrates stories of war babies- babies born off rape. Firdousi features Sudhir, whose mother was a 'Birangana' or a "brave" female soldier. She points out some very pertinent questions,

> Why call a forced victim of rape a 'soldier" at all"? Did she choose to become one or want to become one? She was forced into this life of ignominy and ostracization which also affected her child born of the rape? What is the use of a title that does not take care of the social and financial problems the woman has to face all her life? The title does not mean anything except a living irony of the tragic life she is forced to lead.

Both 'Birangana' and 'Comfort Women' are terms that render these women the identity of a mere "victim" as someone who is "monnolithic, one-dimensional, and ahistorical, denied any opportunity for self-representation" (Henry, Flynn, Powell; 2015). This emphasis on the "necessity" of wartime rape relegates the status of these women as mere wartime functionaries, their bodies as vessels for the enemies to send out messages to the opponents, as a way of exercising their (abuse of) power. The tendency to disassociate wartime rape from the notions of sexual violence carried out in non-conflict zones or in peacetime is problematic because "women's subordinate and unequal status in peacetime renders them predictably at risk for sexual violence in times of war" (Jefferson 153) and hence cannot and should not be studied in isolation. Weaponization of women's bodies do not happen overnight when peacetime changes into a warzone, in reality, women's bodies function as battlegrounds through times of peace and war. In fact, Tanaka's detailed narratives in his book show that the brutal incidents that took place during the war are in actuality manifestations of a broad systemic problem that C Sara Soh studies in her book, *The Comfort Women* and writes about how the Korean women embody "gendered structural violence" in the context of patriarchal colonial capitalism.

Reproductive violence is another feature of war and war-time sexual violence that "has historically received little attention in international criminal law" (Grey 2017). Forced sterilization, forced pregnancy, forced abortion are all products of reproductive violence. In her study on the comfort women, Carolyn Berndt talks of repeated rapes resulting in women's sterility. One of the accounts read,

> After the sterilization operation [...] I was sent to a Japanese military battalion. The "comfort station" was inside the army, and altogether 20–30 of us were placed there. [...] I was called

> by a Japanese name, Kukuko.On average; about 50 Japanese soldiers came a day, and about 100 on weekends. When I fainted, the soldier in charge poured water over me. I was also given the morphine shots. In the morning of weekends, shots were given in advance. This was done by force, whether we liked it or not. My upper left arm still has the burn-like scar, and inside is felt something hard, like a stone.

It is documented that the comfort women were given contraceptive pills to take but many women, like Wei Shaolan never took the pills and when got pregnant had to carry the fetus to term because it was too late to abort. These women mentioned a drug that they referred to as "Number 606" (read: antibiotic terramycin), which was given to them if they got pregnant or was infected with STD. Terramycin would often induce abortion after their bodies swelled up. Many women suffered osteoporosis due to their uterus being removed during their stint as a 'comfort woman'.

Mookerjee cites from *Banglar Bani* noting that "abortions were performed and adoptive families in western countries were found for children born off rape. The [government] rehabilitation centre also tried to marry off the women and gave them jobs". Madhurima Sen's 2022 article on Shaukat Osman's fiction titled, *Nekre Aranya or The Forest of Wolves* (1973) talks about how fiction writing with the backdrop of the Liberation war and its aftermath often overlooked the government's selective consideration and care for the Biranganas. Mujibur Rahman's government sanctioned abortions to retain the "purity" of the nation. He had reportedly given a statement saying, "send the children who have no identity of their father abroad…I donot want to keep polluted blood in this country". The babies born as a result of women getting raped by Pakistani soldiers were called "war babies" or "enemy children". While *Nekre Aranya* leaves out vital strands, Shaheen Akhtar's novel, *Talaash* or *The Search* (2004) talks of the unspoken stories of the violation of the woman's body and the burden they carried as the Biranganas of Bangladesh.

The Bangladeshi government provided resources for the abortion. Dr Geoffrey Davis, an Australian abortion specialist who had volunteered his medical services to Bangladesh that time had participated in performing late term abortions on the survivors of war time rape. It has been reported that close to 23,000 abortions were performed at various clinics located in the country's capital Dhaka. The Biranganas who refused to abort would be ostracised by their family and made to leave their houses. With the help of Mother Teresa and her colleagues at Missionaries of Charity, many war babies after being born were sent to countries in the West, especially Canada to be given up for adoption. Canada also happened to be one of the first countries to adopt these babies. Fifteen war babies were sent to Canada on the 19th of July, 1972 and this initiated a positive message concerning interracial adoption. But what posited as a problem was that these war babies were ready to be raised Christians, and that garnered a lot of hostility back in Bangladesh.

This need to link wartime rape to women's honour and as an extension, to that of their family and community is perhaps what mischaracterizes wartime rape as a grave issue. Being called Biranganas have stigmatized these women even more and their rightful demand to be categorized as "Muktijoddhas" or Freedom Fighters shows how precarious their situation has been all this while. Freedom fighters evoke a sense of honour, respect while Biranganas, sadly, evoke a sense of pity as well as scorn for its phonetic closeness with "barangana". The society's lack of sensitization has a lot to do with how Biranganas have been treated since the Liberation war. They have never received the same honour and governmental benefits (3000 taka/month to 150,000 men who fought during the war) like the freedom fighters. Since 2014 their fight to be recognized as Muktijodhha was triggered when two women's rights organizations—Alumni Association of Saleha Isahak Girls High School and the Bangladesh National Women Lawyers Association started a petition which made Bangladesh's High Court to question the country's government about that stance regarding the matter, the reason for their reluctance to designate the Biranganas (who are by now very old, and many live in extreme poverty) as Muktijoddhas. So far, the government has listed only 448 Biranaganas. Their demand to be given proper respect and dignity is something they are still fighting for. As for the "Comfort Women" survivors, in 1991, Kim-Hak Soon became the first comfort woman to speak out about her experience. This was followed by many more "comfort women" survivors coming forward to narrate their traumatic experiences. And it was only in 1993 that the Chief Cabinet Secretary Yohei Kono of the Japanese government finally acknowledged that the government was closely involved in managing "comfort stations". Before Kono's official statement, the government had repeatedly denied its involvement and instead claimed that women voluntarily worked as 'comfort women'. A joint press conference between the Japanese and South Korean foreign ministers were held in December 2015 in which the Japanese Prime Minister Shinzo Abe apologized without acknowledging the legal responsibility of the government. Shinizo Abe promised to donate around $8.3 million to the South Korean government to set up a foundation that would help the "comfort women" survivors. However, they made it very clear that the donation must not be directly distributed to the survivors because that might seem like legal compensation.

The honour of a community or family is still closely tied to control the sexual activity of women and girls, and this is no different in countries like Bangladesh or Japan, whose government, for the purpose of saving the "dignity" of the wartime rape survivors intact labeled them 'Birangana', or introduced a governmental policy that compelled young girls to get recruited as "Comfort Women" to provide sexual gratification to the military personnel, and it cannot be stressed enough that "combatants the world over know that targeting women and girls both inflicts grave harm on individuals and symbolically assaults the larger community (or ethnic group or nationality) to which the female victims belong" (Jefferson 160). Women are raped during war because the violation of their "safe" status has the effect of shaming them and their communities. The act of homogenizing the experiences of raped women as those who "served" the country during war is probably a way to deflect from acknowledging the issue as not a military strategy but a violation of human rights.

References

Brownmiller S (2013) Against Our Will: Men, Women and Rape. Open Road Media

Campbell R (2013) Emotionally involved: the impact of researching rape. Taylor and Francis
Chang I (2014) The Rape of Nanking: the forgotten holocaust of World War II. Basic Books
Chatterji SA (2018) "Rape as Genocide: 'Born Together' on Children Born of Rape in 1971 War". The Citizen
Chinkin C (1994) Rape and sexual abuse of women in international law
Duscka AR (2003) War rape and political manipulations in survivors. In: Wenona G, de Malathi A, Edith K, Kuluka S, Maja K (eds) Feminists under fire: exchanges across war zones. Between the Lines Press
Fangrad A (2013) Wartime rape and sexual violence: an examination of the perpetrators, motivations, and functions of sexual violence against Jewish women during the holocaust. Author House
Farwell N (2004) War Rape: New conceptualizations and Responses. Sage 19(4):389
Fiumara G (1995) The metaphoric process
Grey R (2017) The ICC's First 'Forced Pregnancy' case in historical perspective. J Int Crim Justice 15(5):2017
Heineman ED (2011) (ed) Sexual violence in conflict zones: from the ancient world to the era of human rights. University of Pennsylvania Press
Henry N (2015) The promise and paradox of justice: rape justice beyond the criminal law". Rape justice: beyond the criminal law. Palgrave Macmillan
Hicks G (1997) The comfort women: Japan's brutal regime of enforced prostitution in the second world war. W.W Norton
Ibrahim N (2017) A war heroine: I speak. translated by Fayeza Hasanat. Bangla Academy
Inal T (2013) Looting and rape in wartime: law and change in international relations. University of Pennsylvania Press
Jefferson LR (2004) In war as in peace: sexual violence and women's status. World Report
Lakoff G, Mark J (1980) Metaphors We Live By
Mackinnon C (1994) Turning rape into pornography: postmodern genocide. In: Alexandra S (ed) Mass Rape: the war against women in Bosnia–Herzegovina. University of Nebraska Press
Madeline M (1996) By force of arms; rape, war, and military culture
Meger S (2016) Rape loot pillage: the political economy of sexual violence in armed conflict. Oxford University Press
Mookherjee N (2015) The spectral wound: sexual violence, public memories, and Bangladesh War of 1971. Duke University Press
Nur S (2020) The struggle this time is the struggle of our independence: a critical discourse analysis of Bangabandhu Sheikh Mujibur Rahman's Historic 7th March Speech
Palmer A (2009) An evolutionary analysis of gender-based war crimes and the continued tolerance of forced marriage
Ramaj K (2022) The 2015 South Korean–Japanese agreement on 'Comfort Women': a critical analysis. Int Crim Law Rev 22:475
Rashid A (2014) Gender and genocide: a research in creation project. Can J Commun 39:263
Ringelheim J (1985) Women and the holocaust: a reconsideration of research. J Women Culture Soc 10:741
Sara Soh C (2020) The comfort women: sexual violence and postcolonial memory in Korea and Japan. University of Chicago Press
Saikia Y (2012) Women, war and the making of Bangladesh
Seifert R (1994) War and rape: a preliminary analysis. In: Alexandra S (ed) Mass rape: the war against women in Bosnia–Herzegovina. University of Nebraska Press
Sen M (2022) On Being Biranganas: passivity, agency, and wartime rapes in Shaukat Osman's Nekre Aranya. J Int Women's Stud 24(6):11
Skjelsbæk I (2012) The political psychology of war rape: studies from Bosnia to Herzegovina. Taylor and Francis
Tanaka Y (2017) Hidden horrors: Japanese War Crimes in World War II. Rowman and Littlefield Publishers
Wadende P (2010) Women and war: A Kenyan experience. In: Solimar O (ed) Narrating War and Peace in Africa. University of Rochester Press

Chapter 6
Sovereign Verse: Jacinta Kerketta's Literary Activism in Rights and Welfare

Subhayu Bhattacharjee and Sinor Lama

In the prefatory remarks to her translation of Mahashweta Devi's *Draupadi*, Gayatri Chakravorty Spivak writes that the self-fulfilling premise of knowledge regarding the objects of critical discourse colours Western observations on the Other although the text of *Draupadi* is potent enough in showing its blatant inadequacies and thus rendering the character of Dopdi Mejhen as neither completely understandable nor 'translatable' (Spivak 381). Translation, in critical discourse, therefore transcends the literal definition of the term as change of diction or language and encapsulates the idea of discursive readjustment as well. Jacinta Kerketta's poems highlight the politics of 'translation' adopted by the modern welfare state in postcolonial India vis-à-vis the plight of Adivasis. While constitutional guarantees and safeguards constitute the benevolently sovereign nature of the postcolonial state, the complexities involved in the execution of these guarantees renders them fallible in co-opting the demands and rights of the Adivasi in the narrative of national progress and other statist goals and objectives. On the other hand, Kerketta's poems serve to offer a literary resistance to the complaisant presumptions of politico-legal discourse and create unprecedented fissures in concepts that are held to be self-explanatory and integral features of the modern welfare state. Since legal discourse, by its very nature, rests on clarity of definition and is premised on the supposedly wholesome articulation of symbolic discourse, the contradictions that existing definitions and conceptual forms engender end up questioning the self-presumed sovereignty of existing legal authority which

---

An earlier theme related to this paper had been reviewed in *Contemporary Voice of Dalit (SAGE)* and had been authored by the same authors of the chapter and this indication is in conformity with SAGE guidelines and the copyright being vested with the author(s). Here what is presented is a more revised and thorough version of the subject.

S. Bhattacharjee (✉)
Department of English, Mirik College, Darjeeling, Mirik, India
e-mail: subhayubhattacharjee007@gmail.com

S. Lama
Department of Geography, Mirik College, Darjeeling, Mirik, India

S. S. Ali and A. Basak (eds.), *Marginal Narratives and the Question of Human Rights in Asian Pacific Literature*, https://doi.org/10.1007/978-981-97-4544-9_6

has the wherewithal to adjust and amend the laws. The fractures which thereby arise on the hitherto unblemished terrain of sovereign authority is tantamount to a form of 'violence' that reveals the true nature of sovereignty as lying in the governed as it forces a change in the existing legal narrative (Guzman 52).

The resistance offered to the easy translatability of Adivasi plight by the linguistic adeptness of Kerketta's poetry renders its nature as an exercise in linguistic or literary activism intact. Just as Spivak considers the character of Senanayak in *Draupadi* with its politico-legal investures and intellectual preoccupations as much more significant from the perspective of his role as the native informant and knowledge-retriever, Kerketta's poetry also addresses the reader strictly in terms of his complicity in existing forms of appropriative practices and kinds of translation. However, this never takes the form of blatant admonition or reproach but emerges as a function served by the meticulous formative structure of the poems. The liminal space of the plight of the Adivasi that resists its compartmentalized reading and/or interpretation is synchronized with the liminality of language that constantly frustrates all attempts to read the poems as either thoroughly symbolic or too literal and accessible from the point of view of semantics. Although this does not mean that the poems transform into abstractions and that the rationale for such linguistic twists and turns is to be located in its conformity with the thematic aspect of non-translatability, the specific mode of reading that the poems call for attempt to serve as a lesson in readership for the participant-reader thereby reversing the hierarchy between the metropolitan expert and the passive Adivasi individual.

In terms of the issue of human rights as a persistent theme of the poems, though they deal categorically with the infringement of tribal rights, their corresponding solutions seem to be missing in the reparative politics of the state as newer forms of surveillance and control emerge as the residual component of the practical enforcement of welfare measures and pronouncements embedded in the symbolic discourse of legal treatises. In consonance with the theory of the 'Event' as advanced by the French Marxist thinker, Alain Badiou, the radical intervention in these normative modes of rupture and reparation lies in the political praxis of actions beyond the framework of the state (Kapila 40). In this respect the poetry of Jacinta Kerketta emerges as the meaningful 'Event' which enables a radical difference from the normative modes of resistance to the encroachment of rights that conceptualizes justice as the provision offered by the state itself. The normative character of such articulations stems from their foreshadowing of the individual or even collective agency of the oppressed in redressing existing infringements and they subsequently reveal their inextricable dependence on statist sovereignty even during the process of articulation of deprivation and exploitation. Kerketta's poems also affirm Badiou's understanding that the nature of the event is neither quotidian nor historical (Kapila 42). While dealing with the historical experiences of Adivasi individuals in their relationship with the state and its agents, the poems reconfigure such relationships to create new modes of engagement thereby differentiating it from all prevailing modes of reparative politics.

6.1 Poetic Resistance to Sovereign Nature of Rights and Safeguards

Born in an Adivasi Oraon community in the West Singbhum district of Jharkhand, Jacinta Kerketta had been witness to injustices of various kinds both inside the family and amongst her community since childhood. Being fluent in three languages- Hindi, English and Santali and possessing the ability to comprehend Ho, Mundari, Kerketta has established herself as a writer of renown in the vernacular dialect in recent times. She is the author of two bi-lingual collection of poems, namely, *Angor* published from Adivani, Kolkata and *Jadon Ki Zameen* published from Bharatiya Jnanpith, New Delhi. Her poems have also been translated into German by Draupadi Verlag.

While Kerketta's poetry is exclusively influenced by the personal experiences over a range of issues, they cease to be merely reflective in nature and scope but emerge as potent sites for transformations of existing socio-political exigencies. In her poem, 'O City!', the description of the act of fleeing the village in the event of modernization and urbanization deploys the possessive pronoun with respect to the soil in order to represent a somewhat autochthonous relationship ('Their soil'). However, a closer look reveals its creation of an 'in-between' space of meaning and identification. While politico-legal discourse defines the existence of common lands and public spaces through the lens of the equality of access (as enshrined in Articles 15 and 16 of the Constitution of India), the specific conditions of tribal lands and their historic expropriation finds in the discourse of equality an inherent bias in favour of those who are better positioned to exploit legal articulations in their favour. On the other hand the negation of the status of the soil as public ground as defined in sovereign terms of legal discourse does not imply a reference to private property as is usually implied, again, in sovereign forms of identification and classification from the perspective of the public/private binaries. The possessive claim over the land does not even mention the word, 'land', and instead uses a signifier ('soil') that is dovetailed with emotional as well as possessive investment. In other words, it transcends the role of private property as accumulative capital and assigns to it the status of personal investment that ceases to be capitalized.

The inherent co-existence of the thanatic and erotic instincts, as Freud's observations on the fable of the hedgehogs, record (Kapila 1) finds its poetic manifestation in Kerketta's poem. The creation of the novel definition of the 'private' necessitates the negation of the sovereign classificatory parameters. The critique of the benevolent standard of measuring accessibility as pivotal to the welfare functions of the state is also significant because it exudes a rationale for an emergent critique of the politics of representation which foregrounds democratic welfare. As Spivak writes, the German equivalent of *Veretrung* defines it as "stepping in someone's place...to tread in someone's shoes" and goes on to define political representation as "speaking for" the disenfranchised thereby thwarting the assertion of their presence in critique (Spivak 108). Kerketta goes on to enquire whether the winds of 'so-called progress' drift equally over the city and the village. The description of progress in such fashion blatantly exposes its dubious role in the narrator's worldview. However, the fact that after such a symbolic interplay of words and concepts, the poem tends to hark back to direct and obvious modes of articulation without symbolic adornments or tacit deconstructive ploys needs to be accounted for in terms of a symmetry between the thematic insistence on resistance to appropriation and its aesthetic counterpart. Like Spivak's imbrications of the urban reader in his complicity with the contentious politics of information-retrieval, the reader is introduced here to the critique of essentialist modes of reading and categorization. The vacillation between more symbolic and more literal modes of articulation frustrates the reader's attempts to 'represent' the poetry of Kerketta—an aspect of elitist readership that mimics governmental strategies of representation. Kerketta's refusal to veil her critique of progress in metaphors or symbolism is a deliberate exercise in literary activism.

In the poem, 'A Madua Sprout on the Grave', the narrator describes the plight of a family driven to despair and suicide owing to the loss of the sole bread-winner. The 'madua' seed which the narrator describes as sprouting from the grave of the husband, Suguna, is shown to be 'soaked in the life-giving dew' in order to sprout. While narratives of tribal existence colour the perception of nature as existing in proximity to the life of the tribal dweller, the fact that the birth of the plant uses the very resource that death turns the mortal being into de-familiarizes such narratives while retaining the complementary existence of the erotic/thanatic concepts. By sprouting from the soil to which Suguna has returned, the seed also assumes the role of the parasite which thrives on the life of the human Other thereby confounding the narrative of natural co-existence as mere symbiosis. The 'madua', also known in popular parlance in India as 'ragi'(finger millet), is a major food crop in many parts of the country. Where its role as the life-giver is affirmed across the nation, the particular situation that the poem describes confronts this national imaginary and holds up the difference in spatial imaginaries, and therefore, refuses to be assimilated in the unequal fabric of the 'national'.

The American critic, J. Hilis Miller, speaks about the role of the parasite as reflective of the unconsidered and unprecedented 'presence' that continues to threaten the wholesome and integral presence of the host while not being visibly antagonistic or adversarial to it (Miller 442). The role of the 'madua' in the poem tends to align itself with the creative role of the parasite in bringing into effect a new conception of co-existence while (in a reversal of Miller's proposition) reclaiming its annihilating façade—the death-causing aspect of its existence.

The desperation leading to suicide of Suguna's wife and children uncannily aligns with the non-dualistic nature of existence of the 'madua'. While bringing about the death and destruction of the family, the explosive potential of the suicide also lies in drawing the attention of sovereign governmental gaze that had hitherto been oblivious of the space peopled by the likes of Suguna. While this forces the state to re-consider its role as the benevolent protector and hence momentarily finds in the death the creative impulse of bringing to light a hitherto neglected domain of relationships, the deepening of surveillance mechanisms and intrusion of the sovereign gaze into the private sphere are its only consequences. The tragic nature of such experiences that attempt to enforce a considerate relationship where it does not exist lies in the vanity of statist welfare at least in its implementation. Shruti Kaplia attempts to locate in her recently published work the creative and subversive instances of the politics of death vis-à-vis some of the principal political thinkers during the Indian freedom struggle across the political spectrum (Kapila 4). Perhaps, Kerketta's poems, when read alongside the same, will serve as a delineation of the vain results of such thanatic modes of engagement that threatens to question the unanimous assumption of the glory of individual sacrifice. As a complementary elucidation of Spivak's response to the uncritical nature of Western discourses of resistance that have in mind 'the subject of the West' (Spivak 24), Kerketta implicitly offers a counter-perspective to Kapila's work on the principal founding fathers of national independence.

The complicated domain of discourses centering on life and death continues to be highlighted in the poem, 'Six By-Lanes of Deceit'. Referring to the activities of various youth clubs formed in Saranda amongst the tribal youth community by multinational corporations who use football as atool to distract the youth from focusing on concrete issues of survival and existence, the narrator writes that the event of birth of every youth in Saranda is immediately accompanied by his induction into some youth club or another. The routine nature of these simultaneous occurrences hint at their ideological stature. The moment of birth is therefore also accompanied by the occurrence of death—the killing of the potential for raising questions and awareness about survival and the problems and issues of everyday existence which could be bolstered through proper education. As a distorted mirror-image of the earlier example of the creative impulse harboured by explicitly thanatic representative modes, this juncture of the poem tends to emphasize the inherently depraved conditions of birth as characteristic of Sananda. While psychoanalytical treatises emphasize the already existing repressions surrounding the act of being born into civilization, the specific conditions of *birthing* in Saranda embody another level of repressive tactics which cannot be easily comprehended through any universal reference point or example. Closely resembling Marcuse's theory of 'surplus repression' (Marcuse 35), it strives to posit the effect of an apparently benign act on a potentially ripe yet immature consciousness. The football 'that is given in each hand' emerges as the double agent of repression in an already contentious moment of birth. The critic of 'progress' in unabashed language re-emerges in the subsequent lines when the differences in the positions of those who travel on newly built six-lane roads and those who labour away on 'asphalt and concrete' are starkly highlighted. While infrastructural developments are held to be fundamental to the development of the 'nation', the alienation that it perpetrates locates the abstract metaphor in concrete yardsticks of difference. While the nation represents the 'absolute space' of appropriation and utilization, the associations with the space are only relatively defined in accordance with socio-cultural and economic positions (Harvey 6–9). Where the roads and lanes represent the case of communication and conveyance for those who are not the denizens of Saranda but who rely on its resources (human and material) and their 'use-value', the inhabitants of Saranda associate these marvels of modernity with alienating objects which further removes them from the privilege of accessing the equally accessible space in sovereign discourse. Therefore the articulation of the ideas and corresponding metaphors of progress in the metropolitan centres of the liberal nation-state are disseminated differently and have differing resonances across various parts of the nation-state even at the moment of their articulation (Bhabha 293).

The metaphor of the road is also potent in its critique of a theory of modernism as 'motion and dissonance' (Kaliney 19). While the linkages across local and global spaces symbolize mobility, the lack of contemplation in a climate of obsession with utilitarian mobility gives birth to its corresponding anxiety. In the narrator's understanding, this is further complicated by the opposing standards of mobility itself that modernization brings forth—namely, the seamless movement forward on concrete roads and the displacement of populations and their subsequent relegation to the toiling space of the 'asphalt and concrete'. Owing to the differing ramifications of modernization itself, the need for a contemplative critique is more 'visible' and unconcealed in nature in the case of tribal existence than in the case of urban anxieties and apprehensions. Despite such anxieties, the linguistic potency of the poem attempts to uncover the concealment of repressive mechanisms by de-familiarizing he terrain of the concrete and familiar such as the dichotomies of birth and death. In other words, the poetic activism of Kerketta lies in the appropriation of the status of the un-moulded and the raw ('asphalt and concrete') thrust on the tribal worker in order to build a new politics/poetics of the un-concretized that reveals the concealed contradictions of the concrete. The poetic thrust therefore attempts to 'dialectically overcome' the hierarchical relationship between the client and the worker by enabling a recognition in the former (and his alias in the reader) of the creative potential of the un-moulded and the latter who is perpetually associated with the same—a reciprocal recognition that is prerequisite for any ethical action (Kojeve 184). The novelty of critique accompanied by its creative intervention through the conception of discourses that are not allowed to be revealed in a simplistic dichotomous reading (mimicking the bureaucratic clarity that legal action requires) also present themselves in the poems, 'Ears of Paddy Tied Bound By the Dams' and 'Closed Door'. The discourse on light and darkness in both these poems seem to create binaries between the natural source of light represented by the sun and the artificially engineered light produced by hydroelectric innovations as represented by the shining lights of the town on the other side of the dam in 'Ears of Paddy'. Both poems are characterized by a violent turn of action in their concluding sections—the violence being representative of the aim of destruction of all existing inequities and leveling of the situations of those who explicitly benefit from engineered projects sponsored by the state and those who are perpetually alienated from the same. The second poem entitled, 'Closed Door', however, has the domain of the domestic sphere as its setting. This difference symbolically represents the redundancy of the practice of differentiating between the private and public domains. This is further made explicit by the interpretative confluences between the two poems in terms of the question of reconfiguring the discourse of the public sphere. The direct and unabashed recourse to violent action as the concluding themes in both these poems, if viewed explicitly in terms of the physicality of violence, would tend to occlude the more potent and poignant case of epistemic violence which the narratives actually engender.

Describing the plight of the tribal inhabitants displaced from their lands owing to the construction of the dam, Kerketta highlights the violent encroachment of technological modernity not only on the territories of the Adivasi but also on the terrain of traditional livelihood forms. The concluding section of the poem rests on a proposal of reclamation of both these territories—one of space and the other of modes and forms of livelihood. Although the lights in the homes of the shining towns are a symbol of allurement, it is not a claim over these symbols of privileged existence sponsored by statist agency which guarantees the narrator's perception of what constitutes the good life for her brethren. Instead the primary cause of unease seems to lie in the exposure of the practical consequences of the implementation of a constitutionally guaranteed proposition on 'public property' and the nature of the state as a welfare state in politico-legal discourse. As a 'sovereign, socialist,…democratic' state, the legal guarantee of equal accessibility of public property is constitutionally enshrined and incorporated. Nevertheless, as a representation par excellence of the nature and character of public welfare, the dam seems to question the very nature of such discourses of statist welfare insinuating, vide the unequal character of its utility, the fissures that lie deep within the sovereign legal enshrinement of rights and public welfare.

Heidegger's distinction between the 'World' as the signifier of the disclosure of meaning of all that appears before the thinking-consciousness (*Dasein*) and the 'Earth' as the space unblemished by semiotic occupation but also pregnant with myriad meaningful possibilities (Heidegger 174) is an useful point of reference in this case. In 'Closed Door', the narrator describes the plight of a housewife who feels stifled in the confines of her home marked by ever-amplifying darkness in stark contrast to the bright sunlight of which she is able to catch only a slight glimpse through the door left ajar. As a natural source of light (in contrast with the marvels of modern engineering and technology as in the earlier poem) it presents a possibility of appropriation by statist discourse on both the nature of public and private property. Thus, laying claim over the sun's light as the entity that symbolically represents a genuine example of the equally accessible as opposed to the manipulative 'World' of 'public' property, the narrator associates the natural with the untarnished image of equity. The apparently innocuous statist reflection on 'public' property is therefore represented as the technological maneuver that aims at the systemic negation of any case for promoting equality. Thus, the natural co-existence between the tribal individual and 'nature' is acknowledged here but not in the terms in which a metropolitan imagination of tribal simplicity looks upon it. Rather it is modeled on the idea of re-configuring 'nature' as the un-appropriated realm of meaning and all meaningful possibilities (Heidegger's notion of the 'Earth') in opposition to the 'public/private' delusion of demarcating commodities. The act of breaking open the door to allow sunlight to penetrate the room represents the true nature of the claim made by the poet-narrator through a new model of equal accessibility. The deep-seated suspicion of human agency (the state is also a human(ist) institution in its welfarist guise) and the relegation of truth to the domain of nature also constitutes the critique of human agency and locates the posthumanist impulse of Kerketta's poetry.

In direct contrast to this, the violent destruction of the dam in 'Ears of Paddy' does not necessarily imply the appropriation of resources and possessions that belong to others but represents the negation of the sovereign narrative of equality. By not subscribing to the idea of snatching away private possession (such as the lights of the urban homes) or unlawfully appropriating the gifts bestowed on others through the process of modernization, the narrative resists its being co-opted by the prevailing discourse of modernization or its characterization as the 'illegal' in the lens of sovereign understanding of criminality (theft, pillage or illegal acquisition—the last of these being its own charge against statist measures). Instead it gives birth to a new discourse of rights and a new narrative of survival where the natural order of existence remains untainted by manipulative statist models of property rights. In other words, the radical nature of its articulation lies in its ability to avoid a glib mimicry of the sovereign norm of acquisition and displacement. The lacunae that it opens up in the existing paradigm of the 'legal' and the 'illegal' marks its radical intervention and is pivotal to the nature of epistemic violence it perpetrates vis-à-vis the question of natural rights, public property, and the right to life.

6.2 Conclusion

In conclusion, it could be said that Kerketta's poetry while being circulated across all mainstream channels of reproduction and while being translated globally, carefully presents a self-reflexive stance regarding the politics of appropriation and representation. While one paradigm of global literary representation fails to conjecture the inability of certain discourses to emerge in the 'global', and another precisely conceives this inability as a testimony 'against world literature', Kerketta demonstrates a third stance global representation with a steady and unflinching vigilance aganst simplistic categorization both aesthetically (through visible differences from various models of postcolonial representation) and politically (through the questioning of statist sovereignty). While representation is not an easily avoidable issue amidst the myriad networks of global circulation, Kerketta's narrative seeks to re-present the already existing politically normative forms of representation of Adivasi plight. It does so with its 'event'ful stature of situating its reasoning outside the boundaries of statist discourse of political conflict and resolution. Where Suguna in 'A Madua Sprout on the Grave' through his death, and Phulo in 'Ears of Paddy' are unable to resist the appropriative gaze of statist benevolence despite the initial radical impulse of the politics of death and destruction, Kerketta takes up their cause to discursively unveil the fissures in sovereign narratives, and hence presents them in a potent light. She thus re-presents the radical sphere of political action in her quest for the representation of subaltern struggle through her globally circulated poetry. It is her literary activism and its concomitant 'violence' that urgently needs to be brought out in critical reflections. Perhaps this could serve as a standalone rationale for the global circulation of such critical essays on the same.

References

Bhabha HK (1990) DissemiNation: time, narrative, and the margins of the modern nation. In: Homi KB (ed) Nation and narration. Routledge, London

Guzman L (2014) Benjamin's divine violence: unjustifiable justice. The new centennial review. vol. 14. Michigan State University Press, (Fall 2014), pp 49–64

Harvey D (2004) Space as a Key Word. In: Marx and Philosophy Conference. 29 May, 2004. London, England. Unpublished Conference Paper. Institute of Education, London

Heidegger M (2008) The origin of the work of art". In: David FK (ed) Martin Heidegger: the basic writings. Harper Collins Publishers, New York

Kalliney P (2016) Modernism in a global context. Bloomsbury Academic, London

Kapila S (2021) Violent fraternity: Indian political thought in the global age. Princeton University Press, Princeton

Miller JH (1977) The critic as host. Critical inquiry. vol 3. University of Chicago Press. pp 439–447

Spivak GC (1981) "Draupadi by Mahasveta Devi". critical inquiry, vol 8, Writing and sexual difference. (Winter, 1981), pp 381–402

Spivak GC (1988) "Can the Subaltern Speak?". Marxism and the interpretation of culture. In: Cary N, Lawrence G (eds) Macmillan, London, pp. 271–313.

Spivak GC (1990) The PostColonial critic: interviews, strategies, dialogues. In: Sarah H (ed). Routledge, New York

Yadav A (2016) The anger of young Adivasis turns to poetry of anguish and hope in a young woman's hands. Scroll.in. June 5, 2016. https://www.google.com/amp/s/amp.scroll.in/article/808591/the-anger-of-adivasis-turns-to-poetry-of-anguish-and-hope-in-a-young-woman-s-hands

Chapter 7
Behind Bars: Systematic Violence and Human Rights in *the Plague upon Us*

Sk Sagir Ali

Emerging from the tumultuous milieu of 1990s Kashmir, Shabir Ahmad Mir's novel, *The Plague Upon Us* (2020), inaugurates its narrative with a distorted mathematical formulation of revolution. This is epitomized by the confrontation between enraged masses and khaki-clad forces seeking to quell dissent with bullets. Situated within the backdrop of Kashmir's bloodshed and strife, Mir's debut work, acknowledged on the shortlist of the JCB Prize and published by Hachette India, adeptly encapsulates the pervasive suffering and melancholy inherent in life within the Kashmir Valley. Against the contemporary backdrop, the narrative unfolds the chronicle of a blind pandemic enveloping the protagonist Oubaid's homeland. Through the juxtaposition of the narratives of Oubaid's four childhood friends, all inhabitants of the beleaguered region, the novel evokes the poignant longing for peace, shedding light on the dire circumstances prevailing in Kashmir. Traversing the terrain of treachery, militancy, massacres, loss, and friendship, the narrative intricately follows the lives of Oubaid, Sabia, Tufail, and Muzzafar.

The study delves into the relentless cycle of human rights violations and the valley's political objectives, intertwined with ruthless insurgency, violence, and militarization in Kashmir. Addressing staged recognition failures, the paper navigates military strikes, informers, and the army's impact on slippery human rights along the valley. Moreover, it elucidates how surviving tropes of human rights abuse pose a perilous confrontation with the past, accentuating fractured relationships in a violent and conflict-stricken land. As articulated by Pramod K. Nayar, this analysis aligns with "literary texts where the human subject's social ontology is eroded, implicitly demonstrating how the subject can only develop and grow in conditions that sustain life." (2016, xiii).

Shabir Ahmad Mir follows Oubaid as he witnesses violence and insurrection tearing through the streets of Kashmir, his home. He is confronted with the tales of

S. S. Ali (✉)
Department of English, Midnapore College, Midnapore, West Bengal, India
e-mail: skali661@gmail.com

S. S. Ali and A. Basak (eds.), *Marginal Narratives and the Question of Human Rights in Asian Pacific Literature*, https://doi.org/10.1007/978-981-97-4544-9_7

four boyhood friends from his past: a young man embroiled in war, the daughter of a social climber, the son of a landlord, and a militant. The unfolding narratives vary as they surface, uncovering a poignant reality. Oubaid confronts his historical backdrop in this chronicle of fractured connections within a tumultuous and conflict-laden region, guided by a resonating voice within his memories. Oubaid originates from a lineage of shepherds, and Mir adeptly portrays and examines the societal schism that permeates Oubaid's existence. Comprising the novel's narrative are four stories, each centered around the lives of four pivotal characters. Oubaid becomes ensnared in a complex tapestry woven by ties of kinship, familial bonds, interpersonal relationships, and an unending struggle. Journalist Iftikhar Wani and his son Muzzafar pay a visit to Oubaid's house following the announcement of his father's demise, a consequence of tending to his livestock in the highlands.

Muzzafar, progeny of the journalist Iftikhar Wani, assumes a pivotal role in the narrative, serving as the pivot for the novel's unfolding storyline. In these tumultuous times, veracity emerges as a potential harbinger of justice or retribution. Oubaid, a youthful denizen of Kashmir, witnesses the ravages of violence and insurgency coursing through the thoroughfares of his homeland, with the lamentable sight of young men wounded by pellets manifesting the grim reality. A compelling inner voice imparts to him an awareness of the individual culpable for introducing this affliction into their lives. Acknowledging this truth compels Oubaid to confront the atrocities inflicted upon those he holds dear. Yet, the persistent voice lingers, compelling Oubaid to reluctantly delve into his own history. Consequently, four resonant narratives, recounted by erstwhile childhood companions from the Kashmir Valley, unfold in his mind, shedding light on a collective tale echoing through time.

Albert Camus's *The Plague* allegorically portrayed the ominous grip of the totalitarian regime during the era of the Third Reich, using a cholera outbreak to underscore the corrupting influence on individuals' minds. In the inaugural chapter of *The Plague Upon Us*, Mir adeptly employs the symbolic hues of red and black to encapsulate the prevailing mood among Kashmiris. Black signifies the pervasive melancholy, unspeakable horrors, the burden of trauma, the collective unease in an environment fraught with instability, and a darkness that envelops everyone in the abyss of uncertainty about the future, with this obsidian hue following the trail of red in a dance of helplessness.

Penned amidst the civil unrest and widespread curfew of 2016, the novel's inception traces back to Mir's exploration of the Greek myth of Tiresias, ultimately metamorphosing into the author's profound engagement with the brutal contemporary history of Kashmir, all the while accentuating the resilience of the ordinary populace. It maintains the issue of collective truth raised by the false narrative perpetuated by the defense in Kashmir. It offers a powerful vision of collective pain and its capacity for testifying. Aziz Pohl and his son Oubaid are introduced in the first story. Since everything took a terrible turn and he lost all of his friends, Oubaid has been plagued by a voice in his head that is unrelenting. Aziz Pohl was a menial shepherd who enjoyed taking his herd of sheep into the highlands. Before his father's lifeless body is brought down from the mountains one day, everything was going according to plan for Oubaid. The deceased had his teeth smashed, nails pulled out, and burns from cigarettes all over his body.

Local journalist Iftikhar Wani proves that a fake encounter resulted in the death of Oubaid's father. In an attempt to probe, he is quickly apprehended, subjected to torture, and ultimately shot. Iftikhar's son Muzzafar meets Ashfaq, an enthusiastic teacher, and becomes friends with Oubaid upon enrolling into Ashfaq's institution. One day, when word spreads about the rape of two Kashmiri girls, protesters storm the building, and Asfaq is also killed. Afterwards, Muzzaffar joins the armed movement with the organization Tanzeem-e-Islami. Later on, he emerges as a key figure and becomes increasingly significant. Major Gurpal, the army's chief strategist, calls Oubaid since he is Muzzafar's close friend. The Major is rarely left in the dark about anything. He has close allies who can keep him informed about current events. He has a lot invested in both fronts: his sources among the natives and his weapons. People work with him willingly or are coerced into it without their consent. The Major is a vicious murderer and rapist. He effectively cultivated a climate of fear by punishing anyone who showed sympathy for the Tanzeem. During the torture, Oubaid divulges to the Major everything he knows about Muzzaffar and pledges to help again in the future. Major Gurpal eventually forces him to ally with the outlaw Brotherhood. To destroy the Tanzeem, a group of former militants called the Brotherhood (modern-day Ikhwan) is founded. They are incredibly powerful since they follow no laws and can do anything to anybody. Oubaid confesses to his militant friend Muzaffar that his only goal in life is to persevere by whatever means necessary. He says, "I was trying to save myself. To survive. That is all I have been doing since I was born—trying to survive. I never wanted anything else." (Mir 2020, 159) In *The Plague Upon Us*, survival is a topic that comes up early as Mir tries to suggest that, at its most fundamental level, survival is a person's primary impulse.

As "the truth is perhaps the only justice we can have; the only vengeance we can wreak," (Mir 2020, 126) Mir masterfully explores the forbidden zones of human desire in post-1990s Kashmir that is frequently tainted by polarization. We witness informants and accomplices monitoring the developments throughout the novel covertly. While women are denigrated, dishonest guys like Altaf Firdousi trick his people into joining forces with Major Gurpal Singh and establishing a new political party. He determines that "if he could no longer sell heartbreak, then he would sell patriotism" (Mir 2020, 73). The dehumanization of actors and the acted upon comes out in nude reality in the torture chamber of TALK1, "the cesspool into which all the surrounding camps dumped their sewage of detainees" (Mir 2020, 71). Mir does not, however, categorize these individuals into tidy groups. Always sly and swearing, Russian literature is Major Gurpal Singh's passion: "I wish we could fight our wars like they did in the old times. Fight during the day and sleeping peacefully at night.... You could even drink with your enemies once you were done with the killing. There is nothing of that now.... No honour.... It's a disgrace..." (Mir 2020, 120). Conversely, young Muzaffar discovers the reality about terrorists in Ashfaq's home:

> Contrary to his expectations, they did not talk about strategies, ambushes, attacks and escapades, but joked and quipped about ordinary things, like a recent cricket match between the arch-rivals in the subcontinent, their old maths teacher of whom they were still afraid,

> how they craved for a decent bath while hiding somewhere in the mountains or missed a hot cup of nun-chai on cold mornings. (Mir 2020, 141)

The well-known tales of torture, army kidnappings, raped youngsters running to join rebels, rape scenes, boiling anger, chattering voices, and conversations that make it hard to accept the direct relationship between informers and security personnel is the crux of the novel. The author confirms every preconceived notion that the public may have regarding Kashmir. Here, all suffering is considered true—each one's suffering is unique. The army major suffers due to his commitment to the false narrative of his state, which he is using to further his investment in shredding ethics and other such concepts. To understand how the horrific violations of human rights are remembered at the individual and collective levels as well as how these memories intersect to produce a monolithic truth about the post-1990s Kashmiri psyche, it is important to understand the events of the midnight raids of AFSPA,[1] wails, sobs, azaadi, resistance, guerrilla praxis of the Tanzeem, struggle for *azaadi*, and *mukhbir* or a supporter of militants. The symbolic events and episodes of *The Plague Upon Us* document the state's violation of human rights and the tale of misguided youths from a relatively broader perspective in Kashmir. Major Gurpal, in the novel, serves as a symbol of institutionalized violence within the military and the government apparatus. The absence of the concept of Zoe[2] becomes starkly evident in the treatment of Kashmiris, where arbitrary arrests, torture, and the ruthless suppression of dissent result in a dehumanized state, rendering these individuals unrecognizable as entities possessing intrinsic humanity. Consequently, this dehumanizing process effectively precludes the cultivation of empathy from observers. In so doing, Gurpal's tropes of strategic violence designed to immobilize and paralyze Kashmiri civilians unsettles the mainstream political narratives about Kashmir and reorients the readers' ideas about what this violence means to Kashmiris. Major Gurpal, who considers Kashmiri civilians as "strangers, foreigners", and "occupiers", asked Muzzafar "to be his ears" (Mir 2020, 45) and to disintegrate the Tanzeem. The army had taken Oubaid prisoner at the interrogation centre, or TALK-1. TALK-1 decided what to do with the prisoners after the various army camps had finished questioning the people they had taken in for preliminary interrogations. They could have been left to remain in hiding, given to the police to be arrested and put on trial, subjected to more questioning, or even made to vanish forever. Mir argued that only bodies—some dead, others barely alive—returned from TALK-1, not men: "Stripped down to the most primeval instincts of man—savagery and survival—TALK-1 was a space–time singularity in the fabric of the cosmos where the laws and lusts that governed men fell apart or morphed into putrefying horrors" (Mir 2020, 71). Gurpal Singh was Hamid's only hope; he had been elevated to Major and was now in charge of making TALK-1 a lethal and efficient counter-militancy nerve centre. Though he was cautious not to overdo it, Hamid had maintained a consistent relationship with Gurpal Singh throughout the years. To Major, the boundary line between "friendship and animosity was a very thin" one (Mir 2020, 71). With its testimonials of Kashmiri victims of state atrocities, *The Plague Upon Us* lucidly captures the tension between the growing sense of national belonging to India and rootedness in India and the young Muslim people's essence of detachment from and visceral anger against the Indian nation-state.

Oubaid, in his final year in college, took up the gun and became a *mujahid*[3] fighter. Soon after wishing to become a *mujahid* but not being accepted by his family, Oubaid becomes an Ikhwani. The laws and desires that kept humanity in check crumbled or turned into rotting horrors at a "space–time singularity" (Mir 2020, 71) in the fabric of the cosmos, reduced to the most basic human drives of "savagery and survival" (Mir 2020, 71). In such an atmosphere, Hamid's almonds, walnuts, apples, and saffron would be worthless, like sobs in a graveyard. The Kashmiri exists or ceases to live here according to the "whim of the state" (Agosin and Molloy 1988, 187). The thanatopolitics of slow violence under the institutionalized politics of death in Kashmir brings out the contemporary forms of dehumanization, thereby questioning the Kashmiri body, the space, and the relationship between the subject and its natural world under different conditions of violence. The long conflict in postcolonial Kashmir emphasizes the biopolitical and necropolitical violence with the numerous forms of horror and hauntings in the landscape of Kashmir with Mir. Furthermore, the Brotherhood posed a dualistic challenge to the Tanzeem as a "tanzeem against the tanzeem" (Mir 2020, 71). Its responsibility was to ensure that the elections—meant to be held to weaken the *tehreek*[4]—took place.

The desire for *azaadi* would be meaningless if people could argue that if they could vote, they had freedom. The Brotherhood ensured that anyone who attempted to criticize the elections would be publicly humiliated by staging a violent demonstration. Mir describes the shift from the fight for *azaadi* to jihad with a rather expressionless visage and a detailed drone:

> Gradually, these new arrivals, the foreigners, took over the Tanzeem. The struggle for azaadi was now a jihad – the holy duty of every Muslim to fight for his brother's faith and his own when it was in danger. Lines began to blur, and identities to clash. As the battlefronts multiplied, it became increasingly difficult to say what all the violence was about. The violence had lost its purpose. Who was to pay the price for this outcome? Why, the people, of course. (Mir 2020, 156)

Mir explains, not passing judgment, by probing deeply and incisively. It was the "mere instinct for survival" (Mir 2020, 156) that man needed in this situation. And everything else—*tehreek*, *azaadi*, resistance, elections—obeyed this impulse without question. Consequently, whether or not they cast ballots, the people of Kashmir saw little value in the elections. Voting would only take place if it meant living to see another day. The only lesson the electorate learned from the elections was that, after the results were declared, they had no more justification to play hide-and-seek with death (Mir 2020, 157). And they now feared the Tanzeem more than any other group because of their survival instinct. The sovereignty of the primal instinct surpassed the sovereignty of the nation-state or even that of political ideology.

Mir presents this conundrum bluntly as he negotiates a settlement in the valley between guilt and fear. He can see past resistance movements and authoritarian regimes as he wades through the unstable circumstances of Kashmir. Mir observes that legal authority and operational guidelines govern the fierce street fights in Srinagar and other places between the "Boys who don't have permission to be angry and men who must do their duty. Boys who throw stones and men who must shoot back" (Mir 2020, 168). Major Gurpal, who loves to read Dostoevsky's *Crime and Punishment*, tells Iftikhar, the journalist:

> See, we are at war here, make no mistake about it. But we are not going to win this war by killing the enemy who has the gun in his hand. No, it is not as simple as that. We are up against something very complex here. Something that pits us against everyone out there – those with guns and also those without. So we need to fight on other fronts as well. The timber trade is a seed that will grow into a weapon which will fight battles for us where we ourselves cannot – and it is those unacknowledged battles that will win us the war. (Mir 2020, 132)

Major Gurpal captures the essence of the entire strategy in a timeless statement to Hamid Puj, "I don't need people out there to like us, I just need them to need us. And I see nothing that can prevent you from benefiting as much as you can from it" (Mir 2020, 61). Mir incisively captures the existential divisions of Kashmir that entail a commitment to ending the cycles of violence and accountability for past and current human rights violations and abuses. His portrayal of the attempt at humanization through pellet guns is remarkable: "Not bullets this time, but pellets. Hundreds of them rushing out of each shotgun in a single burst like hungry vultures who no longer wait for death but peck at whatever they can—arms, thighs, shoulders, chests, cheeks, eyes…" (Mir 2020, 168). Stripping of individual rights results in a meaningless, fragmented show that reveals the cold-blooded, purposeful banality of state violence as a means of control—what Marjorie Agosin and Janice Molloy describe as "[t]he body in pain as property of state" (1987, 181). This kind of violence is unmistakably indicative of "the structural relationships of power [and] domination" symptomatic of government corruption (Bunch 1990, 491). These convincing narratives suggest an alternative to the suffering-centred mode of advocacy based on the corporeality, victimization, and physical pain of sufferers of human rights violations similar to imprisoned animals. The barriers, checkpoints, and mutilated bodies as a result of several sieges, arbitrary closures, and frequent blockades may uphold the trope of the "body in pain" (Scarry 1988, 47). Mir's portrayal of contemporary brutalism is a way of drawing a parallel with a history which consisted of the banalization of violence is the resurgence of nationalism as the recent reconfigurations of identity politics.

The Plague Upon Us delves into the conundrum of using historical ignorance to support political beliefs, as Professor Ashfaq Ahmad Bhat, a popular young assistant professor of history famous for his unconventional teaching at Muzzafar's college, narrates non-controversially. Bhat uses the story of Suyya as a metaphor. Suyya, who lived during the reign of Raja Avantivarman—one of the greatest monarchs of all time, found a solution to the "royal problem" (Mir 2020, 138) of the river Jhelum's frequent flooding by throwing "pots of silver and gold coins from the royal treasury" (Mir 2020, 138) into the Jhelum at the gorge in full view of the people. Suyya announced that the coins might be kept by whoever lost them. En masse, the crowd retrieved the coins by diving into the water, clearing the path of the river of any obstacles like dirt, silt, and rocks. The residents were no longer disturbed by the waters inundating their land since the gorge had been cleared of obstructions, and the Jhelum flowed freely out of the valley. According to the history professor, "engineering" to solve problems is the need of the hour (Mir 2020, 138). The issue of Kashmir with the actual contours of *azaadi* is neatly explained by the professor to his student Muzzafar, who joined Tanzeem. The young professor assists Muzzafar in realizing that Kashmiris are lost at "the crossroads of history" (Mir 2020, 143). Since then, they have been journeying without Moses to lead them, much like the ancient Israelites did after fleeing Egypt. Kashmiris have had to make so many bends and detours throughout their history that they have created their maze. Kashmiris yearn to return to *azaadi*, the place beyond the labyrinth where they truly belong, now that they are in the centre of this maze. Later, during the widespread protests that resulted in the police curfew and widespread police violence on the college premises, Ashfaq Bhat, the young lecturer, was struck in the head by a tear gas shell and died instantly. The event of Azaadi and the subsequent death of the history professor highlight the penetration of human rights language into everyday discourse as it draws attention to its sustained relevance within the contemporary Indian-administered Kashmir.

In the annals of the 1990s, Kashmir found itself immersed in protracted mass demonstrations, echoing with the fervent call for *azaadi*, signifying freedom, resonating across its streets. Following the garnering of widespread acceptance and support from the populace, the Jammu and Kashmir Liberation Front (JKLF) and Hizb-ul-Mujahideen (HM), no longer relegated to the periphery as fringe militant entities, spearheaded an armed guerrilla insurgency against the Indian state within the valley (Bose 2003, 48–50). In a show of defiance against the policies of the government, young Muslim men from Kashmir joined militant groups during this time. As a result, the Indian security forces began to target them, unlawfully arresting them and torturing them regularly in an attempt to stem the rising tide of defiant militancy (Peer 2010, n.p.). The diplomatic markers of Plebiscite Front politics were defined during this period by the collective consciousness of Kashmiri youth, and organizations such as Al-Maqbool, Jamiat-e-Tulba, Islamic Students Organisation, and People's League enabled the staging of relations of care and solidarity under the banner of the Tehreek movement. This evocation of exclusion and precariousness facilitates the Tanzeem organization's new visibility in promoting the political dimensions through chosen tales. A new coalition of opposition groups, the Muslim United Front (MUF), attracted youth attention during the 1987 assembly elections by acquiring political traction. The MUF, based in New Delhi, praised the Indian government as an adversary of Kashmiri autonomy and independence. Later, the *azaadi* demonstrations, marking Black Days on August 15 and January 26, validated the introduction of an official curfew.

The fundamental component of human rights activism, the appeal for solidarity for peace, is sparked by Mir's narratives, which highlight the connection between fear and violence. Mir promotes the value of historical events and fulfilling memories as tools for fostering bonds of solidarity and igniting human rights movements instead of depending solely on a shared sense of "human vulnerability" and a terror of violence (Butler 2006, 42). Redefining the shared "humanism" (Butler 2006, 42) that underpins human rights work is necessary for reframing the Kashmiri subjecthood. The violence, instability, and the perpetuation of precarity surrounding Kashmiri lives by the recent abrogation of Article 370 have been reinforced through innumerable patterns of hatred. The brutal deaths of Oubaid's father, Aziz Pohl, Professor Ashfaq, and other Tanzeem members not only become a way of undermining the status of any young Kashmiris who wage war against the mighty Indian army but also reinforce, in Arjun Appadurai's (2006) words, the superiority, inviolability, and authority of the Indian nation-state. The erasure of individuality, which targets people seen as endangering "the purity of the community," is the most significant facet of agonizing sovereignty in Jammu and Kashmir (Appadurai 2006, 7). Given the unresolved assimilation issues since the Partition, when Maharaja Hari Singh abandoned the Jammu and Kashmir valley on the faultlines that would eventually become the new border between India and Pakistan, Appadurai's remarks make sense. Numerous deaths have resulted from this incomplete process of integration since that time. An insightful observation made by Appadurai is that minorities might serve as a helpful reminder to the majority of the "little gap which lies between their condition as majorities and the horizon of an unsullied national whole, a pure and untainted national ethnos" (Appadurai 2006, 8).

The confluence of violence and resistance engenders a stringent equilibrium, compelling all involved parties to reassess their actions. The establishment of a dynamic balance hinges on the inclusion of all pertinent individuals within the system, with the preservation of human rights and dignity being contingent upon such inclusivity, particularly when they teeter on the brink of collapse. On one front, actors animated by racist ideologies systematically pursue the annihilation or severe disempowerment of the "other". In response, the opposing faction is resolute in utilizing all available means to thwart the aggressor, ensuring their failure or demise. Given that one faction seeks the utter eradication of the other while the latter exacts a considerable toll for the former to realize its objectives, the goals of each side are inherently incompatible. The nation-state, wielding exclusive authority over the use of force, emerges as the principal violator of human rights, surpassing the cumulative strengths of individual, and collective entities within society. To rectify this power imbalance, legal safeguards for civil society organizations, the delineation of legislative and judicial functions from the executive branch of government, and transformations in society's ineffectual moments of barbarity collectively contribute to the restoration of a balanced power structure. Moreover, an exploration of additional sociopolitical theories, such as those advanced by scholars like Michel Foucault or Hannah Arendt, could enrich the understanding of power dynamics within such contexts. Additionally, a nuanced examination of historical precedents and global case studies may offer insights into successful strategies employed to redress power imbalances in similar scenarios.

Notes

1. The Armed Forces (Special Powers) Act (AFSPA) is a controversial piece of legislation in India that grants special powers to the armed forces in designated "disturbed areas" to maintain

public order. Enacted in 1958, initially in the northeastern states of India, and later extended to Jammu and Kashmir and other regions, AFSPA has been criticized for its broad powers, including immunity from prosecution for security forces personnel involved in operations. It has been a subject of debate due to allegations of human rights abuses, including extrajudicial killings, torture, and disappearances. Proponents argue that AFSPA is necessary to combat insurgency and maintain security in conflict-affected areas, while critics contend that it has led to violations of civil liberties and undermined the rule of law. The ongoing debate surrounding AFSPA underscores the complex challenges of balancing security imperatives with human rights concerns in conflict zones.

2. In biopolitical theory, "Zoe" typically refers to the concept introduced by philosopher Giorgio Agamben in his work "Homo Sacer: Sovereign Power and Bare Life." Agamben distinguishes between "Zoe" (ζωή) and "bios" (βίος) to explore the relationship between sovereignty, power, and life. "Zoe" represents bare life, the biological existence shared by all living beings, while "bios" refers to qualified or politically recognized life, encompassing the rights, privileges, and identities granted by society. Agamben argues that modern states exercise sovereign power by differentiating between "Zoe" and "bios," effectively excluding certain individuals or groups from the realm of political life while subjecting them to control and domination. "Zoe" is thus positioned outside the sphere of political recognition and protection, making individuals vulnerable to state violence and exclusion. This distinction between "Zoe" and "bios" serves as a critical lens for analyzing the mechanisms of power and control in contemporary societies, particularly in contexts where certain populations are marginalized, oppressed, or subjected to forms of biopolitical governance.
3. "Mujahid" is an Arabic term meaning "one who engages in jihad," which translates to "struggle" or "striving" in English. In Islamic contexts, a mujahid is often associated with someone who participates in armed struggle or warfare in defense of Islam or against perceived oppression. Historically, the term gained prominence during the Soviet-Afghan War (1979–1989), where Afghan resistance fighters, known as mujahideen, fought against the Soviet Union's occupation of Afghanistan. In contemporary usage, "mujahid" may refer to individuals or groups engaged in armed conflict for various ideological or political reasons, often within the context of Islamist movements or insurgency. It is important to note that the term "mujahid" can have different connotations and interpretations depending on the specific cultural, religious, and geopolitical context in which it is used.
4. "Tehreek" is a term commonly used in Urdu and Persian, meaning "movement" or "revolution." It signifies a collective action or effort aimed at bringing about social, political, or cultural change. In various contexts, "tehreek" can refer to movements for independence, social justice, political reform, or cultural revival. These movements often mobilize individuals or groups to challenge existing power structures, advocate for rights, or promote a particular ideology or cause. The term "tehreek" encapsulates the dynamic and often transformative nature of collective action in pursuit of change.

References

Appadurai A (2006) Fear of small numbers: an essay on the geography of anger. Duke University Press

Agosin M (1987) So we will not forget: literature and human rights in Latin America. trans. Molloy. J Hum Rights Q 10(2):177–192

Butler J (2006) Precarious life: the powers of mourning and violence. Verso

Bunch C (1990) Women's rights as human rights: toward a re-vision of human rights. Hum Rights Q 12(4):486–498

Bose S (2003) Kashmir: roots of conflict, Paths to Peace. Harvard University Press

Mir SA (2020) The plague upon us. Hachette India

Nayar PK (2016) Human rights and literature: writing rights. Palgrave Macmillan
Peer B (2010) forever war. Granta Magazine, 27 Sept 2010, https.granta.com/kashmirs-forever-war/, accessed on 4 Mar 2024
Scarry E (1988) The body in pain: the making and unmaking of the world. Oxford University Press

Part II
Cinematic Echoes: Mnemoculture and the Visual Discourse of Human Rights in Asia

Chapter 8
Frames of Memory: Mnemoculture in Human Rights Films on Cambodia and Vietnam

Farddina Hussain

The words of assurance of a father to his little son that nothing bad would happen in Khaled Hosseini's illustrated book *Sea Prayer,* commemorates the dead Syrian boy whose body was washed ashore in Turkey in 2015. The world woke up to the horrifying image of the three-year-old Alan Kurdi among many others lying by the sea, and the sight had raised ethical questions on human rights and our mapping of the world. One of the poignant responses to our failed responsibilities to protect children and resolve refugee crisis finds expression in the words of the father who looks at his sleeping child remembering home on the eve of their perilous journey in search of safer places. Khaled Hosseini, a diasporic Afghan writer is moved by the incident perhaps due to his own childhood memories of war and how he had to leave Afghanistan for good to live in the United States. This is just one of the many common stories of men, women and children who migrated from war zones like Afghanistan, Myanmar, Vietnam, Cambodia to secured places and in the last decade this had been true of people in Syria and Iraq where they leave their homelands with few amenities consequently escalating the refugee crisis in Europe. There had been many tragic cases of boats being capsized as families tried to escape torture, hunger, death and war traumas to cross over vast water bodies, and these perilous journeys were mostly fatal. Few of these migrants who could successfully reach land carry the memories of home and culture. They cling on to the past as return is never possible, and carry photographs, write memoirs, make films in fear of that feeling of oblivion or amnesia. They attempt to keep these personal memories alive by 'telling' them and very often these memories get commemorated in literature, art, cinema, photographs, museums or memorials. They recall, what Nguyen calls as 'ethical memory' both of one's own as well as of others' stories and experiences in his "Just Memory" (Nyugen, *Memory* 144). The survivors shared experiences for two reasons: to heal and to preserve it for posterity. On the corollary, remembering entails

F. Hussain (✉)
Department of English, Gauhati University, Guwahati, India
e-mail: fardina1ster@gmail.com

S. S. Ali and A. Basak (eds.), *Marginal Narratives and the Question of Human Rights in Asian Pacific Literature*, https://doi.org/10.1007/978-981-97-4544-9_8

imagination and a certain perspective in reliving the past and so it becomes more of a storytelling, a construct although one wants to showcase the accounts of the past following a neutral, natural trajectory. These memories, at times get commodified and is distributed as in the case of cinema. The past is represented, communicated, illustrated, and promoted through the visual tool with its social-cultural-political configurations.

The plural geographical locations and identities of various survivors add multiple perspectives to the telling and construction of the narrative. It reveals how war can be experienced differently by different people and so, the narratives of war remain multifaceted as every teller brings his/her perception and lived-experiences. In their writings the nomenclature, naming a war can be an political issue too like the US-Vietnam war which for the Americans is "Vietnam war, what Vietnamese call the American War, and what historians sometimes call the Second Indochina War (1960–1975)" (Nguyen *Nothing*). Viet Thanh Nguyen elaborates this in one of his books as a tactic of hiding the cruel realities of war:

> To argue over the Vietnam War or the American War is thus to argue over false choices. Each name obscures human losses, financial costs, and capital gains, as well as how the war also blazed through Cambodia and Laos, something both the Vietnamese and the Americans wish neither to acknowledge nor remember. The North Vietnamese sent troops and material through Cambodia and Laos, and the U.S. bombing of these efforts, as well as the civil wars that flared up in both countries, killed approximately four hundred thousand in Laos and also seven hundred thousand in Cambodia during what the journalist William Shawcross sarcastically called the "sideshow" to the war. (Nguyen *Nothing*)

There is a large body of memory narratives of the European experiences of the two world wars in comparison to the South East experiences of civil war and dictatorial regimes in the context of Vietnam, Cambodia and Laos. Instability in any of these countries effect the whole geographical region including Japan and Korea. The long US-Vietnam war and the Khmer Rouge regimes in Cambodia had changed the demography and lives of the people living in these nations. These narratives add a personal attribute to the public memorabilia of the state.

8.1 Human Rights and Cinema

Any expression on Human Rights (HR) based on our understanding of 'being human', always depict how it has been violated in terms of "corporeal unmaking and abuse" (Anker 3–4). These torture narratives show erosion of social ontology and demolition of a human subject as shown in films like *First They Killed My Father* (this film was released worldwide on Netflix in September, 2017) and 1982 film, *Boat People* which is available for viewers online on YouTube. These films depict how subjectivity is denied by regulating the body to gain control over the victim. These are pervasive forms of violence that are built into structures and institutions is what Gultang terms as structural violence in his 1969 path-breaking article "Violence, Peace and Peace Research".

In South East Asian nations like Cambodia and Vietnam, war had led to massive demographic changes where cities and town were evacuated or destroyed by bombs and as a result new camp sites for refugees and the displaced grew in numbers:

> War also only touched a small minority of civilians and women, except in their more common roles as mourners or as workers in the war machine. But the Vietnamese experience of war was total. War took place in the homeland and was inescapable. Civilians endured famine, rape, massacres, bombing, illness, the destruction of their farms and homes, endemic forced relocation into so-called strategic hamlets that were essentially concentration camps, poverty, the deaths of relatives, and becoming internal or external refugees, among other things. Hundreds of thousands of civilians died from these experiences, including many elderly, women, and children. (Nguyen 146).

The ethics of recalling one's past along with the others in the family or community and creating a fellow feeling of shared experiences creates tolerance and empathy. In a similar fashion ethical memory or memory, itself is dynamic and mutable in nature. It can be threatened by its own forgetting trait; it can be deeply political but the narrator is not ready to admit it. Jolie's film based on the autobiography of a survivor of Khmer regime is an instance where memories are constructed as witness to life under dictatorship and are passed on to the next generation and to the world in order to document and save it for posterity.

From *Apocalypse Now* to the sequence of *Rambo,* Hollywood told mostly American stories of heroism and sophisticated weaponry and tactics, although in literature there has been few books that have the Vietnamese perspective as in *Tree of Smoke* (2207) or *A Good Scent from a Strange Mountain* (1993). In *Black Virgin Mountain* Larry Heinemann can only appreciate the brave Vietnamese soldiers retrospectively when he revisits his old battlefields and makes peace with the very soldiers they fought against during the war. Whether it be literary texts or cinema, the act of memory and forgetting plays a crucial role and so the narratives highlight multiple perspectives on the theme of war and its experiences. In addition, the discourse of history and conflict is documented by the state offering their version of the war in museums, for instance Fine Arts Museum of Hanoi and in the war remnants Museum of Saigon.

After the fall of Saigon, the communist government created new economic zones which in reality were camps designed to use human beings as machines or objects (by overlooking the apparent dangers that denied subjectivity) to detect and diffuse landmines in open fields, forests and countryside. Strong men would be dragged from the city roads, markets or alleys into the trucks and taken to the centers where they had to search for landmines and diffuse them continuously putting their lives at risk. Ann Hui director of the Hong Kong based film *Boat People* (1982) depicts the initial years of the Communists' governance and their crimes in Vietnam. The film not only raises HR issues but also projects the structural violence against fellow citizens and the control of foreign reportage. In neighbouring Cambodia similar issues of organized violence during Vietnam war and also during Pol Pot regime against its citizens are mentioned in research reports, memoirs and films. The war spilled over to the northeastern and southern parts of its border where under a secret war strategy of the Americans, bombs were sprayed heavily along the Cambodian-Vietnamese border causing 300,000 deaths and leaving many wounded and homeless (Khamboly 2007). Many Cambodians ran into the jungle to join the communists' fight against Lon Noi (military general) backed by United States of America which instigated a civil war. Once the civil war started the Americans left Cambodia and their embassy. This helped Pol Pot to come to power in 1975. When the Khmer Rouge took over the country, they evacuated cities and towns and used deportees in agricultural fields in the countryside. The Khmer Rouge implemented Maoist and Marxist-Lenin ideologies to transform Cambodia into a classless, non-hierarchical rural society. These programs caused the death of "nearly two million Cambodians during the period of 1975–1979 owing to disease, lack of medicines and medical services, overwork, execution, starvation and torture" (as quoted in Khet 2). Another film *First They Killed My Father* documents these human miseries and deaths of the Cambodians through the lens of a personal story of a survivor.

The civil war in Cambodia ended in 1991 but the memories of atrocities remained. The Khmer Rouge Tribunal was formed between the Royal Government of Cambodia and the United Nations to provide justice to the dead and the survivors. The past conflicts and cases were presented before the Extraordinary Chambers in the Courts of Cambodia (ECCC). As noted by Khet in his thesis, the Cambodian state started the process of "preserving the skulls and bones of the dead to show the world the atrocity" (Khet 5). It was an opportunity for the survivors to confront their painful memories of the past and also bring them to the public. Khamboly too records in his book that "there are around 388 killing sites with 19,744 mass graves, 81 memorials and 196 prisons" as mentioned in Khet's thesis (Khet 4). Although the Khmer Rouge government after sometime was trying to play a role in the peace keeping process and stay in power, these concerns were focused by the next party in power to further political gains and control.

First They Killed My Father is one of the many attempts made by the survivors of the Khmer Rouge regime to add to the collective mnemoculture of Cambodians by revisiting their personal experiences. It is a 2017 Cambodian-American biographical film based on the life of Loung Ung in Khmer language directed by Angelina Jolie. We cannot evade the fact that it has been directed by a rich-white-famous-successful actor of Hollywood, while the cast in the film is hardly known to the world. It is quite a surprise that this film 'even exists' as noted by the Pulitzer award winner critic, Seitz (Seitz *Review*). Jolie adapts Loung Ung's memoir which she picks up randomly during one of her shoots in the country while taking a walk. The writer (Ung) recalls her experiences under the Khmer Rouge regime. Later Ung left Cambodia and migrated to the United States. Jolie and Ung together collaborated to write the script. The narrative framework brings in the perspective of a young Ung to posit the reminiscences as innocent and neutral. It also allows the necessary distance Jolie needed as a director and the cultural load the film carries. Ung is shown as a seven-year-old child trained as a combat soldier by the Organization (Angkar) while her siblings are made to work as labours in the agricultural fields. *Angkar* is the organisation headed by Pol Pot and is also known as 'Brother No. 1' and 'Brother

No. 2' which are the codes for Pol Pot and CPK deputy secretary Gen. Nuon Chea (Kiernan 33).

The plan of Khmer Rouge leaders was "to attack and liberate Phnom Penh, and to evacuate the people out of Phnom Penh, temporarily" (Kiernan 33) and this evacuation plan was decided by Pol Pot (as mentioned at a conference after two years of evacuation) in February 1975. The vision of the regime was of an agricultural rural Cambodia but it was also a strategy to gain total control over the citizens by keeping them on their toes in the country in guarded sites. They first circulated the narrative that the Americans might bomb the cities next. Announcing this made it easier for them to legitimized their act and except a few intellectuals, no one doubted their intentions. Everyone thought their deportation to be temporary. The Pol Pot Organization did not reveal their plan of evacuation to all its members or to the state Information Minister until two days after it had started off. The order took time to travel to different parts of Cambodia and it travelled in many versions; undoubtedly it was chaotic with large numbers of people moving on the streets walking with the hope of returning to their homes soon.

But they soon realized their status as homeless deportees under the control of *Angkar*. They were ordered to work in the fields in the scorching sun and heat of April, the hottest month in Cambodia. The film has close visuals of the children working all day long and having their meagre amount of broth at mealtime. They were constantly monitored; the guards and supervisors move around with guns and threaten them if they try to disagree or relax during work. All the deportees wore a uniform made out of very rough material. Young Loung was taken to a training camp where she was taught to fire AK-47. The medical conditions as the children fell sick were inadequate and they died without medicines or treatment. The elder sister of the survivor in the film meets a similar fate. The film on the communist rule of Vietnam, *Boat People* too depicts the lack of medical facilities and the use of human beings in the fields. In this case, men are used as detectors of landmines and the close shots show their extreme fear and apprehensions of being blown up the next very moment. They have no respite and have to stay after the day's strenuous work, in tiny cylindrical tins without any space for free movement. One of the inmates plans an escape with his friend by bribing an official. But the friend gets killed by the landmine while digging just hours before the D-Day. Although the inmate reached the crowded boat in the dark of the night to escape, all were fired at by government police. The film repeatedly shows the individuals dreaming of and making plans of fleeing the country by sea routes to countries like Australia or the US. The award-winning Australian film, *Mother Fish* showcases a story of two sisters who fled Vietnam. The director Khoa Do is a Vietnamese -Australian who left his country by boat. The term 'boat people' refers to the Vietnamese refugees who fled Vietnam after the fall of the South Vietnamese government in 1975, by boat or ship. The migration and the humanitarian crisis that rose to its height during the period from 1978 to 79 continued for several years following the fall. The boats and ships were crowded and on their long arduous journey, the people mostly suffered from dehydration, starvation and death by drowning.

Hui's film *Boat People* documents the problems, exploitations, starvation and death as children are kept in the so called New Economic Zones; these enclosed zones are far from the city which have small rooms made of tin where hundreds of children are put together without supplying the basic amenities by the Communist Organisation.

The Japanese photo journalist who is also the protagonist of the film discovers a room filled with children, one on top of the other lying and gasping for water and food and are too weak to get up. Nguyen in a research article calls the film as docudrama and presents it as a seminal film to understand and know Vietnam (after the fall of Saigon) and its structural violence and crime against the citizens. It presents several cases showing the lacuna in governance and negligence of HR. This disregard for Human Rights issues and poverty made them dream of other places. These Vietnamese preferred the turbulent sea and uncertainty to staying under the control of dictatorial government officials who were themselves corrupted:

> Hui's film depicted why so many people braved the open seas—where they experienced storms, starvation, disease, pirate, attacks, and death, among other hardships—in search of a different life. (Nguyen 94)

The film offers a "rare visual text" on Vietnam and the atrocities on the citizens who can be taken away or killed at any time for any tiny reason. The young men or the prisoners in the New Economic Zones are called by numbers and they are brutally beaten or shot at for every little dissent. The men in authority treat them as dehumanized beings with no rights whatsoever.

8.2 Memory, Representation and Narrator

Although the conflict is between the citizens and the communist government as it unfolds in both the films, Jolie has a different narrative structure. It is shot through the eye of the young child who survives to tell the experiences of her family. This helps Jolie to maintain a neutrality which otherwise would have been difficult to maintain being a white woman.

It begins by showing the bourgeois family headed by a Government police officer who seems worried for the withdrawal of the Americans and begins to think of leaving the city. He provides every possible comfort and luxury to his seven children in a beautiful home. The furnishing and the costumes of all the seven children present them as the elites of the city. Amidst the hustle and bustle of window curtains, beautiful dresses and movements of several characters in the household, the visuals slowly go slow and grave. The father feels betrayed by the Americans as the Khmer Rouge regime decides to vacate cities. He arranges a truck for the family to leave the city leaving behind the beloved dresses and toys, to proceed towards a friend's house at first. But the friend's wife becomes apprehensive of possible threats from the Khmer Rouge soldiers for sheltering them and therefore the family sets out walking on the streets. The film depicts the struggles and pain of a powerless and homeless family who tries everything to stay together with the hope of survival. From this scene of citizens walking on the street, the film becomes a survival story and, the slightest communications are done with precaution and tension, in fear of being separated, tortured or murdered. The close shots on the faces of the parents show their helplessness in anticipate of the impending gloom with the fall of the government and the march of the communists on the street. The film depicts life in Cambodia under *Angkar*.

The filmmaker's constant portrayal of close shots communicating anxiety and dread makes it more of a human story than treating it as a sentimental issue. Empathy is aroused in visuals and not in mushy dialogues. At the same time Jolie avoids the usual excitement or glorification of modern weapons like other Hollywood action films. There are a few aerial shots to display the geographical context and overhead shots to evoke an indifferent God towards the victims. The shots otherwise documents the characters' movements in the vast open fields with very less dialogues. Most of the time the camera represents what Loung sees. The scenes alternate between past time showing flashbacks, the delight of the past life in the city and the present miseries. Loung remembers when the family was happy, healthy and carefree. The use of repetitions and same angle shots intensifies the routined imprisoned life with no chances of escape. Loung and her family knew it was futile to protest or escape, so they begin to accept the crisis as they come.

This particular family becomes representative of the plights of the many Cambodian families who were separated and who left their comfortable homes in the cities to work in the fields in summer:

> Youk Chhang director of the Documentation Center of Cambodia (DC-Cam) called Cambodia "a broken society—we are broken people living in a broken society— "all victims and survivors are like broken glass that you try to glue back together' (as quoted in Khet 3).

In contrast to the initial scenes of sober colours and privileged lifestyle, the survivor's family would be left with one uniform upholding the communist regime's vision of a homogeneous society. The freshness of colours in the first scenes like white, pink gets replaced by grey, brown and yellow. Thousands of families in the cities join the deportees of other provinces as they leave their beautiful homes and belongings. The tension increases as the screen gets filled with thousands of Cambodian citizens moving with children and ailing elderly people; the deportees stumbling and wavering through the streets, keep going while being severely guarded by the Khmer Rouge soldiers. They were taken to the country side where they build their sheds of bamboos and leaves to live in, which will eventually become their agrarian work-houses. The only respite from these were to look at the family photographs they carried of the good times at home. As a controlling strategy of the government, the family members were separated and in this case, the two boys had to go to another camp for work and the photographs were shared in a desperate attempt to keep the memory of the family intact, to remind themselves of their identity and belongingness. Photographs not only keep memories alive but also give a meaning to their miserable present; but they had to look at the photographs of the happy days secretly with the fear of being discovered by the soldiers. No personal space was allowed and they feel observed/being seen at all times. The father who was previously a police officer particularly remains anxious along with his wife in fear of being discovered. One night the father roasts a fat beetle and offered it to the family as chestnuts. They have these tiny moments of pleasure till the next day when the soldiers come and take away the father. Although the killing is off-screen it was obvious that they would kill the father for being an ex government employee.

Despite the many poignant emotional scenes, the film reaches its tragic height when Loung is most distraught; it does not fall into sentimentalizing the brutalities like the other biographical Hollywood film released in the same year, 2017 from Hollywood: *The Glass Castle.* In the newspaper *The Guardian* the reviewer, Peter Bradshaw gives two stars out of five and calls it a "tiresome film which sentimentally neutralizes parental abuse into a supposedly fascinating angel/devil split" (Bradshaw). Most of its reception rejected its manner of sentimentalizing the issues although the casts were praised for their performances. It is based on the memoir of Jeanette Walles' bestselling memoir of the same name and is a tale of poverty, trauma and nomadic life of the young girl who grows up to be a journalist writing gossip column for *New York* magazine.

8.3 Visuals and Sound

The film directed by Jolie deals with crimes against the citizens, HR cases and the survival of a little girl; it raises more serious issues of governance, authority, power, denial of personal identity and crime. As seen through Loung's eyes, the family do not lament the loss as it is beyond a girl of five to make sense of the geopolitical issues or humanitarian needs. Jolie shows a child's lived experiences in such conditions:

> we can feel her fear, understand her confusion, rejoice in her reunions with family members. The cinematography of Anthony Dod Mantle makes the most of this perspective (Brusatt).

Although Loung experiences rage and panic at certain situations like the landmine scene, she does her best to adapt to the situation. She was at first horrified as her mother informs that they cannot carry party dresses on the road, or at the camp workers anger at a child for stealing a vegetable or at a group who kills, skins, roasts and eat a snake. The film maintains cultural neutrality taking the position of the little Loung. It may also be a precautionary framing since Jolie belongs to Hollywood that glorifies US marines. Jolie shows us how it feels to live during the initial years of the Khmer Rouge regime; it does not offer or debate political issues. The diegetic sounds helps the director to focus more on a human story. The sounds of authority and violence brought in through marching boots, helicopters, gunshots, bombs, along with sounds of nature of birds, insects and water flowing in the river. The interference of human sounds like the cheering crowd and propaganda are pitted against whispered conversations of the deportees.

Although visual narrative speaks of violation of human rights and total control of the masses, the visuals of children playing and smiling compliments the primary narrator Loung's role in structuring such visuals. There are images that focus on the innocence of a child by showing a hand that stretches towards a military helicopter soaring overhead or enjoying the soft clang-clang of a teakettle. At the same time, Loung's stare at the brutalities of Khmer Rouge troops haunts the onlooker. She learns to plant landmines, fire an AK-47 and draw a spear on the chest of a Vietnamese soldier during her training in the camp where there was constant propaganda of Angkar meaning the Khmer Rouge organization. The film includes documentaries and news clips showing American carpet bombing along the Cambodian borders towards the closing years of the war. The Americans showed little concern as they incinerated forests. The US President then, President Nixon denied having any kind of war in Cambodian soil, whereas the Secretary of State callously mentions a final solution to the region. The reportage is carried on throughout the film and the colour on screen and its treatment reminds us of the distant past events and the film after all is a revisit to the past. The cinematic time is continuously brought to the present by recalling past experiences. Although Jolie avoids certain political positions of the Cambodians, the training reveals how they view Vietnamese as enemies.

In addition, the ideals of a homogeneous, classless society is undermined by the visuals of the rice and vegetables being carried away from the farms to the frontline combat soldiers leaving the workers feed on broth instead. The low level soldiers humiliate the weak workers and sometimes behave as sadists simply because of their allegiance to *Angkar*. Even the weak soldiers gain in power to humiliate the slaves at the camps. The film projects the "sense of dislocation and uncertainty, the deprivation and fear, the artillery shells tearing through treelines at night and jolting sleepers awake; the mines blasting bodies into the air and setting them down without legs"(Seitz).

The same issues are projected in Hui's film on Vietnam. The scenes alternate between the adult world and the activities of the small children, humanitarian issues and innocent thoughts, pathos and smiling kids, gunshots and sounds of nature(as in Jolie's film). The children in both the films bear the brunt of violence, they starve, see deaths almost regularly. They know that the adult with the gun standing over there would kill their sister, mother or father for no reason at all. While in Jolie's film, we can feel the story like Loung does; in Hui's film we desparately want to turn our eyes from the gory scenes of crime and atrocities on children and youth of the nation.

These visuals have the potential to foster a better understanding of Human Rights and desolations that war leaves behind. In addition, it is also true that in the process of remembering a lot has been forgotten. It has rightly been observed by Nyugen that "All wars are fought twice, the first time on the battlefield, the second time in memory" (Nguyen, *Memories* 144). No representation can ever write these realities in totality. The issues faced by the world today in terms of refugee crisis, humanitarian aids, education of children, sanitation, employment and the use of modern weaponry shown in the films undoubtedly raise queries on spectatorship and 'politics of pity' as both the films project communist regimes and violation of HR in those nations. But is it enough to understand and view the distant suffering both in time and space? How is the viewer supposed to react or is charity enough in response to such viewings? How do we develop empathy in viewing these films as world citizens? Are political protests- in -solidarity the solution to atrocities and violence? These issues need further considerations on Human Rights Cinema and viewership.

References

Bradshaw P (2017) The Glass Castle Review: treacly tiresome family-in-peril drama. The Guardian. Culture: Drama Films. 6 Oct 2017. https://www.theguardian.com/film/2017/oct/06/the-glass-castle-review-woody-harrelson-naomi-watts-brie-larson.

Brusatt F, Mary A "First They Killed My Father". Film. Spirituality and Practice. https://www.spiritualityandpractice.com/films/reviews/view/28497/first-they-killed-my-father.

Galtung J (1969) Violence, peace, and peace research. J Peace Res 6(3):167–191

Khamboly D. A History of Democratic Kampuchea (1975–1979). Documentation Center of Cambodia. Phnom Penh, Cambodia. Print

Khet L. Initiating a way to address legacy of memory in Cambodia. Action Research Paper. Documentation Center of Cambodia. Phnom Penh. Cambodia. Print

Kiernan B (2002) "Cleansing the cities". The Pol Pot Regime, 2nd edn. Yale University Press, New Haven and London

Nguyen V (2016) 6. Ann Hui's Boat People: Documenting Vietnamese Refugees in Hong Kong". Looking Back on the. Rutgers University Press, Vietnam War, pp 94–109. https://doi.org/10.36019/9780813579962-009

Nguyen VT (2013) Just memory: war and the ethics of remembrance. Am Literary History 25(1):144–163. https://doi.org/10.1093/alh/ajs069

Nguyen VT (2016) Nothing ever dies: Vietnam and the Memory of War. Harvard University Press, p 2016

Seitz MZ (2017) "Reviews, first they killed my father". 15 Sept 2017. rogerebert.com/reviews/first-they-killed-my-father-2017.

Chapter 9
The Spectral as the Political: Dystopia, Myth, and Horror in Patrick Graham's *Ghoul*

Rishiraj Pal

The Indian horror miniseries, Ghoul (2018), is set in a near dystopic future which envisions India at a time when Muslim–Hindu tensions have gone past the pressure-point and have led to state-sanctioned persecution of Muslims. The first episode opens with the following lines: "The near future. The country has changed. Sectarian violence has reached its crisis point. Secret detention centres are established. A military clampdown is in effect" (*Ghoul*, S1:E1).[1] The chapter will analyse the emancipatory and moralising function of ghoul vis-à-vis the concept of spectropolitics which evokes "both nightmarish scenarios of dehumanization and dreams of revolution" (Blanco and Peeren 93), emerging as the site of potential change, and would discuss how the spectral has been used to initiate a rupture within the well-guarded system—the detention/execution centre—that turns into a haunted space in which the drama unfolds.

9.1 The Patriot and the Traitor

As this *Netflix* series opens, the military appears to have assumed absolute power and anybody questioning the state or not abiding by the dictates of the government is being sent for reconditioning to a detention cell, Meghdoot 31, which is supposedly an "advanced interrogation centre" (S1:E1). Lt. Nida Rahim, a fresh NPS recruit trained in advanced interrogation, is posted in this high-security facility where she is enlisted to interrogate a notorious and menacing prisoner, Ali Saeed, and learns in the third episode that the (suspected) terrorists brought to the detention centre are all killed after being mercilessly tortured.

R. Pal (✉)
Department of English, Centre for Distance and Online Education, Rabindra Bharati University, Kolkata, India
e-mail: rishirajpal.rp@gmail.com

S. S. Ali and A. Basak (eds.), *Marginal Narratives and the Question of Human Rights in Asian Pacific Literature*, https://doi.org/10.1007/978-981-97-4544-9_9

When the course of events reveals that Nida's father, Shahnawaz Rahim, had also been brought there for interrogation (and not particularly for any sort of reconditioning), and was eventually killed, she loses all faith in the authoritarian nationalist regime that she has been serving and prepares to avenge her loss by summoning the ghoul, the monster from the Arabic folklore, with her blood as did her father within the confines of the detention centre. Saibal Chatterjee offers a succinct thematic summary in his review:

> *Ghoul* is a subversive horror tale that places a majoritarian state at the centre of the plot and then proceeds to explore the themes of political tyranny, betrayal, guilt and revenge through the unsettling goings-on in a secret detention centre set up for elements suspected of waging war against the government of the day. (*NDTV.com*)

The tension between the good and the bad citizen is evoked when the ethical parameters are set through state sanctioned orders: "As per the revised ethical actions of First May, all residents have been ordered to surrender all dangerous articles which have been prohibited" (S1:E2). Muslim religious literatures are declared seditious and artefacts and books, contraband. Shahnawaz laments over this predicament to his daughter:

> They took away all our belongings. Our legacy, our books. They took away our stuff saying it was sacrilegious. They said our books are anti-religious . . . First, they closed the universities and now the schools. (S1:E1)

Nida was the "highest scorer in Advanced Interrogation" and Colonel Dachuna, who is in charge of Meghdoot 31, appreciates her sacrifice for the country as she went beyond her duties and turned in her father; Dachuna believes that this act would serve as a brave example for all the civilians and officers. She has been a "consistent top performer" (S1:E1) of her batch and seems to have been brainwashed into subscribing naively to the state mechanism that champions jingoism in the name of national security to such an extent that she fails to understand her father's fears and frustrations. Colonel Dachuna, while addressing the NPS cadets, reminds them that.

> the enemy has not yet been completely defeated. External powers and false ideologies have resulted in the spread of terrorism from within. To eliminate such traitors, the government has instituted some tough policies. Recent terrorist attacks in our country have proven one thing: the enemy is not an outsider. He is one of us; the one who is easily misled. Anyone can be a terrorist. Our neighbour, our friend. (S1:E1)

To her father's utter disbelief and agonising warning, "What you are doing is wrong, my dear, absolutely wrong" (S1:E1), Nida ended up betraying him as she herself believed that her *Abbu* has surely subscribed to some kind of "anti-national" ideology and needs an urgent reconditioning. She too perhaps believed that her father might be a part of some terrorist organisation or supported their cause as Nida noticed in the tense car scene that he could not let go of the "seditious literatures" and his lecture notes (S1:E1).

Nida falls under the ideal "nationalist Muslim" category while Shahnawaz is looked upon as a traitor. Despite being a second-class citizen of India, she earns her identity as a nationalist by subscribing to the dominant ideology. Even then, Major Das, kept on suspecting her and seemed to be convinced till the very end that Nida was solely responsible for causing the bloodbath in the detention centre, perhaps because Ali Saeed whispered Nida's name while he got caught in the very first scene. But there is no denying the fact that "Nida's nationalism—never mind her unwavering loyalty—is always suspect, for she belongs to the category of the "hyphenated citizen": the Indian Muslim" (Magazine).

The present right-wing ruling government in India does not seem to tolerate any form of dissent and often uses coercive forces and draconian laws like The Unlawful Activities (Prevention) Amendment Act (UAPA) that criminalises dissent to silence any form of anti-government statements by putting the dissenters behind the bars. Activists Arun Ferreira and Vernon Gonsalves in their article simplify and explain what these kind of laws imply:

> Like the TADA [Terrorist and Disruptive Activities (Prevention) Act] and POTA [The Prevention of Terrorism Act], UAPA also criminalises ideology and association. By virtue of declaring an organisation 'unlawful' or 'terrorist' and banning it, these Acts have *de facto* criminalised their ideologies. Hence mere possession of any literature of such an organisation or even upholding an ideology common to that organisation in the absence of any violent act is construed as an offence. On the other hand, mere membership or association with such an organisation too becomes an offence. It is by this logic, that very often, organisations advocating the rights of a certain minority community or that of oppressed sections are easily labelled as fronts of a proscribed organisation under the schedule of the Act. Their activists or members get arrested and remain in prison for years, and are denied bail. (*TheWire.in*)

Patrick Graham describes the miniseries as a "slightly skewed alternative reality to what we know today and the dystopia is kind of generic in that it looks like your archetypal right-wing, fascist, totalitarian government" (qtd. in Jhunjhunwala, *Scroll.in*). The horror resides less in conjuring up of the mythical demon than what can be located in the affairs of a dystopic everyday life, a sector controlled by the state machinery that tactfully deigns its totalitarian nationalist "self" pitted against its ethnic "other."

The officials at the Ministry of National Protection programmatically deports Shahnawaz Rahim to Meghdoot 31 betraying Nida's innocent faith in the system's nationalist/patriotic claims (S1:E1). Being a Muslim, Shahnawaz is denied any kind of rights both as a free person and even as a convict. His life is reduced to a recorded confession archived by the interrogating team. In Episode 1, when the camera zooms in and shows the names on the confession tapes, "compiled through…years of hard work," as Colonel Duchuna puts it, one cannot miss the fact that all the names on the tapes are essentially Muslim ones and the Colonel, at that point, explains that these are confessions extracted from "all kinds of terrorist; students protesters, opposition party leaders, religious fanatics. Dangerous anti-nationals" (S1:E1). It is suggestive of the systematic oppression and ethnic cleansing based on a homogenizing principle of the nationalist imaginary. As Tanul Thakur explains in his article,

> horror here is not just visceral but also political. It comes alive in situations both extraordinary and ordinary – in the dim hallways of deep dungeons; in prison cells; in random interrogations and later, during the arrest of a (Muslim) professor who is told, "You've no rights"; in the

> systematic ethnic cleansing carried out by the state, which orders burning of minorities' religious texts and symbols. In *Ghoul*, horror resides in the hearts of people, in casual bigotry encouraged—and rewarded—by their country. (*TheWire.in*)

The dystopic futuristic setting of *Ghoul* is no less horrific. For this speculative narrative functions within and engages with the current Indian discourse on anti-nationalism. Strategically inserted terms like "*wapasi*" (deportation) and "*adarsh nagrik*" (ideal citizen; rather, law-abiding citizen) immediately connects the speculative mode of story-telling with the controversial policies and polity of the current Indian government such as Citizen (Amendment) Act combined with an abuse of the aims of National Register of Citizens. An article in *Human Rights Watch* records these ills:

> [W]hether it is the decision to revoke the special constitutional status of Jammu and Kashmir, or to bring in the discriminatory Citizenship Amendment Bill, or indeed the rising cost of onions, people will write letters, send petitions, and hold protests. But if there is criticism these days, there is every chance that the mighty will take umbrage enough to denounce it, or even retaliate with vicious abuse of power. (Ganguly, "Dissent Is 'Anti-National' in Modi's India")

With students being charged with sedition and any voice of dissent against the government being painted as "anti-national," the show tethers the spectral to the political from the very onset and functions as a cautionary tale that finds almost no realistic element to fight the systematic destruction and denial of human rights and, therefore, brings in the mythic as the only recourse. Joyojeet Pal and Ankur Sharma in their well-researched article, "From 2016 to 2020, Growing Use of 'Anti-National' in Political Discourse on Indian Twitter," shows with adequate statistical data that "the most dramatic increase in the use of 'anti-national' happens in 2019 starting with the dilution of Article 370, and peaking thereafter during the CAA protests" (*TheWire.in*). Much before the paranormal is introduced, the system stripping the Muslims of their constitutional and human rights seems scary enough, especially to a Muslim professor whose religion goes against all his credentials and makes him an obvious suspect.

9.2 The Mythic Corrective

Patrick Graham handpicks the monster, "ghoul," a mythical creature originating in pre-Islamic Arabia, to offer a spectral route to reveal the shameful, scandalous, and darkest of human secrets that violate human rights. He explains, "I wanted to take a monster from mythology that hasn't been seen before. Zombies, vampires and werewolves have been done to death, so I wanted to bring a new, old legend to the forefront of modern horror culture" (qtd in Jhunjunwala, *Scroll.in*).

Here the spectral is endowed with an ethical principle, a moralising purpose: to "finish the task" and to "make the sinner realise his guilt and then eat his flesh" (S1:E2). The ghoul (like a devilish *ginn*), however monstrous, is summoned by the betrayed professor as a last resort when the reality around becomes hostile and life-threatening, paving the way for the supernatural to intervene and bring about a rupture within the established status quo. According to Ashish Nandy, a political psychologist, “the legend or myth is a different kind of moral and political statement, which is deliberately non-historical, in which ethics are privileged over scientific objectivity” (Devare 185). As he puts it while discussing the differences between historical and ahistorical cultures, “All myths are morality tales. Mythologization is also moralization; it involves a refusal to separate the remembered past from its ethical meaning in the present. For this refusal, it is often important not to remember the past, objectively, clearly, or in its entirety” (Nandy 47). Some cultures do not live in history; some societies live outside a sense of historicity. “Myths,” as Nandy would argue, “are the predominant mode of organizing experiences of the past” (47) in such societies.

This miniseries takes the demon out of its pre-Islamic Arabic context—"Arabs used to think that ghouls appear to human beings in the wilderness where they change their shapes” (qtd. in Ahmed K. Al-Rawi 292)—and appropriates it to manifest a transformative political manoeuvre. For here it is the mythical that aims to restore the violated natural order, and by offering a corrective, unleashes an ahistorical moralising force that debunks the ideological underpinnings of a totalitarian state—be it the disproportionate share of human rights within a democratic nation or the repudiation of the Constitution that legitimizes those rights and expects its citizens to uphold its aims—in this case, through chaos, confusion, and horror. Ashis Nandy argues that the “mythic societies sense the power of myths and the nature of human frailties; they are more fearful than the modern ones... of the perils of mythic use of amoral certitudes about the past” (47).

Meghdoot 31 is a bunker that was “built after the first Emergency, in the event of a nuclear attack” and “there is no mention of it in any official records; no information at all” (S1:E1). This speculative futuristic narrative refers to historical events and, in trying to achieve a sense of historicity by providing such familiar co-ordinates, betrays it because despite all the confessions being archived and the State is actively involved in the whole process, the slaughterhouse, as it were, is not supposed to go down in any recorded form of history. This very fact aligns the detention centre with the nature of everyday life of the citizens who do not participate in the State’s conscientious efforts of building a *Hindu Rashtra.* Existence itself in such a belligerent setting becomes volatile. The historicity of such cultures gets nullified as the nation-writing project of the *Hindu Rashtra* has a well-defined method of selection. And, one can well imagine, glorifying the patriotic “nationalist self,” would involve an act of disavowal—the disavowal of the ethnic “Other.” It is perhaps the ahistoricity of ghoul as a mythic creature that allows this seamless adaptation into a narrative that involves a complex triadic relation between myth, history, and speculative fiction.

The term “ghoul” stems from a verbal root “ghãl” meaning “to kill” (Al-Rawi 292). Ibn Manzür opines that the “ghoul is one of the ‘most fearful génies and devils’ because ‘Arabs used to think that ghouls appear to human beings in the wilderness where they change (yataghawalün) their shapes’ (Ibn Manzür 2005, 2953)” (qtd. in Al-Rawi 292). In his philological study that attempts “to show this monster’s delineation in Arabic culture, including Arabic folktales" (291), Al-Rawi concludes that "according to Arabic folk belief, the origin of the ghoul is unknown, an idea that has persisted down through the centuries and to the present day" (293).

Moreover, many narratives of Arab Bedouins refer to the ghoul as a figment of imagination conjured up by the weary minds of the wanderers. What imagination is able to manufacture in the mindscape, myth doubles that in the spectral order. Myth is a cognitive paradigm. And it is perhaps because of this, Graham manifests the ghoul not as a ghostly entity but as an overwhelming transformative phenomenon capable of metamorphosis and of invoking nightmares marked by one's guilt; the realities and dreams of the guilt-ridden souls are affected by the ghoul's pervading presence even before it has begun to punish the guilty. The moralising principle of the myth is thus extended to the cinematic unconscious, thereby making the spectral a projection of the guilt-ridden, weary conscience of the nationalist brave-hearts who get to taste their wrath when their friends and neighbours take the shape of a life-threatening monster: "The Ghoul is among us right here" (S1:E3).

9.3 Towards a Radical Spectropolitics

Working through the question of ghoul as an emancipatory mythical being summoned to destabilize the order using a radically violent procedure, one needs to consider its social, political, and ethical implications. As Avery F. Gordon argues in *Ghostly Matters,* "the ghost is not simply a dead or a missing person, but a social figure, and investigating it can lead to that dense site where history and subjectivity make social life" (8). What circumstances would justify the violence that the "task" of the ghoul involves? Perhaps the radical reformist nature of such spectral formulation entails such extremist *modus operandi*: to reveal their guilt and eat their flesh.

The corporeality of the ghoul renders the menacing quality it has because it becomes what it feeds on, echoing the popular nutritional proverb: you are what you eat, or, you become what you eat. The body uses the consumed material for its own construction and sustenance. The corporeal continuity of the ghoul is perpetuated by a relentless hunt of the guilty humans with blood on their hands. This lack of ghoul's fixity of being is a result of its "ambivalent multiplicity[,]... the liminal form of being (and thinking) encompassing life and death, human and non-human, presence and absence" (Blanco and Peeren 91–92).

At the end of Episode-3, it is perhaps due to this complex metaphor of the eating the flesh along with the ambivalence of the spectral existence that it becomes almost impossible for the audience to know for sure whether the flesh-and-bone figure Nida shoots from a point-blank range is the "decorated war hero" (S1:E3) Colonel Dachuna, who is no less a monster to Nida—"an evil spirit" (S1:E3)—for he has tortured and killed her father along with many other Muslim citizens, or the ghoul who has now taken the shape of Dachuna by eating his flesh. The episode ends with Nida, now behind bars, preparing to summon the ghoul with a blade she has kept in her mouth. The officers at the Ministry of National Protection remind her, "It was not the unit that was operating illegally. It was you... Lieutenant Colonel Dachuna and his entire division were all just following the state policy. And by terminating his command you have proved one thing, Ms. Rahim, that the daughter of a terrorist can be nothing but a terrorist" (S1:E3).

To arrive at such conclusions without fair trials and investigation speaks volumes about the human condition in such a dystopic landscape. The need for a radical "spectropolitics" thus emerges in this context. As Janice Radway argues in her foreword to Avery F. Gordon's *Ghostly Matters*, spectropolitics can work to "revivify our collective capacity to imagine a future radically other to the one ideologically charted out already by the militarized, patriarchal capitalism that has thrived heretofore on the practice of social erasure" (xiii).

This explains how the ghoul attains a political valency and creates a bizarre situation of hope even in a dreary scenario of despair. As María del Pilar Blanco and Esther Peeren put it,

> a "spectropolitics" is an attempt to mobilize spectrality to more precisely designate the diffuse operations and effects of present-day globalization, as well as to critique the way its processes produce certain subjects as consistently disenfranchised or, in Judith Butler's terms, forced to live in extreme precarity as "would-be humans, the spectrally human." . . . A necessarily confused and confusing concept capable of evoking both nightmarish scenarios of dehumanization and dreams of revolution, spectropolitics reveals, first of all, the increasingly spectral nature of the political. (93)

Besides Nida's handing over his father, what remains significantly disturbing is the kind of inhuman torture Ahmad, one of the inmates, had to endure when Chaudhury and Gupta, the two intemperate officers slaughtered his wife and his small child in front of his eyes during a maniacal confession procedure. Ali Saeed (who enters the scene as an embodiment of the ghoul) sitting on the confession chair in the torture cell alludes to the faint sound of a child crying. He obliquely asks the two officers whose idea it was to kill Ahmed's wife and child in front of him; repeats the tensed and aggressive private conversations between Dachuna and wife, who has apparently turned bitter towards the hot-tempered Colonel; and calls out to Nida in the same affectionate way as her father used to call her. They are all spooked and haunted by the nightmares and their past deeds that cannot be repressed or forgotten.

What summoning the ghoul signifies in the spectropolitical plane, recalling the events from the past does that in the psychological plane. The ghoul haunts not only through jump-scares and other such familiar devices of visual horror but also through a subterranean moralising inducement that works at an unconscious level throughout. "To be haunted," as Avery F. Gordon puts it, "is to be tied to historical and social effects" (190).

The ghoul is neither dead nor living; there is no definite ontological basis to its form. It is shaped by one's grief insofar as it pathologises the grief by making manifest one's guilt. In Graham's depiction of the spectral as the political, the carceral space—a spatial extension of their despair and anguish—seems to be a repository of wronged, dehumanized, and grieving souls bereft of their basic human rights. And in that space, the spectre gestures towards a still unformulated future marked by terrorizing totalitarianism pitted against a paranormal dissent as the guilt of the perpetrators attains an anthropomorphic dimension in the ghoul incarnate.

Note

1. Abbreviations S and E refer to Season and Episode respectively. Therefore, S1:E2 signifies the second episode of the first season of the *Netflix* miniseries, *Ghoul*.

References

Al-Rawi, Ahmed K. "The Arabic Ghoul and its Western Transformation." *Folklore,* vol. 120, no. 3, Dec. 2009, pp. 291–306, www.jstor.org/stable/40646532. Accessed 30 April 2022.

Blanco, María del Pilar, and Esther Peeren. "Spectropolitics: Ghosts of the Global Contemporary." *The Spectralities Reader*, edited by María del Pilar Blanco and Esther Peeren, Bloomsbury, 2013, pp. 91–102.

Chatterjee, Saibal. "Netflix's *Ghoul* Review: Radhika Apte Plays A Conflicted Soul As Only She Can." *NDTV.com,* 20 Mar. 2019, www.ndtv.com/entertainment/netflixs-ghoul-review-radhika-apte-plays-a-conflicted-soul-as-only-she-can-3-5-stars-out-of-5-1905911. Accessed 26 Apr. 2022.

Devare, Aparna. *History and the Making of Modern Hindu Self.* Routledge, 2011.

Ferreira, Arun, and Vernon Gonsalves. "Fifty Years of Unreasonable Restrictions Under the Unlawful Activities Act." *TheWire.in,* 09 Mar. 2017, thewire.in/rights/uapa-anti-terrorism-laws. Accessed 28 Apr. 2022.

Ganguly, Meenakshi. "Dissent Is 'Anti-National' in Modi's India." *Human Rights Watch,* 13 Dec. 2019, www.hrw.org/news/2019/12/13/dissent-anti-national-modis-india. Accessed on 29 Apr. 2022.

Ghoul. Created and directed by Patrick Graham, Blumhouse Productions, Phantom Films and Ivanhoe Pictures, 2018. *Netflix*, https://www.netflix.com/watch/80245092?source=35.

Gordon, Avery F. *Ghostly Matters: Haunting and the Sociological Imagination.* University of Minnesota Press, 2008.

Jhunjhunwala, Udita. "*Ghoul* director Patrick Graham: 'I wanted to bring a new, old legend to the forefront'." *Scroll.in,* 22 Aug. 2018, https://scroll.in/reel/891355/ghoul-director-patrick-graham-i-wanted-to-bring-a-new-old-legend-to-the-forefront. Accessed 28 Apr. 2022.

Magazine, Aakshi. "*Ghoul*: Challenging the Category of the 'Nationalist Muslim'." *Economic and Political Weekly*, vol. 53, no. 45, 17 Nov. 2018, www.epw.in/engage/article/ghoul-challenging-category-nationalist-muslim. Accessed 28 Apr. 2022.

Naahar, Rohan. "*Ghoul* review: *Netflix*'s *Sacred Games* follow-up is even braver, scary in unexpected ways." *Hindustan Times,* 14 Jul. 2020, www.hindustantimes.com/tv/ghoul-review-netflix-s-sacred-games-follow-up-is-even-braver-scary-in-unexpectedways/story-I2MqNEZ4OVxvfq019XSpAP.html. Accessed 29 Apr. 2022.

Nandy, Ashis. "History's Forgotten Doubles." *History and Theory,* vol. 34, no. 2, May 1995, pp. 44-66, www.jstor.org/stable/2505434. Accessed 31 Jul. 2012.

Radway, Janice. Foreword. *Ghostly Matters: Haunting and the Sociological Imagination,* by Avery F. Gordon, University of Minnesota Press, 2008, pp. vii-xiii.

Thakur, Tanul. "*Ghoul* Is a Horror Story That Speaks Truth to Power." *TheWire.in,* 30 Aug. 2018, thewire.in/film/ghoul-netflixreview-radhika-apte. Accessed 28 Apr. 2022.

Part III
Borderless Struggles: Narratives of Marginality and Social Injustice in Asia

Chapter 10
Borders and Boundaries: Resituating *the Tiger Claw* in the Current Times

Indira Chakraborty (Bhattacharya)

Many scholars have defined the current times as an "Age of Migration". Yet, it cannot be said that migration is a twentieth century or a twenty first century phenomenon exclusively. Migration is perhaps as old as human civilization and is usually comprised of geographical movements. These movements entail a series of economic, political, cultural, and social circumstances that lead to migration. In other words, it is because of these structural forces that drive one's mobility, thereby controlling the mechanisms which channel and limit the migrants. Movements transform all the elements involved, not only the structural circumstances that affect the mobility, but also people who do not migrate, for instance, the inhabitants of the host country or anyone for that matter who encounters these migrants. They get affected indirectly by forces induced by migration. Migration changes people and their approaches and perspectives. Ostensibly, this question then comes in, who is a migrant and when can one say one has 'stopped' being a 'migrant' and has been assimilated in the mainstream culture and society. This is a very complex maze of possibilities without much hope of retrieval, even though most countries have subscribed to the UN definition of a migrant. A migrant can be defined as someone living outside his/her homeland/own country for a year or more. But the issue is more complicated. Nevertheless, to tag one as a 'migrant' is not only difficult but tricky too, since that involves three basic things—first, migrants cover a wide range of people without proper compartments to distinguish, secondly it is difficult to count migrants and to determine how long they have been abroad. Finally, it is equally or even more difficult to define when one "becomes" and "ends up" calling oneself a migrant. Around the world when almost all nations are closing borders to consolidate and strengthen its sovereignty, making strict vigil on who comes in and goes out, citing 'terrorism' as 'terror' being reasons for the strictness, it is of utmost importance that

I. Chakraborty (Bhattacharya) (✉)
Department of English, St. Xavier's University, Kolkata, India
e-mail: indira.cbhattacharya@sxuk.edu.in

S. S. Ali and A. Basak (eds.), *Marginal Narratives and the Question of Human Rights in Asian Pacific Literature*, https://doi.org/10.1007/978-981-97-4544-9_10

the procedures of transformation that determine a person's 'becoming' a 'migrant' or a 'citizen' or one's return to his/her homeland be considered with prudence.

The very narrative of 'global war on terror' as has been designated by various postcolonial scholars has certain parallel metanarratives which sought to undermine their subtle differences, and the reference to this inadvertently reminds one of the reigns of terror during the Second World War. This prospect drives to relocate the relevance in certain texts that were primarily written as a response to abovementioned events of political turmoil not as immediate reference but for resurrecting the general human experience. This brings to the major concern of the essay. The essay intends to consider the text *The Tiger Claw* by Shauna Singh Baldwin published in the year 2004 in the immediate backdrop of the 9/11 incident, also taking into consideration (as its content) the times of holocaust broadly. Probably the relevance in "rereading" the text (*The Tiger Claw)* vis-a-vis this context therefore lies in the need to rethink about the larger history and the political forces at play especially at a time when borders all around the world are closing. The essay will try to address how the text serves as a metaphor and the author strives to justify that stance to resituate and redress certain issues. The text then, also acts as a token and tries to resurrect these larger political histories to probably "rememorialize" the machinations of these forces at play that are ubiquitous and reiterative. The closing down of borders literally and metaphorically is not a sudden occurrence, it can be considered as a cumulative consequence of socio-political events which materialized in the form of stringent citizenship laws and the compartmentalizing of immigration policies.

The global politics is driven towards a regime which has now started closing and narrowing the definitions of what comprises a 'nation' by consolidating the 'border(s)' and controlling who can access the resources. This has become extremely active because of the socio-political forces of globalization that are into play, which to an extent is considered to have downplayed the sovereignty of a nation-state. At a time when nations are no longer defined by maps and cartographies, these invisible forces or lines of web constantly shape and define the notions of 'nation', most Western and powerful nations (sometimes non-Western countries too) have restricted movement across borders through security agents and mutual agreements with neighboring states, leading to devastating consequences for people who want to move.

Shauna Singh Baldwin, an Indo-Canadian author (currently based in Milwaukee) had tried to represent the socio-political dynamics in the texts *The Tiger Claw* (2004) and *We are not in Pakistan* (2009) as an expression of angst and as immediate and remote response respectively, trying to juxtapose the individual and the global. In the text *We are not in Pakistan* a collection of disjointed short stories, sketched in the backdrop of diverse and assorted cataclysmic histories Baldwin has tried to juxtapose the individual in the global too. While the last century has witnessed World Wars, colonialist attacks, counterattacks, wars for supremacy, et cetera, it is without doubt that perhaps the most convoluted legacy remains of Colonialism which stems another (or a few) complicated history/(ies) across the world. Immediately after World War II and a changing world scenario, the colonial ruler does not exist in the true sense of the term, and modern-day concepts of the 'empire' has drastically changed the political map of the world. 'Empire' is no longer a 'metaphor' to demonstrate the resemblances and disparities between "todays' world order and the empires of Rome, China and Americas" (Negri and Hardt n.p.), but as a 'concept' which "calls primarily for a theoretical approach" (Negri and Hardt n.p.). It is a force that encompasses every "civilized" country within its "spatial totality" and whose periphery is not restricted to any territorial or topographical limitation. It is a process of subsuming "social life in its entirety" (Negri and Hardt, xv). Therefore, today either there isn't or cannot be any 'one' nation that can project or can proclaim itself in the sense as it once used to be in times of European Colonialism and hence, power is distributed across borders and frontiers through networks. As such, the modern-day construct of globalization has tried to dissolve boundaries by catalyzing accessibility, thereby seamlessly assimilating notions of identity. Amidst this process of dissolution, a necessity to redefine nation through borders may seem to be at best feigned and imposed, thereby generating the need to be sorted in terms of definitions of identities. In a similar vein, notions of freedom have also altered in this scenario of global accessibility and seamlessness. Thus, the onus is on history to define and delineate the identity of any individual, in various pseudo-concrete manifestations and essentially such notions of identities are mapped against certain established parameters. Also, such frameworks too are trajectories of a post-postcolonial globalized world order where human identity is no longer just limited to categories of social sciences but also technicalities, where life is mapped too, indicated by parameters like application and applicability of Internet of Things and post-humanism.

Interestingly, in *We are not in Pakistan* Baldwin places the narratives in diverse histories, communal or personal, past, or present, spanning locations as diverse as Ukraine and Costa Rica. A wonderfully kaleidoscopic world, the protagonists of the ten stories are male or female, young and old, rich, and poor, affable, and detestable, Jewish, Christian, or Sikh, as well as American, Canadian, Pakistani, Costa Rican, Ukrainian, Mexican, or even Greek. Life altering events such as 9/11, or the Chernobyl disaster, and the Indian Partition become the background as also smaller-scale individual and 'insignificant' tragedies. True to her previous works, themes of fear, foreignness, and the essential question about identity bridge cultural chasms and there is an apparent stillness covering the deeper turmoil. Interestingly, there is a superficial quietness muting the deafening cacophony of jumbled emotions as well a subdued simplicity airbrushing the fierceness of life's unforeseen blows. And very ingeniously and very efficiently, Baldwin maintains this narrative status quo throughout her book, making the unseen intrigue, the layered baffle, the half-glimpsed tantalize and the promised mystify in every sense. The author, however, does not allow the invisible, the not-to-be-seen and the intangible to manifest involuntarily and hence the aim of this essay is to propose the idea that, Baldwin strikes at the very fundamental notion of freedom and pursues a single thread of connection, questioning the very essence of the meaning of the term freedom.

In the text *The Tiger Claw*, Baldwin retrieves the historical data of the Indian princess Noor-Inayat-Khan, who happened to have served in the Second World War in a clandestine operation as British spy in France under the terror seize of the Nazis. It was a chanced discovery as Baldwin might put it, especially in a context when she was a living witness to the aftermaths of one of the most politically and otherwise most critical events in the history of United States of America—the terrorist attack on the World Trade Centre, which happens to be a financial locus point. Strategic destruction of such a point seems symbolic to have struck a blow at the very fundamental belief of being a controlling agency. The text begins in the form of maintaining records, giving the details of the location of characters during a specific period stretched over meaningful places connected by dots. Baldwin in her book *Reluctant Rebellions* mentions how non-fiction has its own limitations of not being able to represent every truth, therefore the necessity of fiction to resurrect 'silences'.

If one has to define the world order in terms of the socio-political changes, then post the dissolution of Berlin Wall and unification of Germany any event that might have affected the world order to a similar scale is the terror attack on the World Trade Centre on 11th September 2001 and can possibly be the one which shaped certain perspective on the world order. The world view on many things had been shaped and changed by this cataclysmic event. The way emotions are manipulated is used in the evolutionary politics of the cultivation of national and social narrative. This narrative politics further shapes the way individuals are viewed as. In the light of such an incident, individuals are identified on the basis of physical features, skin colour or even their cultural practices and sometimes such practices become the basis of cultural and political attack. Their bodies then become the primary site of violence as well as resistance.

In one of her essays in *Reluctant Rebellion* mentioned earlier, "Ruthless Terrorist or a Valiant Spy?" Shauna Singh Baldwin talks at length in detail about how she came across the name and life of Noor Inayat Khan. This sudden encounter with her life, triggers in Baldwin the urge to conduct detailed research about her life and her times, sifting through books and scholarly writings, about her work and her associates. She also gives a detailed account of how her quest led her to various places and people and her encounter with different individuals who were witnesses to Noor's times. This information led her to better insights as she herself has claimed "More information, better insights." (Baldwin, *Reluctant* 43). But apart from giving insights, this information also provided the link to certain kinds of questions, queries and introspections which probably forced her to talk about Noor in great detail in the book *The Tiger Claw* and that too at a time when geographical locations became geo-political locations, moving towards a devastating phase of challenge. A challenge that had thrown open new concerns and consequences.

Baldwin's encounter with Noor's story made her question Noor's position. On a closer observation of Noor as an individual, she occupied a very complicated position not only in terms of her historical location/identity but also her geographical identity. Her inclinations, influences and inheritances shaped her into a certain kind of an individual who could not be easily fit into any perfect mould. Such insights also led to more questions for Baldwin which she expressed in detail in the essay "Ruthless Terrorist or Valiant Spy?". Questions pertaining as to what could probably be going on in Noor's mind when she decided to join the SOE forces. Especially at a point of time when belonging from an Indian family known for its rebellious nature against the British crown, was considered threatening how difficult it might have been for her to prove her loyalty to the British government during her training and operation despite best efforts and efficiency. Noor's identity has always been marginal in terms of her ancestry, her citizenship and her ideological inclination, her inclination towards any of these categories were difficult for her. This is because, her selection would have affected her position and that she could not afford to jeopardize her travel or her assignment to Paris. It was a difficult choice that she had to make between choosing her love for her Jewish boyfriend at the time of war in France and her sense of loyalty to her family and her nation (British Government).

Noor's character is also more interesting because ideologically she has been shaped and influenced by an extremely syncretic system of faith, adopting her father's musical taste and Sufi ideology, despite belonging from a conservative Muslim family whose opinions starkly differ from Sufi philosophy. Having descended from an ethnically mixed family, Noor's position at a time during madness of "ethnic purity" that raged high in Europe and wartime France has been particularly speculated by Baldwin in this given essay. Her position vis-à-vis her backdrop of being a colonial subject, with brown skin, with too much of oriental features, too much of "Abbajan" in her as Kabir her brother (in *The Tiger Claw)* would like to put it, had also aggravated the concern of being tagged as the "other" who is a perennial threat to the system. Baldwin speculates about such a situation in the text referring to the imagination of Kabir "Noor. Abbajan's favourite. Abbajan was open and warm with Noor in a way he never was with Kabir, teaching her how to play the Veena, allowing her to touch her feet when he returned from touring..." (Baldwin 32). Noor's formative years under the philosophy of Hazrat Inayat Khan made Baldwin also conclude in the essay mentioned earlier stating how,

> ...she must have been both and that exclusivity and single path solutions would have been foreign to her very being (Baldwin, *Reluctant* 42).

Here of course by both, she tries to draw upon the fact that Noor was not just an Indian with a royal ancestry and rebellious history, she was also a child of a mother with an American descent. A woman, with so many layers of identity at a time when the world turned against each other for power worked for a nation where she was not born. Despite several odds she also involved in clandestine operations where multiple identities might have been operational on field—speculations such as that make the fiction a more readable one. For Baldwin as a writer of fiction and not history, the work became extremely difficult since she had to distance factual history and fictional character. It is through these lines in-between history and fiction through the fissures that Baldwin tried to contextualize the current political state of affairs in United States especially with the onslaught of the political upheaval owing to the events following the incident of September 11, 2001. This one particular incident unleashed a global war on terror, in the long run actually terrorizing people across and may be the entire world.

In another of her essays, Baldwin "Writing in the Time of Terrorism" talks about how she conceived the idea of writing about Noor at a time when the world turned against each other in the name of consolidation of borders. She confesses,

> Hours After the Attack on World Trade Centre in 2001, my horror and grief for the victims gave way to the realization that a backlash was in progress against the members of the Sikh Community and other minorities (Baldwin, *Reluctant* 47).

The basic contention of the article is formed from an insight (by sifting between fictional Noor and the real Noor through her biography) that what Baldwin tried to do with an extremely popular tale of a valiant spy, is simply an attempt to contextualize representation in contemporary America and by doing that she tried to draw a parallel to what was happening in war-torn Europe during Second World War. Noor, being a woman and that too, a liberal, Sufi, Muslim, with mixed genetic inheritance, the nuances of her identity has been explored here in *The Tiger Claw.* The complexities in the markers of her identity have successfully augmented the possibility of her body being the site of all kinds of aggression and stereotyped impressions. Scholars like Peter Morey and Amina Yaqin in their book *Framing Muslims: Stereotyping and Representation After 9/11* have written at length how gender or religious or any kind of 'stereotyping' happens, how it is reiterated, how various social forces operate to materialize that image. Now the nuances that Baldwin tries to explore or project through Noor's character becomes metaphorical because such an image not only debunks assumptions or breaks down stereotypes at all levels, but also threatens such attempts. For Noor it was always the position of a state of a limbo, always to do a tight-rope walking, always at the edge of things. Baldwin by doing this is actually trying to draw attention, is trying to "speak truth to power" (*Reluctant* 53). She feels it to be more essential she wanted to invoke the character of Noor and root her to the current times. This is probably one of her ways of speaking "truth to power" how much ever they provide the readers with an analogy of resistance, irrespective of the dangers associated with her. And this she does by characterizing her "Noor" in *The Tiger Claw*, by providing her at times, without deviating much from 'history' (perhaps!) some sort of agency to act upon her wishes sometimes.

The point of entry of Noor as a metaphorical textual element at such a disturbing time was to invoke the complex image of Noor associated with one of the most complex times of history of the world. Baldwin very successfully accomplishes to metamorphose the two time lines and tries to provide a strong message as to how irrespective of the world which has apparently changed yet resonates of a very traumatic past. It is as if the timelines are a continuum, fused and blended seamlessly.

> We are told that the world changed dramatically on 09/11/01, that racial profiling, random search and seizure, and invasion of privacy are non-permissible. The secrecy is the mode of operation for the government. The crime seems to have given an excuse to redefine the very basis of morality, beginning with the dictionary definition of *torture.* Words like *freedom* and *democracy* are up for redefinition. (Baldwin, *Reluctant* 47)

Baldwin opines how the crimes that were perpetrated on that day gave license to those who "wished to dismantle international law and set aside the law of the land…" (47). It somehow legitimized powerful institutions and politicians to profile "others" very conveniently and label minorities as "immigrant "terrorists" and "sleeper spies" and lock them at random. This "racial profiling" or "stereotyping" is something that helps us invoke the thread of Noor whose context is in reference to "stereotyping" and "othering" of "Muslims" and "Sikhs". Morey and Yaqin in their aforementioned book, talks at length about several politically motivated personnel in the US government for instance Christopher Hitchens, who with his vitriolic blogging and cheerleading the mass hatred against Islam and followers of Islam, instrumentalized this. He also channelized the "Islamic Rage Boy" image popularized in a certain context in another part of the world to drive out Muslims or at least was able to make a subtle justification of the perpetuation of hate crimes and arson against followers of Islam.

During the course of the argument, Morey speaks of Jaques Lacan's *Ecrits*, who talks of the "armor of identity" and goes on to expand as to what would that probably mean. It entails a carefully concentrated notion of the "other" and popularizing the same and also a definitive effort being made to construct and safeguard identity from the possibility of contamination from the "other". He says,

> This distinctive outline of such constructions having to do with matters such as visible difference, cultural practice, the role of religion in personal life and motivation, and alien moral bearings, is what persuades us that thinking about stereotypes and stereotyping is legitimate –indeed essential –as well as timely (29).

This is precisely why Noor's character has been invoked at this crucial juncture. Noor epitomizes an allegory of everything that opposes such racialization. Her character walks on the very edges of whole process of breaking stereotyping.

Stereotyping is a very convenient method of perpetrating and justifying any crime committed against any set of individuals/communities. Noor's character uniqueness posited to stand against such attempts and resist such practices of essentialization. This is particularly true post 9/11 because it somehow reflects the same myopic vision that was induced during the Second World War, which brings to the current discourse about the relevance of unraveling such a character that would be emblematic to the resistance (which is what Baldwin is trying to invoke and unravel through her) at this point of time. Also, such political discourses help to give form to stereotypical representation as something historically made infamous by the Holocaust. Even though it is essential to recognize the invidiousness of negative prejudiced stereotyping yet stereotyping is somewhat to some degree essential to making sense of certain things. But racial stereotyping is a phenomenon that was prevalent during the Second World War. Not only was it cheered but such stereotyping of that kind was circulated and perpetuated. "Stereotyping", if anything is closer to that of essentializing the known traits of a community, was popularized or used in order to probably as a means to "know" that community but "Knowledge" about anything/anyone can always be created in order to accommodate the justifications. These attempts both at individual level or state level may have overlapping functions—not just "social causal" function as Henri Tajfel has put it in his book *Human Groups and Social Categories* (1981) but as "social justificatory" function and "social differentiation" (254) function.

The point being made is an effort to draw parallels to the similarity in operation and the kind of the tools that were used during Noor's time in the name of racial cleansing in the sheer "madness" to compartmentalize "difference" and "otherness" and the mere similarity in these efforts were as valid as what happened before 9/

11/01 and is still relevant and in the current time. The sheer contemporaneity of it being validated by the kind of violence perpetrated in the garb of religion, all veiled owing to the reluctance to share resources is worth reflecting on. In order to break stereotypes, artists and writers often "speak truth to power" and as some would opine "... power doesn't listen" (Baldwin, *Reluctant* 53).

The factual data encountered by Baldwin which researching on Noor Inayat Khan has to an extent been fictionalized. The account used in this article is about this fictional Noor who is mostly based on this historical figure Noor Inayat Khan, used as a metonymy of resistance emblemized in this rare historical figure and that too with the baggage of identity as that of hers. The precarity of her position and her identity provides a fine line to define the possible instance of rebellious spirit. The book *The Tiger Claw*, as conceived by her as is read as a kind of a response to the cataclysmic conditions prevailing in the United States and perhaps had forced her rethink in certain ways. It can also be deciphered that historical data has not been exactly transpired/translated into the book. There is a difference when it comes to expecting ratifiable history in a work of fiction. But there is an undercurrent of politics that has probably led her to do that. No other character than her, more specific a Sufi, syncretic, Muslim woman, could possibly have posed a mere challenging question. During Noor's involvement with the war troops also called into question several aspects of her identity—all the categories with which one defines individual identities. Questions of nationality, ancestry, appearance, language, religion, state (whether nation of ancestry or that of citizenship), everything that defines individual identity, posed questions about locating Noor's identity as well. So, at a time when the entire world almost is fraught with such parochial limited notions of identity, perhaps Noor's existence, otherwise slipped into oblivion, could have perhaps provided a new avenue to look for inspirational resistance albeit in a subtle manner. With this primary contention, the current article tries to project a metonymic representation of Noor. Noor's selector Colonel Buckmaster as far as Baldwin has portrayed in the fictional work, had never wanted to keep faith in her as an SOE operator positing highly biased opinions regarding her truthfulness. Her ancestry and her resemblance to her father provoked him with regressive remarks.

> A glance at the documents from...have told the Colonel that she was an Indian colonial, a refugee,...was from the princely state of Baroda, where rulers had never been conquered in, either by the East India Company or the Raj. Baroda was a British ally, subjugated yet independent and Noor could describe herself similarly. But Colonel Buckmaster wanted a pliable, eager woman, bilingual in French and English, with harnessable energy, ... (Baldwin, *Tiger* 50).

However, her religious identity was ambivalent too, being a descendant of a Sufi practitioner and a man who revolutionized Europe at a time when people lost faith in humanity after the First World War. Her syncretic faith testified by her love for Armand (apparently a fact that remains unchanged, with fictional names) and her floating identity like that of a "stranger" figure of modernity as probably Zygmunt Bauman would have put it. Bauman in his book *Modernity and Ambivalence* describes about how a stranger figure invades and disrupts the cozy insider–outsider binaries through which modernity constructs its social order.

In a very similar vein, the image of a Muslim, Sufi, woman, apparently all contradictory paradoxical terms which do not somehow complement each other creates a self-image of normalized secular society. Seen in the similar light Noor's image is metamorphosed into that of Bauman's "stranger" image who invades, cuts across, boundaries, debunks categories/social orders and at times deconstructs them. Noor's position had always been on the margin, periphery on the edge. And this position can probably be read as vantage point—apparently a point not just because of her skillsets, but also her ambivalent position can be used to understand how from the periphery/margin one can gauze the contemporary situation the US seeing from the similar lens as that of Noor.

Sara Ahmad in her book *The Cultural Politics of Emotions* informs us about how various social and scientific thinkers have tried to explain the context of evolution of human emotion and how various social forces are at play. Ahmad builds up the argument stating how two kinds of touch "soft touch" and "hard touch" determine an "object"/individual's attribution whether masculine or feminine and that is also being assigned to nation's/state's permeability and penetrability.

> The risk of becoming a 'soft touch' for the nation, and for the national subject, is not only the risk of being feminine, but also becoming less white would involve moving backwards in time, such that one would come to resemble a more primitive form of social life or a lower and animal like condition (Ahmad 3).

Therefore, Noor's overtly manifesting Brown identity resembling her father, accounts for her 'becoming' a "soft subject"—one who could have been gullible and therefore easily abuseable, but for her training as a war operative. Noor was closer to her father Hazrat Inayat Khan in her whole disposition. Kabir, Noor's brother envied her (depicted in *The Tiger's Claw*) stating her as "Abbajan's favourite" and referring her as the rightful owner of Hazrat's mantle.

> Noor. Abbajan's favourite. Abbajan was open and warm with Noor in a way he never was with Kabir, teaching her how to play the Veena, allowing her to touch her feet when he returned from touring…
>
> And he did'nt need Mr. Freud to tell him what the dream meant, hatred for that part of Noor that was most like himself. Yes, it had taken Kabir years to name it, but he knew it now. It was that shared part that was "too damn Indian" (Baldwin, *Tiger* 33).

It was also probably because of this profiling that forced Noor to face discrimination about the process of selection as SOE agent.

> A glance at the documents from the Bettersea Reception Centre in her file would have told the Colonel that she was an Indian colonial, a refugee, like everyone else who had fled the German Abbajan was from the princely state of Baroda, where rulers had never been conquered in was either by the East India Company or the Raj. Baroda was a British ally, subjugated yet independent and Noor could describe herself similarly. But Colonel Buckmaster wanted a pliable, eager woman, bilingual in French and English, with harnessaeble energy, he wasn't interested in the rest of her life, talents or language (Baldwin, *Tiger* 50).

The body of Noor, both at the physical and corporeal/ethereal levels, becomes the emblem of resistance. Her whole being, from the level of her spirit to her whole disposition reflected her language of resistance. Both fictional and historical characters of Noor were writers of children's stories, some of these stories written under incarceration addressed as "ma petite" to a fictionalized unborn child of the couple. She resorted to several of her Sufi learning and Indian mythological narratives for metaphorical references. Baldwin has very clearly woven Noor's moorings and the story very beautifully and expresses why Noor must have written what she could, interpellating them in italics,

> I write, not because this story is more important than others, but because I have so great a need to understand it. What I say, is my truth and lies together, amalgam of memory and explication. I write mostly in English, mostly, ... Other languages often express my feelings better—French, Urdu, Hindustani.... But all my languages have been tainted by what we've said and done to one another in these years of war. (Baldwin, *Tiger* 3)

Noor's reflections on her Sufi training that she inherited from her father led her to such writings and she "progressively fashioned" her personal reflections and tried to incorporate them in her writings. Noor's writings also incorporated her "factual reconstruction of the larger social and political contexts within which she experienced them" as Lara R. Curtis maintains in her book *Writing Resistance and the Question of Gender* (66). For Noor, she maintains, resistance also was expressed in "a variety of ways in which Noor tends to write resistance in relation to "questions of gender and identity" (66). Drastic political changes across the world forces her to join resistance forces and that there have been several indications both at spiritual level and her writings of how she espoused the ideals of her father's Sufi teachings. In the same book Curtis also opines that.

> ...her writing strongly indicate that she tended to weigh issues in contemporary writings strongly indicate that she tended to weigh issues in contemporary politics in terms of the moral lessons of Sufism. In some of her narratives, thematic notions of resistance resonate autobiographically, especially when she associates herself with her female characters who are sacrificing their lives for values they believe to the honourable and morally correct (66).

Curtis contends that Noor (historical character) had a tendency to invest her writings by blending various spheres of her influence to give shape to her core ideals and narrative from Sufism.

Noor's body bears the mark of torture and resistance, and both her body and spirit therefore become, not just the site but also the emblem of resistance. Noor's remarks (in *The Tiger Claw*) written on the walls, within the confines of the Pforzheim prison of Dachau Concentration Camp bear testimony to that, even after her death, as her brother Kabir could discover. Her statement invoked that very statement of existence which possessed the seed of Western Enlightenment philosophy, "I resist, therefore I am" (Baldwin, *Tiger* 544).

The historical character Noor witnessed the drastically deteriorating political climate throughout the world, she understood here "resistance" should be nurtured, which led her to join the forces. Even her writings (composed both during the imprisonment as well as a SOE operative) strongly indicate her influence by Sufism and how she tried to weigh politics in terms of the moral lessons she learnt from Sufism.

Curtis also mentions in her book about how Noor's (historical character) stories "…resonate autobiographically" (66) narratives of her female characters that she created in her writings, those characters in fact seem to personify her ideology. Curtis refers to this tendency of Noor "to invest her modes of writing resistance" as a consequence of "…blending of traditions," (66). Her writing illuminates the subjective position and her nature of her being." Curtis even concludes by saying that Noor's "spiritual self-awareness matures along with the increasing gravity of her experience, especially with regard to the ways in which her opinions as well as her actions reflect her keen perception of resistance as a core value of human nature" (67).

These words of Curtis actually sum up the character of Noor represented here (both the historical as well as fictional), and hence comprehends the whole discussion in one statement. The necessity to invoke the character of Noor in this context and interpret her very existence as a trope of resistance is testified by such evidences. Baldwin's efforts of resurrecting history also is justified and relevant against the backdrop of the political turmoil, as has been contended in the current essay. Thus Noor, transcends both characteristically and metaphorically as an emblem of resistance, who still continues to remain a potent symbol of it. In fact, she teaches us how to "…speak truth to power…" (Baldwin, *Reluctant* 53) as Baldwin phrases it in "Writing in the Time of Terrorism" in *Reluctant Rebellions.*

References

Ahmad S (2014) *The Cultural Politics of Emotion.* Edinburgh University Press

Baldwin Shauna Singh (2004) *The Tiger Claw.* Penguin

Baldwin SS (2016) Reluctant Rebellions, Centre for Indo-Canadian Studies

Basu S (2006) *The Life of Noor Inayat Khan: Spy Princess.* Roli Books

Bauman Z (1993) Modernity and Ambivalence. Polity Press

Bond E (2018) *Writing through the Body.* Palgrave Macmillan

Curtis LR (2019) *Writing Resistance and the Question of Gender: Charlotte Delbo, Noor Inayat Khan and Germaine Tillion.* Palgrave Macmillan

Lucas B-M (2019) Masculinity in the Metanarrative of the Global War on Terror: Shauna Singh Baldwin's Transnational Critique. Revista Canaria De Estudios Inglesias 78:125–139. https://doi.org/10.25145/j.recaesin.2019.78.09

Morey P, Amina Y (2011) *Framing Muslims: Stereotyping and Representation after 9/11.* Harvard UP

Tajfel H (1981) *Human Groups and Social Categories.* CUP

Van der Veer P (1995) *Nation and Migration.* U of Pennsylvania Press

Chapter 11
Marginalised Lives in Assamese Literature: Saga of Loss and Longing in Assam's Chars

Parvin Sultana

The Muslims of East Bengal origin comprise the second wave of migrants brought to the Northeastern region as a part of the colonial endeavour. The discovery of tea and the movement of tea garden workers to the state of Assam led to an increase in the demand of foodgrains. A depleting population because of the Burmese wars and epidemics created a vacuum in the workforce in the state. Amalendu Guha in *Planter Raj to Swaraj* talks about the migration of peasants from East Bengal. This migration transformed the unused lands to food producing revenue generating lands. But it also changed the demography of the region with more people coming to that area. This migration started figuring prominently in post independence politics. Boundaries earmarking the new nation made the dates of migration crucial, an issue that continues to simmer in the state politics of Assam. The Muslims of East Bengal origin on the other hand worked towards assimilating with the larger Assamese community accepting the Assamese language. Renowned Assamese poet Jyotiprasad Aggarwala named this community *Na-Axomiya* or *Neo-Assamese*. The larger Assamese society have constantly engaged with issues concerning this community and Assamese literature is no exception. While works on this community continue to be few—renowned Assamese author Syed Abdul Malik wrote *Rupabarir Palash* focussing on the lives of people from this community. Few other works have followed.

However, this community which comprise a substantial part of the greater Assamese society continues to be marginalized in terms of representation in literary works. Nonetheless they are also perhaps one of the most visible communities across platform. Their image is often used to portray alleged illegal immigration across a porous border, population explosion and encroachment of government land. Interestingly, this community is often portrayed as being responsible for many problems that the state faces. If we look at popular literature, the treatment is almost similar to an extent. The community is portrayed as a 'problem', even writings making a case

P. Sultana (✉)
Pramathesh Barua College, Gauripur, Assam, India
e-mail: parvin.jnu@gmail.com

S. S. Ali and A. Basak (eds.), *Marginal Narratives and the Question of Human Rights in Asian Pacific Literature*, https://doi.org/10.1007/978-981-97-4544-9_11

of reform also often strip the community of basic human rights. The tone is patronising. Writings from within the community have emerged which have tried to address this lacuna. Starting from late Ismail Hussain to Dr Hafiz Ahmed, Khabir Ahmed to Shalim M Hussain and others—poets and novelists from the community have highlighted the problems of the community and presented a larger case of assimilation. There is a need however to look at the gaze from outside.

The Muslims of East Bengal origin with their distinct language and culture comprise the majority of Muslims in Assam. Their presence in every aspect of Assam's socio-political life is a reality. While the community has largely believed in assimilation, it has also faced prejudice, hatred when the state indulged in sub nationalist politics. The six years Assam Movement saw unprecedented attacks on the community. The community has also asserted itself from time to time through politics and poetics. This paper will look at how the larger Assamese society perceive this community through two novels—Rupabarir Palash by Syed Abdul Malik and Kahibunor Malita by Rudrani Sharma. Both the books look at the lives of the Muslims of East Bengal origin and engage with the community on multiple levels. While the books are set apart by the periods they cover—Syed Abdul Malik's book talks about the earlier days of migration, Rudrani Sharma's novel takes us through the lives of three generations and shows what the state politics in contemporary times did for the community—there is some continuity among the two books. Both the authors are writing from outside the community and bring forth how the larger Assamese community looks at these people and their struggle for a dignified existence. The novels touch upon issues of migration, assimilation and even identity politics that the Muslims of East Bengal origin faced from time to time. The two books were selected keeping in mind the fact that both the books revolve around the 'contested' community and reflect on issues that have shaped the state's politics over the decades. The social location of the respective authors were also considered as this paper aims to also study the reflection of this community with respect to human rights in mainstream Assamese literature.

This paper with the help of the two novels will reflect upon the question of the right to a dignified life and the right to have rights (Arendt 1994) of a community which is often found entangled in binaries of insider/outsider and are often forced to lead a life in a legal limbo.

11.1 Situating the Miya Muslims in Assamese Discourse of Belonging

Assam along with the northeastern region is a microcosm of diversity. Home to a large number of indigenous tribes which share cultural traits to the South East Asian countries, this region and the state of Assam have also been a theatre of multiple contestations. Be it linguistic, religious or ethnic faultlines—the region has had its fair share of conflicts. The northeastern continues to witness homeland and secessionist movements that precede Indian independence. The modern world's oldest movement for self-determination unfolded in Nagaland.

The contestations did not end with independence. Nation building has been a tumultuous affair in the region. Starting from hill districts to autonomous and separate statehood, the region and the state of Assam have witnessed many geographical and political changes. And the question of identity have also gone through myriad transitions. The literature of the region is also mired in these transformations and have responded to the larger changes. Such contestation is evident even in the perception of the community. Through a literary movement that surfaced recently an educated section of the community started addressing themselves as Miya Muslims, the urdu word which was initially used as a slur. This is their effort on asserting their identity. (Daniyal, 2019)

Literature from the region have reflected on these issues. While literature may not bring about significant socio-political change, it does the crucial work of illuminating aspects of our collective existence often left untouched by political and economic practices. And of the various literary forms, fiction is the most privileged site (Hasan 2000). Assamese literature is also abundant with accounts of secessionist movements, rise of extremist organisations like ULFA and the turbulence that the state went through during the years of the Assam Movement. Apart from this, the stalwarts of Assamese literature like Lakshminanth Bezbaruah, Rajnikanta Bordoloi, Jyotiprasad Agarwala have also written about different tribes. Their owrks have on one hand paved the way for assimilation and formation of the greater Assamese Society, on the other hand it has also faced criticism from authors writing from the margins about the patronizing tone and the tendency to smoothen over and downplay the conflicts that these tribes has had with the mainstream Assamese society.

Many contemporary authors like Arupa Patangia Kalita, Rita Chowdhury have also written about the movement years. While Arupa Patangia's *Felanee* have problematised the very question of identity and put forth the varied experiences of the people of Assam including the assertion that was evident amongst tribes, Rita Choudhury's *Aei Xomoy Xei Xomoy* gives an account of an Assamese middle class woman who actively participated in Assam Movement and was later disillusioned with it.

Books written about the movement touches upon the issue of alleged illegal immigration as it was the central issue, the reference to the alleged illegal immigrants who were largely from the *Miya* Muslim community was tangential. Their voices continued to be marginalised. Mainstream academic works also referred to this community as an 'outsider' and a group of 'land hungry aggressor'. On the spectrum of belonging, the question of the Miya Muslims were always precarious.

The identity of the '*other*' continued changing from time to time. Scholars writing on the Assam Movement and Nellie Massacre have pointed out the shift to this 'other' that took place during the Movement. While it was initially any body from outside Assam, during the movement it slowly turned into largely a Muslim of East Bengali origin. (Pisharorty 2018, Kimura 2013)This was a problem as the state did have to undertake the burden of refugees who left Bangladesh during its war of liberation. This was also a time when the first non-Congress government came to power at the Centre and parties like Jan Sangh made its presence felt in the corridors of power.

Many political leaders affiliated with right wing politics took an interest in the Assam Movement and tried to give a communal colour to the insider–outsider divide.

The spectre of an outsider is that of an individual who is denied citizenship and the rights to have rights (Arendt 1994). Post 2005 and the discard of the IM(DT) Act which safeguarded people from spurious accusations of being a foreigner, there is a spurt in cases marking people as D voters and detaining them for failure of proving citizenship. The last decade is a saga of deprivation of rights of people from marginalised sections. And this very systemic deprivation have urged people to revisit history to understand and situate the Muslims in Assam in a proper perspective.

11.2 Representation of Muslims in Assamese Literature

Muslims comprise an integral part of Assam's greater society. Assam's syncretic culture is a product of the humanism of Srimanta Shankardeva and the Sufism brought by Azaan Pir from Iran. However popular literature have not engaged adequately with the community. Few mainstream authors wrote about the lives and livelihood of the Muslims of Assam. One needs to remember that the Muslims of Assam are not a homogenous group and there is a distinct cultural and linguistic difference between the Muslims who converted from the local indigenous communities and Muslims who came from erstwhile East Bengal during the British colonial rule mainly looking for land.

It is the Muslims of East Bengal origin whose representation in Assamese literature is of concern here. Mainstream authors have engaged with the community but in a limited way. Birendrakumar Bhattacharya wrote *Kabor Aru Phool* (*Blossoms in the Graveyard* translated by Mitra Phukan) just around the Bangladesh War of Liberation. However this book largely looks at refugees who fled Bangladesh because of the war and pine to go back to a free country. This did not look at the experience of the Miya Muslims who stayed in Assam and had to face discrimination for being alleged illegal immigrants. Homen Borgohain in a short story *Ismail Sheikhor Sandhanot (In Search of Ismail Sheikh)* published in 1958 gave an idea of what the community went through. The picture he portrayed is of utmost relevance even today. He talked of the Miya Muslims who came to Assam even before independence owing to a colonial policy but faced discrimination and harassment as the first years of independence saw communal polarization and manifested into large scale displacement.

The story written by Homen Borgohain is about a government official who oversees the eviction of Muslims of East Bengal origin who are victims of land erosion and squatted on government land. A person called Ismail Sheikh requested him time and again to not break his home as his children were unwell. But the official did not pay heed. Later the official was informed that both the children of Ismail Sheikh died because they were exposed to cold and rain. Remorse hit the official hard and since then he has been searching for Ismail Sheikh for penance.

These are some of the examples in which Assamese writers engaged with the Miya Muslims community. The engagement has been limited. But as one of the most defining factor of Assam's socio-political life is related to this community, it becomes pertinent that books written about this community is studied and discussed in details. The following sections will reflect on the two books selected for this paper.

11.3 Rupaborir Polosh

The first book is *Rupaborir Polosh* written by veteran Assamese author Syed Abdul Malik. Malik is an Assamese Muslim. Assamese Muslims are Muslims who were converted by Azan Pir and have a close cultural and linguistic proximity with the Assamese Hindus. In this book he gave an elaborate account of the entire journey undertaken by Muslims of East Bengal origin. The story revolves around the character of Babar, a young boy whose father is a fisherman working for the Zamindar in one of the provinces in East Bengal. The very first scene resonates whiplash on Babar's father's back because the fish he caught were not of the desired size. Babar witnesses this wrongs with gritted teeth. His entire life, he has seen his father toil away without a second to spare but still he could not provide adequately for his family.

The systematic exploitation of Zamindari system is reflected in details. The peasants have no land rights and are at the mercy of the zamindars. There are also instances of sexual harassment perpetrated by the landlords' family. Saving two young girls from sexual assault at the hands of the Zamindar's son, Babar and his friend run away fearing the wrath of the zamindar. Left with no option, they start for Assam—another province of erstwhile British India. Along with the fear of punishment, the hope for better opportunities of livelihood led them on this difficult journey. They start along with a group and undertake a tedious journey to reach Assam. Once they reach the new place with hopes and dreams, they are left to work with people from their country who have come earlier. This points to the fact that migration have taken place in waves across years and pushed by the exploitation of zamindari system and a hope for better livelihood opportunities. M Kar's work Muslims in Assam points to the waves of migration that saw a gradual increase in the number of Muslims in Assam.

Babar also aspired to escape these hardships but leaving behind home and family was difficult. He however met people who has left earlier and being with them helped him overcome the longing for home. An elderly Sorif Gaonburha (village headman) took Babar under his wings and allowed him to mend his fields. Babar also took to the kindness of this person and worked for his family. Around this time, the Second World War started leading to an acute increase in demand for goods. Most people started accumulating more and more land lying vacant and cultivating them. Babar did the same without understanding the consequences. This was also the time when the Muslim League was strengthening its hold on minority areas of Assam and reached Babar's village. The colonial government encouraged the people to turn the wastelands into food producing fields.

Babar not only had to look after Sorif's lands, but he has acquired few bighas of land for himself. Along with this, he was also working as a supplier with the

British Army. He in fact has become a person with means in his village. He was later induced to campaign for Muslim League. As many Muslims vouched for the League, the concerns were of local level as opposed to the larger politics. For Babar, more than Muslim League's demand for a separate homeland, issues of land rights and the right to a dignified life meant more. He was also distrustful of those aligning with the Congress as they had a notorious reputation in the village. It should be noted that Babar's opponents who fought elections from Congress were also Muslims showing the inherent differences in terms of political choices amongst Muslims. Babar's political life was however short lived. When Muslim League lost in the election, Babar distanced himself from the party and its agenda.

This book then further moves to the period around partition. A communal polarization has taken a concrete shape and demands were made for people of East Bengal origin to return to their homeland. But for Babar, home was Assam. He belonged to that group of people who have almost assimilated linguistically and culturally to Assam. However the urge to revisit his village was strong. A visit back home made him realize the nexus between the political and economic power in the newly formed state of Pakistan. The exploitative zamindars were the political masters of the new country. Disillusioned with this state of affairs, he returned to Assam. However in Assam, the crackdown on alleged illegal immigrants baffled Babar. His identity, belongingness was put on perpetual doubt. Both the nations in the throes of their birth drew rigidified ideas of nationhood and citizenship. Legality scarred families and the border divided nations as well as lives and families. Through the life of Babar, the book gives a glimpse of the politics that would grip the nation for decades to come.

The book ends on a hopeful note when Babar's daughter starts studying Assamese and is growing up to accept this as her home and hearth. The book also focuses on the hardships that this community faces owing to floods and erosion. Through the characters of Girin Master and his relationship with Babar, the author tried to pinpoint images of peaceful co-existence across communities. However the seething tension is also reflected when Girin Master wants to sell his lands to Babar but is not able to because of the stringent policies of government. This pinpoints to the Line system which tried to ensure that land ownership does not pass from the indigenous people to the Muslims of East Bengal origin. Financial hardships however ensured that this was not followed completely and the Line System was flouted in many instances.

11.4 Kahibunor Malita

The second book selected for this paper is *Kahibunor Malita* written by Rudrani Sharma. The book revolves around the life of Ramij Master and is an intergenerational tale of immigration, displacement and the question of belonging. The book starts with the story of Ramij's grandfather who comes to Assam much before independence fleeing the exploitation of zamindari system as well as the plight brought by famine in the years of 1897–98. In this new land he was however lucky enough to find respite in the kindness of one Madhu Mahajan who allowed him to work in his fields. Basir

Miya was so indebted to Madhu Mahajan for saving their lives that he named his son after him—Madhu Miya.

Through the relationship between Basir Miya and Madhu Mahajan, the mood in the earlier years of the twentieth century is reflected. The available land lying barren welcomed these new entrants. The local people were also accommodative of these hardworking people who ensured a flow of cheap labour. However a continued migration created an atmosphere of conflict—not just amongst the local people and the fresh entrants but also amongst people who came a few years earlier and those who came later. The idea of who rightfully belongs in this place and who is a encroacher was even then being decided by the time of entry.

The first few chapters while elaborating the stories of Basir Miya and others also reflect on the role of British colonialism. The British encouraged the first wave of migration once tea was discovered and tea plantations were set up. To provide food for this increased population, the British initiated the next wave of migration—this time peasants from Mymensingh and other parts of East Bengal. These people also brought the art of jute cultivation and soon turned the fallow lands into food producing fields. The author portrays the picture of a people moving from their homeland looking for new opportunities. Basir Miya settled in today's Barpeta with his family. His children also started working at the fields of Madhu Mahajan.

Ramij is the youngest son of Madhu Miya. Through the lives of Madhu Miya, his wife Rahima and his sister Amina—the author portrayed the problems that the community faces even today. Amina was married very young and was also widowed early. She was forced to come and live with her brother's family. Even Madhu's wife Rahima had to face a lot of criticism because she failed to give birth to a son first. The community which was yet to benefit from education suffered from rampant misogyny. This was reflected in practices like child marriage, polygamy, son preference etc. Madhu however struggled hard to make a difference. His life was marked by hardships. Theirs was a life marked by frequent floods, river erosion and displacement. This was often accompanied by accusations of being fresh illegal immigrants from across the border which was now a different country.

While Madhu himself could not get a proper education, he hoped to educate his children. However only Ramij—his youngest showed some interest in getting educated. From his childhood, Ramij was different. He was observant. He belonged to a generation which was born and reared in Assam and believed in the need to assimilate. Ramij also did his bit to be a part of the greater Assamese society. However he was not blind to inherent discrimination which was deep rooted in the society. Instances like being given food in different utensils in Hindu homes bothered him and he did not shy away from pointing it out. Nonetheless he did find good friends amongst Assamese Hindus.

Responding to the socio-political changes around him, Ramij wanted to fight elections in his college. It was only then he was made aware of his ethnic identity when he was abused for being a 'Miya' and still wanting to fight elections. This was an eye opening experience for Ramij. He realized that there were differences which he could not wish away. But should he be ashamed of who he was? How was he a lesser Assamese despite loving the language and land? Why was his ethnic identity an obstacle on the path of assimilation?

As his young mind grappled with these questions, Assam was in the grip of the Assam Agitation. Communal violence was at the peak when the state was rocked by massacres carried out at Nellie, Chaulkhowa, Gohpur and other areas. Many innocent people lost their lives. Bina, who was the younger sister of Ramij's close friend Jagadish Sharma, was widowed when her husband was killed in cold blood. The loss of lives across communities was disturbing. This episode reiterated that in such conflicts there is no winning side. Rather deep faultlines were drawn in the society.

Post violence, the state and people like Ramij Master tried to pick up the broken pieces and build a bridge of unity across communities. Ramij was aware that his community must assimilate with the Assamese community to strive in an atmosphere where their identity is always under suspicion. To ensure this he formed a cultural association to inculcate assamese values amongst the youths of his community. Ramij faced a lot of opposition from within the community. There were those who did not like his stand and believed that the community was well off being with the Bengalis as they are anyways criticized for being of 'East Bengal origin'. They even believed that assimilation was not possible as they will be asked to prove their loyalty at every situation.

Through Ramij's life and struggles, the author on one hand gave an account of the struggle of a community across generations and on the other hand reflected on the aspirations of a upward mobile class emerging in the community. The author also gave a glimpse of the inherent diversity of the community even on issues of language, identity and allegiance.

11.5 Identity, Sense of Belonging in the Two Novels

Read together, both the books give an account of the history of the community of Miya Muslims who moved from one part of British India to another to escape a difficult life. Exploitation, hardships and famine pushed these people to distant lands. However once they reached the new place, they worked towards assimilation. Syed Abdul Malik's book *Rupaborir Polosh* gave an account of the earlier years especially around the time of independence and the conflicts that took place in the early years. In a lucid account and through the life of Babar, Malik showed how common people made sense of issues like war, partition etc. For Babar encroachment on government land was not illegal because it was for supporting the government during war. For a young Muslim man trying hard to make a life for himself and his family, questions of legality took a back seat. Survival became the primary concern. Similarly Babar initially saw Muslim League promising development and rights for Muslims and not as a party working towards a separate country. Uprooted once, Babar had no interest to be pushed to another country again. As a result, his disillusionment with the politics of Muslim League was soon to set in. Babar also dreamt of a life for his daughter as a part of the greater Assamese society and this was reflected in her education and early life.

In the second book the period covered focuses more on the Assam Movement and the following years. Through the life and work of Ramij Master, the author Rudranee Sharma again looks at the question of identity of this migrant community. How an upward mobile educated section of the community perceived itself as an integral part of the Assamese community was elaborately looked into. Both the novels shows that on the identity question—the community made a very pragmatic decision. Census after census the community declared itself to be Assamese and accepted the language as their own. It was the allegiance of this community that actually played a crucial role in ensuring that Assamese becomes the state language of the state and parts of the state is not amalgamated with Bengal. During the reorganization of states, this became crucial as India mostly opted for linguistic reorganization.

Both the novels however shows the inherent differences of opinion within the community and acknowledges diversity. Many from the community believed that they should stop adhering to Assamese because they are often ridiculed and their allegiance questioned. The politicization across these lines is also focused in both the books.

Another crucial aspect of both the books lies in the absence of glorification or romanticisation of the choices of the community. The authors rather looked at the agency and compulsions of the characters with all their faults intact. This aspects made the books more realistic and humane as well as relatable for people across generations.

11.6 Saga of Loss and Longing

Both the novels reflects upon the pertinent issues that the community faces on a regular basis. The river is nothing less than a lifeline for this community which continues to be largely engaged in agriculture. They move to fertile lands often left with rich deposits of silt after every flood. However the new lands are always at the risk of further flooding as well as erosion. Every year Assam loses hundred of villages to river erosion and the people living on these riverbanks are pushed to inland towns and nearby areas where they are hounded for allegedly being from across the border. (Sultana 2020).

Losing their homes and hearths to the river, these people squat on government lands and are often targeted as ‘doubtful’ people when evicted. The media portrays these as doubtful citizens and justifies evictions without compensation. There is a history of marking people as D voters randomly which justify these kind of portrayal. (Siddiqui 2019) Questioning the identity of these people, the state is exonerated of compensating them because their very ‘citizenship’ is under doubt. The loss of home, hearth is accompanied with the loss of self. And the lack of right to citizenship further denies them the right to have rights.

Both the novels draw tragic pictures of such loss and longing. Through the lives of Babar and Ramij Master, the authors portrayed the predicament that the community continues to find itself in. Forced to move by colonial politics and policies, exploitative regime, the community was again pushed against the wall in the host country. It is to be remembered that Assam's politics continues to be shaped by the question of alleged illegal immigration from across the border. These people who are largely an agricultural community continue to be left out of the benefits that come from education. The middle class in the community is still nascent. The community continues to form a majority of the educationally and financially backward section but denied any safety net in the form of government policy. Instead they are often used as fodder for communal politics which is at peak around elections. They are portrayed as an alleged threat to the state's security and the rights of indigenous communities.

11.7 The Question of Agency

While both the novels depicted a realistic picture of the community as well as the inherent internal diversity within the community, the projections was however that of the authors in both the cases. The authors do not belong to the Miya Muslims community. While Syed Abdul Malik was an Assamese Muslim, Rudranee Sharma is from the Assamese Hindu community and the novels to some extent reflect what the authors depict to be pragmatic choices for the community.

Somewhere through both the protagonists, the authors seem to be making choices for the community rather than giving ample space to the community to exercise their right. This becomes evident in both Babar and Ramij Master's choices of assimilation of their respective communities to the larger Assamese community. But assimilation comes with a cost of shedding off their own cultural identity and markers which in itself is violent. The choices in front of the community were spelled out as either assimilation to the larger Assamese community or allegiance to the Bengali speaking community. However the possibility that the community might decide to retain its own dialect was sidelined. This becomes crucial because the second book *Kahibunor Malita* was published in 2017 and demands for recognizing the dialect and culture of the Miya Muslims as distinct and a part of larger Assamese culture have been around at that time. Such extreme choices leave the community without a right to decide for themselves.

Both the novels fell short of acknowledging the agency of the community in asserting its own identity and was more keen on legitimizing the tendency to assimilate to the larger Assamese society. However it needs to be taken into account that the earlier years of independence and the language movement made such a decision pragmatic. The Miya Muslims put their weight against Assamese language at the backdrop of Language Movement in the 1960s and it made the percentage of Assamese speakers a majority in the state as opposed to Bengali speakers who comprise the second largest linguistic community. Systematic disillusionment with this choice set in and this was reflected in the decision of many from the Miya Muslim community recording Bengali as their mother tongue in the following censuses. The *Chalo Paltai* (Lets Change) Movement also found many takers amongst the community. (Saikia 2019) The insecurity reflected in the two novels regarding allegiance to Bengali language need to be studied in this context. It further becomes crucial as such preconditions of shedding one's own identity for the sake of assimilation is not imposed on other ethnic groups.

11.8 The Question of Human Rights

The novels engaged in details with the lives of the Miya Muslims who entered Assam at different points of time. Both are intergenerational accounts of people who have faced different hardships—first in the form of exploitative regimes in the parent country and second from polarizing politics in the host country. The novels dealt with crucial aspects of human rights of the community and how they were systematically denied of it. The accounts largely come across from a class perspective. In case of Babar of *Rupaborir Polosh*, the exploitation of a feudal system becomes evident. The bonded labour of landless labourers working in the fields of the Zamindars gets reflected in the lives of Babar's family members. Once Babar settled in Assam, his arrest and harassment with the police showed how communal polarization rendered him stateless and a citizen of dubious origin and denied him the rights that come with the membership of a democratic nation.

Similar human rights exclusion and abuse is reflected when we look at the second book *Kahibunor Malita*. Ramij Master's grand father Basir Miya fled similar feudal assault and took refuge in Assam. While initially they found kindness in the locals, things changed soon for worse with the six year long Assam agitation. Even before that Ramij Master's experiences showed deep rooted prejudice towards the community. This prejudice and hatred took an extreme form in 1983 and almost 3000 people were massacred in Nellie. These were largely women and children. Reports filed during the 1983 massacres showed a gross dehumanization of the people which seemed to justify the violence they were subjected to.

The dehumanization is reflected when these people are evicted from government lands and the eviction is justified in terms of legality as freeing the land from encroachers. It is not questioned by mainstream media also as a violation of rights of citizens. Rather these people are dehumanized as 'doubtful' people and their eviction is rendered legally and morally right.

11.9 Conclusion

The novels revolve around the lives and livelihood of Miya Muslims or Muslims of East Bengal origin. Both the books touch upon crucial aspects of their lives. Migration is a common phenomenon and has marked human history since ages. But a colonial past and fervor nationalism divided cultural and geographical terrain into two nations and criminalized those who did not stick to these borders. These borders divided countries as well as families. The novels show how across generations these communities are held hostage to their history—a history which was more a compulsion of survival as opposed to free choice. The books in varying matters engaged with the problems that the communities continue to face—child marriage, illiteracy, lack of awareness, misogyny etc. The books show the double marginalization of women and children in the community. However they also point out to a slow but steady process of assimilation, a growing middle class which is more articulate in voicing its concerns.

References

Arendt H (1994) The origins of totalitarianism. Harcourt Books

Borgohain H (2000) "In Search of Ismail Sheikh" in Image and representation: stories of Muslim Lives in India. In: Mushirul H, Asaduddin M (eds), Oxford, pp 226–237

Daniyal S (2019) "I am Miya": Why poetry by Bengal origin Muslims in their Mother Tongue is Shaking Assam, available at https://scroll.in/article/930416/i-am-miya-why-poetry-by-bengal-origin-muslims-in-their-mother-tongue-is-shaking-up-assam accessed on 23rd June, 2022

Guha A (2006) Planter Raj to Swaraj: freedom struggle and electoral politics in Assam. Tulika Books

Hasan M, Asaduddin M (2000) Image and representation: stories of Muslim lives in India. OUP

Kar M (1990) Muslims in Assam politics. Omsons Publications

Kimura M (2013) The Nellie Massacre of 1983: the agency of the rioters. Sage

Malik SA (2012) Rupaborir Polosh. Chandra Prakashan

Pisharoty SB (2019) Assam: the accord, the discord. Penguin India

Saikia A (2019) In Assam, campaign urging Bengali Muslims not to list Assamese as mother tongue has sparked protests. Scroll.in, June 09, 2019, available at https://scroll.in/article/926022/assam-drive-urging-bengali-muslims-not-to-list-assamese-as-mother-tongue-could-become-explosive Accessed on 25th Nov 2021

Sharma R (2017) Kahibunor Malita. Purbayon Publication

Siddiqui N (2019) Discourse of doubt: understanding the crisis of citizenship in Assam. Econ Polit Weekly. 54(10):9 https://www.epw.in/journal/2019/10/perspectives/discourse-doubt.html Accessed 25th Sept 2021

Sultana P (2000) The nowhere people: Tale of 'missing' villages in Assam. The News Mill, available at https://thenewsmill.com/nowhere-people-missing-villages-in-assam/ Accessed 27th Nov 2021

Chapter 12
Dead Horses Tell no Tales: Agrarian Revolts, Farmer Suicides and the Right to Cultivate in Neoliberal India

Syamantak Shobhan Basu

12.1 Introduction

The *Kisan Andolan* or farmers' movement that began at the tail end of 2020 and is continuing to this day is perhaps the most significant organised protest to take root in India in the 30 years since economic liberalisation in 1991. It is certainly one of the largest-ever mass movements in India (or indeed anywhere in the world) since independence from British colonial rule. The movement was first organised as mass sit-in on November 26, 2020 to protest against the passing of three Acts in the Indian Parliament which farmers claim are inherently pro-corporate and anti-farmer, and would completely hand over all power of negotiation to large agri-businesses while pushing farmers into neocolonial slavery.[1]

As a networked protest, centred around several static sites, connected through a platform organisation called the Samyukta Kisan Morcha (roughly translating to the United Front for Farmers), the movement's success in capturing the national imagination relied upon its excellent use of cyberspace to reach out to a wider audience, and gain the sympathy and solidarities of people across a cross-section of society. Farmers' movements, consistently a feature of the political life of India, where over

[1] The laws in question are the Farmers' Produce Trade and Commerce (Promotion and Facilitation) Act, 2020, Farmers (Empowerment and Protection) Agreement of Price Assurance, Farm Services Act, 2020, and the Essential Commodities (Amendment) Act, 2020 passed during the Monsoon Session of the Indian Parliament culminating on September 23, 2020. A succinct summary of the implications of the laws and various articles explaining the impact and the protests resulting out of them, from a developmental point of view, is provided in India Development Review, 'The farm acts: all you need to know.'

S. S. Basu (✉)
University of Illinois Urbana-Champaign, Champaign, USA
e-mail: ssbasu2@illinois.edu

S. S. Ali and A. Basak (eds.), *Marginal Narratives and the Question of Human Rights in Asian Pacific Literature*, https://doi.org/10.1007/978-981-97-4544-9_12

50%[2] of all workers are still dependent on farming for their livelihoods and about 18–20%[3] of the GDP is drawn from agriculture, have lost their power to affect the public opinion over the years, as the growth of neoliberalism and the consequent aspirational politics that come with it have turned agriculture from the bedrock of Indian society into an unfashionable profession, seen by many as a relic of an feudal India averse to the discreet charm of the new bourgeoisie. Farmers in India have increasingly begun to be left behind. This particular movement, however, is increasingly seen as a successful protest, one that is influenced changes to grassroots politics in India, after succeeding its initial primary goal[4] after over a year of demonstration and the speculated loss of hundreds of lives. In February 2024, citing unfulfilment of previous promises, especially the provision of a Minimum Support Price (MSP) for crops, farmers started a second round of protests and blockades at the old sites. This present movement is still in its nascent stages, but has seen some spectacular events already, with the police using drones to fire tear gas at protesters, and the latter in turn using kites to bring down the drones in an innovative tactical struggle. (Kataria, 'Kites battle drones as farmers take on police during India protests') The impact of these developments will not be discussed here, but they serve as strong reminders of the lasting power and success of the initial movement of 2020–22.

In order to understand the dismal state that the present crisis has reached over the years, it would be prudent to take a step back from the present period of activity of the farmers' insurrection to a former, more passive state of suffering crystallized over the course of several decades. The years since the liberalisation of the Indian economy and the opening of the Indian market to the world in 1991 by the Narsimha Rao government have been marked by supreme farmer distress, with hundreds of thousands of farmers committing suicide due to low yields, poor prices and lack of systemic government support for agriculture.

---

[2] Minister of Agriculture and Farmers' Welfare Narendra Singh Tomar said in a response to a question in the Lok Sabha in December 2019:

> As per Census 2011, conducted by the Registrar General of India, the total number of agricultural workers in the country have increased from 234.1 million (127.3 million cultivators and 106.8 million agricultural labourers) in 2001 to 263.1 million (118.8 million cultivators and 144.3 million agricultural labourers) in 2011. However, the share of workforce engaged in the agriculture sector (comprising of cultivators and agricultural labourers) has come down from 58.2 per cent in 2001 to 54.6 per cent in 2011.

See the press release by the Ministry of Agriculture & Farmers' Welfare: https://pib.gov.in/PressReleasePage.aspx?PRID=1601902.

[3] According to the Economic Survey of 2020–21, agriculture had cushioned somewhat the shock to the economy delivered by the Covid-19 pandemic, its contribution to the GDP estimated to be 19.9% of the total, up from 17.8% of in 2019–20. See Ministry of Finance, 44.

[4] After a prolonged and sustained protest, the three Farm Bills were recanted in a public address by Narendra Modi, the Prime Minister of India, on behalf of the union government on November 19, 2021. The laws were then repealed through the Farm Laws Repeal Bill on November 29, 2021, which was passed in both houses of the Parliament.

Despite its policy-focused outlook, the farmers' movement has succeeded in utilising popular sentiment in burnishing an element that is important for all mass movements in the digital age—media optics. The key difference between the current farmers' protest, which has sustained for over a year, and agitations in the past, is an emphasis on consciously building a public-facing image, and success in garnering broad-based social support for a movement led primarily by a single section of society. The primary reason for this is of course that the farm laws would have had a domino effect on society at large, with pricing control moving into the hands of a corporate oligopoly implying that costs of essential items would become unregulated. However, the moral acceptability of a mass-movement to a wide cross-section of people often determines its ability to ensure the participation of the wider society. In this, the ongoing farmers' movement has been especially successful.

An astute use of iconography, together with excellent organisational principles and communication tactics, has allowed the protesters to formulate a powerful expression of resistance to the Indian government's disastrous agricultural policies through a language of courageous, non-violent, united resistance and communitarian living. The public rhetoric of the movement is channelled through a need to find recompense for historical injustice meted out to Indian farmers. This rhetoric has been aided by the movement's media-savvy approach. With the traditional media initially ignoring the movement's demands, it took to creative use of social media, expertly using Facebook Live and Twitter (now X) through the movement's official platforms to consolidate public sentiment. At a critical moment, when the movement seemed to be at its end in Uttar Pradesh, Rakesh Tikait, one of the leaders of the movement, refused to allow his protest pavilion to be dismantled, issuing a desperate appeal for support from farming communities and quickly galvanising them into action. For many who entered the protest at that stage, an evocation of masculinity (with the suggestion that the government was emasculating the protestors), and a call for in-group loyalty to the clan leader, were driving forces. This displayed an astute understanding of the latent power of social media to instantaneously enervate and mobilise vernacular spaces. In its most active phase, until the intial repeal of the farm laws and the dismantling of the first protest platforms, the movement used creative means to propagandise, combining town criers, and announcements from local places of worship with decentralised use of social media. Another striking example was the creation of an innovative 'MSP calculator' (Press Trust of India, 'Jai Kisan Andolan launches "MSP loot calculator"') by one farmers' union to demonstrate the extent of losses incurred by farmers due to a lack of Minimum Support Price guarantees.[5] Farmers are using such innovative tactics to push for the implementation of a well-structured MSP bill, together with the policy suggestions of the Swaminathan report

[5] One of the key public debates that the farmers' protest has brought into the public domain is the lack of a Minimum Support Price or MSP for farm produce. Farmers claim that the agricultural laws being pushed by the central government would erode even the informal MSP system present in the country. Since MSP is not legally mandated in the country, farmers are demanding that this be recified. See: India Today Web Desk, 'Explained: What is MSP and why farmers are protesting over it?'

aimed at alleviating farm distress.[6] The Sikh practice of Langar,[7] or the communal kitchen where anyone may serve and all are welcome to eat together regardless of class, caste, religion or gender, was adopted by the movement. This became a much-admired public aspect of the movement as a cornerstone of its affirmative, empathetic, pluralist and inclusive politics. This was held in stark contrast to the government and the supporters of the laws, who were projected as taking away the rights of *annadatas* (literally providers of rice, or feeders). The politics created out of the movement generated polarity and imbibed many of the values cherished in the Gandhian ethos that has dominated the Indian public sphere since the days of the freedom struggle.

However, all of this represents a mature stage of a movement that has been many decades in the making. This articulation of a concrete philosophy of dignity and justice from a common platform of diverse ideologies is in stark contrast to what has come before. There have been sporadic flashes of protests, where spectacles of the terrible human suffering of farmers in India have caught the public attention for a while, before disappearing into the margins once again. This includes the protests by farmers from Tamil Nadu who brought the skulls of their dead friends with them, (Alavi, 'Tamil Nadu farmers return to Jantar Mantar with skulls and chains') or demonstrated with live mice in their mouths. (Biswas, 'Why are farmers in India protesting with mice and human skulls?') Long Marches organized by farmers have passed through major Indian cities to camp in front of Parliament. The spectacle of tens of thousands of farmers marching silently through Mumbai at night, so as to not disturb sleeping examinees, and being greeted with food and nourishments by grateful citizens, created excellent precedents for the dignified and largely non-violent protests of today. (Ghosh, 'Mumbai With Farmers. Food, Footwear, Flowers For Protesters').

Beyond this realm of resistance lies despair. The sheer numbers are terrifying, and the complete apathy that subsequent governments of various political dispensations have shown towards the issues plaguing Indian farmers takes the form of a banal evil, slow-burning and immovable. This paper does not attempt to articulate the modes of protest, or the expressions being used to project the agrarian distress and its consequent anger in present-day India. What it seeks to do instead is reflect on a period of a few decades leading up to this movement, with the aim of illustrating the social background to this seemingly sudden explosion. While farmer-led protests are not new in India, with peasant insurgency from the British raj onwards becoming a

---

[6] The National Commission of Farmers (NCF) was a body chaired by Prof M. S. Swaminathan, which submitted five reports on the agrarian situation in India between 2004 and 2006. The fifth of these reports dealt with farmer distress and rising farmer suicides and made suggestions for the implementation of certain policy decisions to provide relief and sustainable growth for farmers. Incidentally, Prof Swaminathan was also the chief architect of the Green Revolution in India. See this interpretative summary of the report for more details: Sanyal, 'Report Summary Swaminathan Committee on Farmers (October 2006).'

[7] For a description of the religious philosophy and practice of the langar, see: 'Langar: The Communal Meal,' The Pluralism Project, Harvard University, https://pluralism.org/langar-the-communal-meal. Accessed 29 October 2021.

bedrock of the nationalist movement and later shaping the early polity of independent India, the *Kisan Andolan* has transformed farmer insurrections into an entirely new phenomenon, adapted to engage with the modes of production and dissemination of the Information Age. To understand how this developed, one needs to understand the crystallisation of the crisis to which the present movement is a reaction.

In contrast to the 'more intensified class conflict, widespread anti-imperialist struggle and generally [a] higher level of militancy among the masses' prevalent during the later years of the British raj and infusing the nationalist movement, Ranajit Guha says that the 'peasant movements of the first three-quarters of British rule represented a somewhat inchoate and naive state of consciousness.' And yet, he continues, 'we propose to focus on this consciousness as our central theme, because it is not possible to make sense of the experience of insurgency merely as a history of events without a subject.' (Guha 11–12) The Green Revolution of the 1970s and 1980s, while initially multiplying farm produce and holding up a promise of wealth and stability to India's farmers, ended up creating structural inequalities across the agrarian sector, due to the long-term effects of chemical additives and unsustainable farming practices, while setting up inescapable debt traps for small farmers by to raising the costs of agriculture. The resultant distress did not see farmers coalesce around their unions and produce an organised struggle immediately. Compounded by the effects of neoliberalism and the demands of an open market, it created a pressure cooker situation that threw large swathes of the farming population into a confused chaos. The first four decades after India's economic liberalisation has so far seen an inchoate expression of anger from its farmers, which is only now beginning to take the shape of an articulate, mature and popular mass movement with the potential to transform modern Indian society at large.

12.2 In Ancient Rome and Modern India, Everybody Loves a Good Fire

One of the landmark events of Roman Empire was the Great Fire of 64 AD. Numerous conflicting accounts exist of the source of the fire, but it is believed that the emperor Nero allowed the fire to proceed unchecked to gain control over how Rome was rebuilt. Roman historian Tacitus, chronicling Nero's apathy towards the fire, wrote of how Nero burned prisoners in his gardens to illuminate his lavish parties, to which the foremost citizens of Rome were invited: '[O]n the dwindling of daylight they were burned for use as nocturnal illumination. Nero had offered his gardens for the spectacle and he produced circus games, mingling with the plebs in the dress of a charioteer or standing in his racer.' (Tacitus, 326).

Palagummi Sainath takes up the same metaphor almost two thousand years and several thousand kilometers apart to describe the situation of rural India. Sainath, eminent labour journalist, historian and archivist, is one of India's most respected public intellectuals. Sainath is known for his sustained, detailed, empathetic, and insightful reporting on issues plaguing rural India, including rural poverty, structural inequality and farm distress. After years of work as the Rural Affairs Editor of *The Hindu*, in 2014 Sainath founded the incredible People's Archive of Rural India (PARI), which is an online repository of rural India's vast linguistic, occupational, artisanal, agricultural, and cultural diversity.

The social scope of this website, which draws its strength from volunteer writers, journalists and photographers, and is funded through the charitable organisation CounterMedia Trust is truly immense, and has the potential to become a formidable archive for scholars, activists and journalists working on a cross-section of issues in the fields of labour, poverty, inequality and rural studies. Central to Sainath's journalistic approach is his desire to tell the stories of those who have been left behind by modernity's vacuous promises of progress. This paper focuses on his work as a journalist and writer at the turn of the millennium and in particular, his book *Everybody Loves a Good Drought* (1996), which is a collection of his news reports documenting the acute and unacknowledged crises of India 'poorest districts.' It is a scathing indictment of structural inequality, rural distress, negligent governance and the apathy of neoliberal media and society in India. It serves as a reference point for journalists and scholars of poverty and politics alike, weaving together as it does the microhistories of people belonging to differing regions and communities and engaged in various livelihoods. Even as he refuses to shy away from the terrible truths he reports, Sainath wraps his work in empathy for the victims of India's fractious modernity; it is also what he accuses governments and elite neoliberal society of lacking most. Sainath's stereoscopic vision covers several aspects of rural life in the book—education, health, the informal political economy of rural India[8] and crime. Of special interest to this paper is his coverage of drought, the systemic failure of governments to provide support to drought-hit regions, and their subsequent attempts to manipulate the optics of drought events through the provision of 'emergency relief.' Outlining the scale of the problem, Sainath says:

> In August 1995, Prime Minister Narasimha Rao inaugurated an anti-drought project in Orissa. This one will involve spending Rs 4,557 in six years (over Rs 750 crore a year) on just a few districts including Kalahandi, Bolangir and Koraput. Every paisa of that huge sum would be worth spending if it actually fought scarcity and built better infrastructure. That, however, is most unlikely. In part because the main causes of the problems these areas face do not even begin to get addressed. (Sainath, *Everybody Loves a Good Drought* 317–18)

Sainath attributes this to the cruel fact that *everybody loves a good drought*. Not only do state and federal governments budget enormous sums of money, which are either spent inefficiently or end up in the hands of middlemen, but in the age of the open markets and global media, drought becomes an international spectacle. 'Donor governments,' he says 'love emergency relief' since it 'forms a negligible part of their

[8] Incidentally, any sustained study of agricultural distress in India post 2016 has to factor in the effects of Demonetisation—the almost overnight invalidation of Rs 500 and 1000 notes (the largest denominations in Indian currency at the time). Touted as a move to curb 'black money' and transform into a cashless, digital economy, the move was an unmitigated disaster. Besides the loss of life caused by the sudden panic of the situation, the move inflicted incalculable damage to artisanal industries, rural economies and small businesses, largely dependent on cash-based currencies.

spending, but makes for great advertising,' because you can 'run television footage of the Marines kissing babies in Somalia.' This approach deliberately ignores the facts that there are 'more serious issues between rich and poor nations—like unequal trade.' Settling these 'would be of greater help to the latter. But for that, the "donors" would have to part with something for real. No. They prefer emergency relief.' (Ibid. 322).

Sainath is particularly withering in his critique of media coverage of drought, to which he attributes the voyeuristic interest of corporations, which transform it into an event to be monetised. The drought that exists in real villages filled with real people is different from the spectacle of drought in the news media, which allows for the illusion of action, without any actual structural change. The chain of sustenance goes up from 'local stringers' keyed in to the structural issues plaguing a drought-stricken region, through state-wide media and upto the national media, whose understanding of the situation is that 'drought means parched land and, hopefully pictures of emaciated people.' (Ibid.) This then becomes a matter of interest for global news media, particularly those with a saviour complex, who can then provide just cause for 'emergency relief' operations. Sainath's frustrations with these exercises in futility are apparent to see, as he notes how 'many forces including well-meaning sections of the press have been co-opted into presenting a picture of natural calamity. Too often, into dramatising an event without looking at the processes behind it. The spiral works in different ways in different states. But it works.' (Ibid., 323) It may be argued that farmer agitations in the years since the book was written have in fact also utilised this principle to great effect, positioning themselves in public around the media's hunger for a money-spinning spectacle. This, however, would also raise questions about the ultimate effectiveness of this form of agitprop, since expanding the scope of the spectacle serves the interests of globalised capital and its incorporated media, which allows for permissible dissent without addressing the fundamental questions of structural inequality.[9]

The underside of spectacle is of course apathy. Deepa Bhatia's Nero's Guests (2009) follows Sainath as he reports on issues related to farmer suicides in rural India. The narrative form of the investigative documentary provides the necessary freedom to move between first-hand interviews, lectures recordings and personal discussions. The documentary locates the agrarian crisis in the neoliberal turn of Indian society,

---

[9] 'We have long argued that the "naturalness" of these processes, with inconvenient facts allowed sparingly and within the proper framework of assumptions, and fundamental dissent virtually excluded from the mass media (but permitted in a marginalized press), makes for a propaganda system that is far more credible and effective in putting over a patriotic agenda than one with official censorship.' (Chomsky and Herman, lxii).

What is curious is that the difference between a 'marginalized press' and 'mass media' in neoliberal India lies not just in conspicuous silences but in active polemical discourse. Mass media outlets carrying partisan bias towards the government tend to practice silence and erasure of public dissent wherever possible, and when forced into action, covers the same material as the 'marginalized press' but spins it as misguided, destructive, radicalism inimical to 'national unity.' Farmers in India are thus branded 'Naxalite' or 'Khalistani' (since Sikhs make up a majority of the most visible protestors in the current movement), which then becomes the locus standi of the debate, shifting attention away from core issues of socioeconomic justice.

which compounds existing issues that can be traced to the Green Revolution. Sainath and Bhatia re-center the gaze away from the bureaucratic failures of the agrarian economy in India and onto the apathy of elite society, the newly globalised media and the intellectuals of modern India. To do this, they use the analogy of Nero and his guests during the burning of Rome. Drawing upon Tacitus' version of the events, Sainath speaks of how the historian does not directly blame Nero for the fire. He does chronicle, however, how Nero would throw one of the greatest parties known to ancient civilisation, as a means to distract his people from the devastation of the fire. Faced with the problem of illumination for such a gigantic party, Nero resorted to burning numerous criminals and prisoners at the stake, drawn from among the Christians, upon whom he tried to lay the blame. "They were doomed to the flames thereby to provide the nightly illumination," Sainath quotes Tacitus and goes on to speculate, not on Nero's legendary cruelty, but on the guests invited to this party:

> Who were Nero's guests? What sort of a mindset did it require for you to pop one more fig into your mouth as another human being burst into flames? What sort of mindset did it require for you to drop those grapes into your jaws as another pathetic person...burned to provide you illumination? These were the sensitive elite of Rome: these were the poets, the singers, the musicians, the artists, the historians, the intelligentsia…For me, I always wondered: who were Nero's guests? After five and a half years of covering farmers' suicides, I think I have my answer.

Sainath may be accused of anachronisms in constructing his moral argument, and he is most certainly polemical in his approach. Yet his rhetorical device is simple and effective in communicating its core message: If modern Indian society found itself in congruence with the rule of a famously cruel, sadistic, and authoritarian regime in Ancient Rome, how far exactly did the rot actually go?

To wit, Sainath focuses on three aspects contributing to the scale of the farming crisis—(1) government negligence, (2) an apathetic media (3) a hypocritical and disinterested elite and middle class. Each aspect is linked to the other. A retreating government under neoliberalism operates according to market principles, thereby finding little profit motive in supporting independent farmers; a corporate media, controlled by these very market practices, likewise does not see value in reporting dearth and suicide with sensitivity, instead of sensationalism. Therefore, thinking about the true causes for the struggle of farmers, locating it in the inequality of prevalent socioeconomic systems, and formulating effective policies that might mitigate their distress by reconstituting the system is disincentivised by neoliberal market practices. This is where the work of journalists like Sainath comes in, to pierce through the heart of an encrusted apathy and to reflect on (a lack of) human rights in such a society. Through what has now become an oft-repeated motif for his work, Sainath articulates his assessment of the Indian media as 'politically free but imprisoned by profit.'[10] Today, it seems as though this ominous statement has fulfilled its

[10] Many of Sainath's observations on the corporatisation of Indian media have now become gold standards for critical analysis of the industry. For one such analysis, see Samarth Bansal, "The Indian media is politically free but imprisoned by profit": P Sainath,' March 22, 2018, accessed October 25, 2021, https://bansalsamarth.medium.com/the-indian-media-is-politically-free-but-imprisoned-by-profit-p-sainath-5191b331c249.

true potential. Whether the Indian media is de facto 'politically free' in 2024 is a matter of serious debate, due to dropping press freedom metrics and the censorship of journalists and media houses using financial deterrents, vigilante action and legal repression,[11] it is also certainly true that Indian media is much more imprisoned by profit today than it was fifteen years ago.

The documentary works to capture the scale of agrarian distress through careful selection and editing. We are repeatedly told that there are hundreds upon hundreds of suicides documented by Sainath alone, so choosing which story to tell is as difficult as it is important. Bhatia and Sainath, focus on farmers whose activities reflect a sharp consciousness of their situation and a fighting spirit, who choose to kill themselves regardless, to indicate how individual will is not enough to rescue farmers from the enormity of the social and economic crisis facing them. The film talks of Kashi Visvesvara Rao, a former 'Progressive Farmer of the Year' awardee, known for berating his fellow farmers for choosing to give up on life, who killed himself in 2004. It mentions Sudha Mani, whose mother committed suicide and who was yet denied compensation, because society did not recognise women as farmers, but only as farmers' wives. The most striking individual whose story is told in the film is Srikrishna Kalamb. While interviewing his family after his suicide, Sainath and his team discover that he was also a poet, who wrote eloquently of the apathy shown towards farmers, of his own helpless condition and the complete realisation that death was its only logical outcome. Srikrishna Kalamb's poems serve thereafter as a binding element for the narrative of the documentary, infusing the suffering and emotion of the articulate, expressive and despairing farmer into an otherwise dispassionate public discourse that revolves around 'macro' questions of statistics and policy. Kalamb's voice links the damning data to the lived experience of abandonment, neglect and despair that is the story of so many of India's farmers. It is Sainath's greatest triumph as a storyteller that he is able to effectively balance the two, and it is here that his work becomes of archival value—the seed of a living archive, a people's archive.

Structural issues plague the coverage of farmer suicides, as Sainath points out repeatedly. The film foregrounds the statistic that nearly 200,000 farmers had cumulatively committed suicide in India since 1997. The National Crime Records Bureau (NCRB) of India, which collects data on crimes and accidental deaths, places annual farm suicides in 2019 at 10,281 for the year, 7.4% of the total number of suicides

---

[11] India was ranked 142nd out of 180 countries in the 2021 World Press Freedom index by the Reporters sans frontières. The report stated in 2021, as the farmers' movement took root, that 'India is one of the world's most dangerous countries for journalists trying to do their job properly,' particularly after the resounding reelection of the Modi government in 2019, with pressure having 'increased on the media to toe the Hindu nationalist government's line.' The ranking dropped even more alarmingly in the following two years, with the country ranked 150th in the 2022 index and 161st in the 2023 index. This represents a dire state of affairs, especially for a democracy of India's size and importance.

For a fuller report, see https://rsf.org/en/india.

See also Iyer, 'India has launched a sharp assault on press freedom—but independent media is determined to resist.'

for the year. (National Crime Records Bureau, Chapeter 2)[12] It also estimates that 296,438 farmers had committed suicide between 1995 (the year when the NCRB began to record farm deaths in its *Accidental Deaths & Suicides* report) and 2013. The number has edged up to nearly 400,000 since. This is despite allegations of heavy falsification of data, at both the state and the national levels.[13] (Sainath, 'Maharashtra crosses 60,000 farm suicides;' Roy, 50–56) What *Nero's Guests* seeks to do is to put faces to these numbers.

Through an elaborate study of the statistical data and distribution of farm suicides in India by region and year, Nagaraj and Sainath et al. have found that,

> like nature, a socio-economic context abhors a vacuum. The space vacated by the state was taken up by private agents, particularly in areas like credit, supply of seeds and fertilizers, extension services (like advice and help on crops to be grown, digging of bore wells, etc.), marketing of crops, etc. These agents, often combining all these multiple roles, were mostly from the urban centres in the region and, with next to no regulation of their operations, their relationship with the farmers was essentially a predatory one, of exploiting the latter's vulnerability during the period of crisis. (Nagaraj et al, 81)

Farmer bodies saw the new farm laws as exacerbations of this same threat, where the exploitation of middlemen would be replaced by much more heavy-handed exploitation at the hands of a new corporate oligopoly venturing into agri-business, headed by companies such as the Reliance group, the Tata group and the Adani group. Global corporations in the FMCG sector would not be far behind, sniffing a hope of monetising India's vast agricultural wealth. This would take the entire power to independently cultivate crops out of the hands of farmers and place it in the hands of these powerful corporations, who would hold small farmers to ransom and demand the growing of crops to meet the demands of a global market. The solidarity that the movement received from farmers' unions in the US, who warn that the laws would facilitate exactly the sort of corporate takeover that had happened there forty years ago is ample evidence of this. (The Wire Staff, 'Happened in the US 40 years ago') In *Nero's Guests*, Sainath articulates this organised capture of the agrarian system:

> What is this agrarian crisis?
>
> Five words: The drive towards corporate farming
>
> …
>
> How is this agrarian Crisis operationalized?
>
> Five words: Predatory commercialisation of the
>
> countryside
>
> …
>
> What does it achieve?

---

[12] The data on the original link seems to no longer be available for public viewing. However, the may be found at https://data.gov.in/catalog/accidental-deaths-suicides-india-adsi-2019?page=3. I have retained the original record to maintain the paper trail used in my research.

[13] Roy, while pointing out the gaps in the NCRB's data, however, attempts to complicate the issue of farmer suicides, suggesting that it may be a more region-specific issue than a national issue at large. She also says that other factors such as family disputes or mental illnesses may play as big a role, if not more so, as agrarian distress in farmer suicides.

Five words: The biggest displacement in Indian history

The bitter fruit first sowed in the 1990s is being reaped in the 2020s, with India having dropped from 94th to 101st out of 116 countries in the Global Hunger Index of 2021. (Press Trust of India, 'India slips to 101st position in the Global Hunger Index') The number dropped even further to 111th out of 125 countries in the 2023 index. A report based on the index states that India has a level of hunger that is 'serious,' noting that 'India has the highest child wasting rate in the world, at 18.7 per cent, reflecting acute undernutrition.' (Press Trust of India, 'Global Hunger Index 2023: India ranks 111th out of 125 countries'). The report notes that even neighbouring countries Pakistan (102nd), Bangladesh (81st), Nepal (69th) and Sri Lanka (60th have performed better. This despite the state of near bankuptcy of the Sri Lankan economy in recent years, and the GDPs and market sizes of the aforementioned countries relative to India, pointing to a problem of distribution and equity rather than availability of overall resources. In the period between 1991 and 2012, hunger deaths returned for the first time since the 1943 Bengal Famine, which was an artificially-created disaster due to the wartime colonial policy of the British raj and cost around 3 million lives in Bengal alone.[14] Sainath says in *Nero's Guests* that in the 15 years preceding the documentary, 'the fastest-growing sector in this country is not IT, it's not software, it is inequality. It has grown faster than at any time in our history since the time of the colonial raj.' The statement bears out eerily in a study conducted by Thomas Piketty and Lucas Chancel, published in 2017, which found that income inequality in India was its the highest level since 1922, which was the year of the creation of the Indian Income Tax Act. They found that the top 1% of the country held 22% of the income in 2014. They also claimed that between 1951 and 1980, 'at a time when strong market regulations and high fiscal progressivity are implemented' (sic) the rate of growth of incomes of the bottom 50% of the population grew, but that this was reversed between 1980 and 2014. (Chancel and Piketty, 29) The figures are stark, but not unexpected if one has an ear to the pulse of the general populace, and yet the media maintains a stoic silence on all matters of poverty and structural inequality. Sainath notes that at the time of the documentary, 'not a single newspaper or channel has a correspondent working full time on poverty.'

Of all the various facets of rural poverty, the poverty of rural working women is particularly neglected. Journalists-turned-filmmakers Nandan Saxena and Kavita Bahl have made a series of National Award-winning documentaries on the agrarian crisis. For the purpose of this paper, we will look at a film by the duo named Candles in the Wind (2014), which documents the struggles of women farmers of Punjab. The thread connecting each of the women who feature in the documentary is that each of their husbands has committed suicide due to farm distress, and each is therefore a 'farmer's widow.' Sainath had recounted Sudha Mani speaking of her mother, with the wish that she had a single memory of her where she was not working. He had also spoken of how, when he saw Srikrishna Kalamb's wife, he immediately felt as though she was planning to kill herself, an intuition which he says was born out

[14] This is the widely-quoted figure given by Amartya Sen. The historical consensus lies between 2.1 and 3 million. See Sen, 202.

of years of reporting on farm suicides. That the discourse around farmer suicides in India has revolved around men is not just because they are the ones primarily in charge of running farm households, but because in agricultural work, as in any other, women's labour is taken for granted, and they are expected to take up the mantle of a family when the man commits suicide, but given no credit for their struggles. *Candles in the Wind* looks at this idea more closely, and discovers that the situation is, if possible, even more dire for women farmers. Not only are they saddled with the debt of their dead husbands and a tremendous amount of labour both on the farm and inside their homes, but are also forced to bring up young children alone, and to take care of dependent in-laws. They must also fend off unwanted attention from suitors. Mahinderpal Kaur, one of the women interviewed, talks of a 'Chaddar' tradition whereby a widow is handed over to a willing suitor, sometimes even at the funeral ground. She states her desire to remain single, and not be treated like milch cattle. Many women, however, are not in the position to make that choice. What is key is survival.

When the narrator Kavita Bahl asks a few women farmers picking crop stubble for subsistence how they survive, she is met with the half-derisive answer that the work is not enough to ensure survival, but only for what they call 'timepass.' Bahl says that timepass was 'a refrain that punctuated the conversations I was to have with the women we met. For the women of Punjab, timepass is a state of being, a state of loss, depression, and hopelessness.' The situation of the women farmers of Punjab, and indeed all over rural India, is that of perpetual limbo, with little support from either society or governments. The documentary quotes Inderjit Singh Jaijee, a writer and civil rights activist working to document suicides and to rehabilitate the children of victims in the Sangrur district of Punjab, who outlines the work necessary to help the family of a suicide victim. Together with some others, he had set up the Baba Nanak Educational Society, which at the time of the documentary, provided Rs 1000 or 1500 to children of farmers who had committed suicide, on condition that they would continue to study. Jaijee states that even with the capacity of an individual NGO, they were able to look after 110 villages, but the work could not be scaled up due to the continuing apathy of the government. The government, at the time of the documentary provided a widow pension of only Rs 250 a month, an amount that has now been raised to Rs 1500 in Punjab, in no small measure due to the pressures of activists and filmmakers such as Sainath, Jaijee and Bahl. The national pension availability under the Indira Gandhi National Widow Pension Scheme (IGNWPS) is Rs 300 for women between the age of 40 and 79, and Rs 500 for those 80 and above.

For the thousands who have lost loved ones in the years after the Green Revolution and liberalisation, however, betrayal is the emotion that resonates most strongly. A betrayal that fosters a paralysed lack of direction in farming communities, which leads to mass suicides among farmers, which K. C. Suri believes is an entirely new phenomenon:

> Agrarian distress is not new to India; but farmers' suicides are. In the history of the country over the past several centuries, we have heard distress stories due to drought, pest and failure of crops. We have heard of the accounts of farmers abandoning cultivation and leaving their villages during medieval times. Farmers faced worst price falls, crop failures and the burden

> of debt and land revenue during the British rule. But what is happening today seems to be qualitatively different….Earlier, farmers in distress might have become dacoits or rebels, but never did we hear that they committed suicides. (Suri, 1523)

This lack of proactive reaction to distress is depicted profoundly in Gurvinder Singh's 2011 Punjabi language feature film *Anhey Ghohrey da Daan* (Alms for a Blind Horse), based on celebrated Punjabi novelist Gurdial Singh's eponymous novel of 1976 (translated as *Alms in the Name of a Blind Horse*). The film is a social realist reflection on the problems of landless farmers of the lower castes in rural Punjab. Apart from creating a visually striking representation of the fallout of the agrarian crisis, the film registers a crucial difference with the documentaries. The latter attempt to persuade the viewer of a need for action. *Anhey Ghohrey da Daan*, however, does no such thing. It is a quotidian depiction of a single issue—homelessness, both material and spiritual. The iconography of a liberalised India, confused about its newly-forged identity, which accentuates the visual landscape of the film, contributes to a curious paradox that further destabilises the leading characters. At one point, while depicting the insides of a shabby rural home, the camera dwells over a poster of the wrestler John Cena. A jarring note, filled with subtle mockery, not of the subjects of the film, but on the social conditions that have given rise to such humourless irony. The chimneys of a factory loom in the distance. Modernity has come calling, bestowing its poisoned boon upon the countryside.

The film takes the narrative form of a meditation. Its visual aesthetic deliberately tends towards dark, slightly fantastic tones, with reality tinted through the lens of low-intensity, slow-burning horror. The film is equal parts allegory and social realism, and describes a liminal experience at the margins of agrarian society in India. It revolves around the life of a landless farmer in Punjab, and his son, Melu, who has become a rickshaw-puller in the city to escape his life of poverty. The title refers to a tradition of the Mazhabi Sikhs, a section of Sikh society believed to have been descended from three men who carried the dismembered body of the Sikh Guru Tegh Bahadur to his son, Guru Govind Singh, who welcomed them into the fold of Sikhism. However, Mazhabi Sikhs are often segregated into ghettoes and have separate places of worship. While Sikhism does not explicitly practice the Hindu caste system, caste is by no means a non-issue among the Sikhs in Punjab.[15] The title of refers to a story in the Hindu tradition about a demon, Svarbhanu, who tricked the gods and consumed *amrit* (the nectar of immortality). The gods beheaded him, but not in time, and his dismembered body became two immortal beings—Rahu and Ketu, who come riding for revenge on blind horses during every eclipse. This also refers to a tradition among the Mazhabi Sikhs of collecting alms for Rahu's blind horse to appease the rage of the demon.[16] The Hindu caste system treats lower castes

[15] The farmers' movement recently ran into similar tensions with the killing of a Dalit Sikh, Lakhbir Singh, by a group of Nihangs, a martial sect that styles itself as guardians of the *Granth Sahib* or the Holy Book of the Sikhs. What makes this more complicated is that the Nihang Sikhs are not upper-caste by origin.

[16] For a fuller explanation of the tradition and how it connects to the film see Choudhury, 'A Dark Horse Called Hope.'

as the descendants of the ancient demons, and so the tradition speaks to both the systemic oppression and debasement of the lower-caste Sikh farmers, as well as a quiet defiance on their part. The two chief characters of the film, however, Melu and his father, do not share in this tradition. The character of the Father is a silent observer, watching as bulldozers belonging to the rich landlords raze the houses of squatters belonging to his community. Although he does join in solidarity with his community's demand for justice, his role is not an active one. He barely speaks throughout the film, and appears worn down and defeated, only brightening up at the prospect of meeting Melu. His son, a rickshaw-puller in the city, is beset by another form of melancholy. The emptiness of his intense physical labour, and the violence and uncertainty of his station, has sucked out all motivation out of him, and replaced it with what appears to be a mute rage. He shares his father's taciturnity, but his youthful resentment is characterised by anger rather than resignation.

The value of a film such as *Anhey Ghohrey* is that it speaks to the listlessness that has characterised farming communities of India in the years after liberalisation (although the seeds of this disquiet were planted decades before, as the novel shows). This space of inaction, and an attachment to traditions handed down across generations, explains the stultifying impact of a global market on a largely unorganised and sprawling profession that has yet to utilize the technological implements of modernity or to receive its dubious 'boons.' It accurately illustrates the tension between the old and new world orders: the latter not necessarily a beacon of progress, the former not necessarily a haven of prosperity, each refusing to concede to the necessities of the other. In *Nero's Guests* we hear of model farmer Kashi Visvesvara Rao telling his fellow farmers that 'farming is in our blood.' In *Anhey Ghohrey da Daan*, the beggar who goes around collecting alms before an eclipse is accosted by an enraged Melu as he returns to his village to seek refuge: 'Why must we carry on with such fruitless traditions?' he demands. The nameless beggar responds with the only sanguine truth known to him—'It is what our ancestors have done. How should we abandon what our ancestors have done?'.

12.3 A Lament of Despair, a Song of Hope

And yet hope springs from art, and from art flows the fount of resistance. In each of the films, the common element is the use of poetry and folk traditions as a counterfoil to the all-encompassing despair. *Nero's Guests* uses the poetry of farmer-poet Srikrishna Kalamb. In one poem he writes:

> Different I am/ so unusual my life / my death too, will surprise you/ like untimely rain/ Fond of poetry/ I exist like the cotton crop/ its root sweet/ alike the hard stem of sugarcane/ Of my death, they will say/ how it hangs/ like decorations on door frames

And yet another laments:

> Mute calves from Warhad are we/ watching the plunder of mothers milk/ Drenching earth drop by drop/ with our sweat/ yielding pearls/ yet our babies in hunger fret!/ Cotton crop watered by our sweat/ knotting 17 tears on our clothes
>
> …
>
> We farm with our sweat/ on the pyre our bodies will only half burn/ no money to buy the wood!/ Reins of our lives always in the hands of others/ While grinding flour/ the floors will stain without blood!

The poetry is rich in symbolism and speaks eloquently of the condition of the Indian farmer, each line an enunciation of betrayal and anguish, each turn of phrase an indictment of systemic indifference. Scraps of paper meant to be thrown away with the scraps of a life that ultimately amounted to nothing of material value. And yet there is hope in this despair. Kalamb's daughter, Usha, had collected and meticulously recorded his poetry, and they have now been published in book form, inscribing her father's memory in place.[17] Usha had said of her father: 'My father died as a farmer, in perpetual debt and worries. But he lived as a poet, and will remain immortal in his poems.' (Hardikar, 'We Cultivate Pearls, but Our Children Go Hungry').

Kavita Bahl similarly relies on folk music and poetry to convey the pathos of the women farmers of Punjab. She deftly uses Amrita Pritam's haunting poem 'Ajj Aakhaan Waris Shah Nu' (Today I invoke Waris Shah) addressed to Waris Shah, the Sufi writer of the Punjabi epic romance *Heer Ranjha*. Bahl translates Pritam thus:

> When a daughter of Punjab was in distress/ You wrote tomes in empathy/ Today, a million daughters wail/ And implore you, O Waaris Shah!/ Wake up, O comforter of the grieving/ Wake up and look at your Punjab/ The fields are lined with corpses/ and blood flows down the Chenaab[18]

The poem clearly illustrates Bahl's ideological choice as artist and communicator. She is an active interlocutor, often involved in the plight of the women she is interviewing. Her desire is not to be a passive 'archivist,' collecting the stories of unfortunate women for consumption in a so-called 'neutral' media that knows the selling price of human suffering. At the end of the documentary, she helps one family with some money, and breaks down at the show of dignity by the elderly woman of the family, who tells her that the world has turned upside down; that she, as the elder in society, should be offering something to Bahl as a present instead. The question of narratorial distance does not arise. Much like Sainath, Bahl is completely invested in the stories she is documenting. Her narratorial position is also her subject position—not that of a dispassionate analyst of a human rights issue. Her objective is feminist solidarity.

She uses her own poem, written in Punjabi, to bookend the documentary, providing a translation in English that reads thus:

[17] See Kalamb, *Black Earth*.

[18] The poem bears the legacy of the Partition of Punjab during India's independence. For more context on Amrita Pritam's striking poem, and an alternate translation in English, see Dutt, 'When Amrita Pritam called out to Waris Shah.'

> I shall not leave/ My body has become one with this earth/ My soul with this water/ Playing with this earth/ Tiny hands built a doll's house/ Empty hands…a vacant house/ My body has become one with the earth/ My soul with this water/ I shall not leave/ I shall not leave.

The final note is defiant. Even in the face of great suffering, the widowed farmers of Punjab shall not leave their homes.

The symbolism in *Anhey Ghohrey da Daan* is much more direct. The entire film wraps around the allegory of the blind horse of the demonic Rahu, and an approaching eclipse. Before each scene of foreboding—the bulldozing of the squatter's house, Melu's mother complaining about how their richer neighbours no longer let them pick loose mustard to sustain themselves as was once was the custom, Melu's brother sustaining an injury, and his own desolate return to the village—the familiar chant rings out: 'Alms for the Blind Horse, brothers!'

A simmering desire for revenge undercuts the narrative inaction. Melu's friends Dulla and Lakha, fellow rickshaw-pullers, tease and taunt him about his sincere efforts to help his family, all of which lead to nothing, while they enjoy themselves drinking and playing cards. In one sequence, the rickshaw-pullers' union calls a strike which turns violent. Melu Singh too sustains an injury, and is disturbed by the fallout of the violence, and possibly perturbed at his friends' nonchalant behaviour. While drinking cheap liquor together on the ramparts of a ruined fort, Dulla, who seems upto that point never to take anything seriously, apologises to Melu for his flippancy, and suddenly and dramatically declares to the world that there is a terrible anger in him. A rage so great that if he could, he would set the whole city on fire.

Melu Singh says nothing. His fire is internal. When he returns to his village, he berates the beggar asking for alms for the blind horse, urging him to leave the ancient customs behind. The irony is that his father has gone to the city to meet him at the very moment he has returned to the village, possibly after a long gap. Time is at a crossroads in rural India, and to the Mazhabi Sikhs of Bathinda, and the landless farmers of the country at large, there is no safe haven in either city or village.

12.4 Conclusion

The landscape of Indian farming is vast, and its stories innumerable. Yet for years together the mainstream of the country has heard few of its problems and experienced even less of its culture. The issue of farmer suicides remains non-existent in the mainstream media, and is almost always sensationalised when represented. Films such as *Peepli Live* (2010) have attempted to sensitively represent the issue with some popular success, and yet the communication of a complex problem requires a more nuanced analysis than the Indian cinema industry is prepared for at present. The solution lies in amplifying the stories that arise directly out of farming communities and from rural populations. Gurdial Singh, the writer of the novel upon which *Anhey Ghohrey da Daan* is based, himself came from a rural background and was the son of a carpenter who rose through sheer effort and determination to become a college lecturer and a famous author. The epitome of an organic intellectual, Gurdial Singh's works however remained largely unknown outside of Punjab, until they were translated to the screen through a competent film adaptation, for which Gurdial was himself the screenwriter.

It is clear that communicating the stories of farmers in distress with compassion and a persuasive rhetoric can lead to changes in policy. *Nero's Guests* states that the writings of journalists like P. Sainath had a big role in forcing the government into action. Similarly, stories of direct action by farmers become part of the folklore of people's movements. Kuldeep Kaur Kusa, a leader with the Bharti Kisan Union (Ugrahan) talks about the value of solidarity in *Candles in the Wind*. She mentions how, in 2002, when the government was not buying paddy, the women participated in a *chakka jam* (blocking of highways to register protest) and forced the government to accept their demands. Afterwards, to prevent their leaders from being identified and arrested, they closed ranks around them, leaving their homes and sitting in protest till the police were forced to leave. That spark of self-consciousness has blossomed into the fire of dissent at the farmer protest sites, as young and old leaders take the stage and borrow from these successful precedents. The instrumental role that years of organising and documentation of older farm protests has played in the interim success of the present mass movement is clear. The question that arises now is, can the history of farmers' protests in neoliberal India be linked to the growth of public consciousness about agrarian distress and suicides? Do films and literature attempting to represent the extent of the crisis play a significant role in aiding this consciousness?

The farmers' movement of 2020–24 represents a distinctive change in the representation of farmers in the public sphere. Its success in being able to blend ideological rigour, demands for popular justice and a technologically proficient image has resulted in it becoming a distinct pole in Indian politics.[19] This is owed in no small measure to the cultural and communicative aspects of the movement. The building of libraries and cultural centers in the movement spaces[20] represents an awareness among the agitators of their pedagogical role. The *Trolley Times*, which is an indepedent newsletter founded during the early days of the movement by a section of protesters in direct opposition to the politics of the mainstream media, who they claim work in the interests of the government and corporations inimical to the farmers' interests, has now become a powerful archive for this momentous period in modern Indian politics. It functions now as a full-fledged website, carrying stories not only on the current and historical state of the movement but also other issues related to agrarian distress, displacement, government policy and protest cultures. The website

[19] See Nair, 'Will Farmers' Muzaffarnagar Meet Change Political Equations In UP Polls?';

Gupta, 'What Does the Repeal of Farm Laws Mean for Punjab's Assembly Elections Next Year?'; and,

Kumar, 'Farmers stir upsets political equations in Haryana.'

[20] These are stretches of road filled with tents and temporary structures meant to house thousands of protesters. The ideological permanence of the movement's cultural space is therefore all the more remarkable. At the height of the movement, the first protest site, Singhu, seemed more like a separate city than a border space between two states.

maintains a details list of the martyrs of the movement, ensuring that they are kept alive in public memory and not collapsed into a mere number. It allows contributions and also the purchase of materials associated with the movement, thereby eliminating dependence on outside funding and interference. Although the *Trolley Times* is not the official mouthpiece of the Samyukt Kisan Morcha, it provides able support to the platform. It also highlights the importance of decentralized spaces of discourse associated with the movement, that nevertheless worked in close collaboration with it. Gurvinder Singh, the director of *Anhey Ghodey*, also made a film in 2023 documenting the frenzied activity of the movement in the period between 2020–21, also aptly named *Trolley Times*. The media practices of the *Kisan Andolan* are beyond the scope of this particular paper, but they represent an active area of interest for students of social movements in times to come. Even beyond the immediate outcomes of the movement, its effects on an economy struggling to cope with structural inequality, a devastating pandemic and an economic slowdown, and on a culture in flux, uncertain of its ethical bearings in a new world, are worthy of study.

And yet even in the present moment of euphoric celebration of an agrarian protest culture decades in the making, I claim that it is profitable to go back to an older period of uncertainty, despair and disarray, so that we may understand that as Rome burned Nero drew his courage from the guests who sat in silence and watched him set people on fire. It gives us the opportunity to historicise a glorious moment in the present in the context of the immense loss and suffering that has paved way for it. It underlines the importance of the critical organising work done by farmer unions in keeping the spark of resistance alive, and of certain journalists, writers, filmmakers, and activists who kept up persistent efforts to draw the public attention to these burning issues by cutting through the smokescreens of a suborned and apathetic media. The work of all these committed storytellers and social activists helped prepare the public consciousness so that when the proper historical conditions arrived, farmer insurrections could consolidate and explode onto the national stage as a legitimate mass movement. Perhaps the powerful assertion of defiance by the farmers' movement was seeded in Melu Singh's refusal to collect alms for the blind horse of tradition. Perhaps when Kuldeep Kaur Kussa says 'hard times do not befall cattle, hard times befall human beings,' she outlines the determination to 'live through the hard times as human beings' and emerge to a moment of freedom. It is certain that the moment of the *Kisan Andolan* was made possible because countless people of conscience, empathy and determination saw the inhumanity of the situation and echoed Sainath in one voice: 'we will agree not to be Nero's guests.'

References

Alavi AM (2017) 'Tamil Nadu farmers return to Jantar Mantar with skulls and chains.' Hindustan Times, 19 July 2017, https://www.hindustantimes.com/delhi-news/tamil-nadu-farmers-return-to-jantar-mantar-with-17-skulls-and-chains/story-zqRCAUXZr2AITae2GLLoFO.html. Accessed 29 Oct 2021

Anhey Ghohrey da Daan (2011) Directed by Gurvinder S, written by Gurdial S, Gurvinder S, Jasdeep S, National Film Development Corporation of India

Biswas S (2017) 'Why are farmers in India protesting with mice and human skulls?' BBC.com, 21 Apr 2017, https://www.bbc.com/news/world-asia-india-39650496. Accessed 29 Oct 2021

Candles in the Wind (2014) Directed by Kavita B, Nandan S. Top Quark Films

Chancel L, Thomas P (2017) 'Indian income inequality, 1922–2015: From British Raj to Billionaire Raj?' 5 September 2017, World Inequality Database, https://wid.world/document/chancelpiketty2017widworld/. Accessed 18 Oct 2021

Chomsky N, Edward SH (1988) Manufacturing consent: the political economy of mass Media. Pantheon Books

Choudhury BD (2020) A Dark horse called hope: close-up on Gurvinder Singh's Alms for a Blind Horse. Mubi.com, 2 June 2020, https://mubi.com/notebook/posts/a-dark-horse-called-hope-close-up-on-gurvinder-singh-s-alms-for-a-blind-horse. Accessed 22 Oct 2021

Dutt N (2017) When Amrita Pritam called out to Waris Shah in a heartrending ode while fleeing the Partition riots,' Scroll.in, 14 August 2017, https://scroll.in/article/847004/when-amrita-pritam-called-out-to-waris-shah-in-a-heartrending-ode-while-fleeing-the-partition-riots. Accessed 30 Oct 2021

Ghosh D (2018) 'Mumbai with farmers. food, footwear, flowers for protesters. NDTV.com, 12 March 2018, https://www.ndtv.com/mumbai-news/maharashtra-farmers-protest-in-mumbai-mumbai-with-farmers-residents-offer-food-footwear-to-tired-pro-1822751. Accessed 22 Oct 2021

Guha R (1999) Elementary aspects of peasant insurgency in colonial India. Duke University Press

Gupta V (2021) What does the repeal of farm laws mean for Punjab's assembly elections next year?' TheWire.in, 19 November 2021, https://thewire.in/politics/what-does-the-repeal-of-farm-laws-mean-for-punjabs-assembly-elections-next-year. Accessed 19 Nov 2021

Hardikar J (2008) We cultivate pearls, but our children go hungry. India Together, 20 April 2008, https://indiatogether.org/kalamb-agriculture. Accessed 25 Oct 2021

India Development Review (2020) The farm acts: all you need to know. Idronline.org, 24 September 2020, https://idronline.org/the-farm-bills-all-you-need-to-know/. Accessed 28 Oct 2021

India Today Web Desk (2020) Explained: what is MSP and why farmers are protesting over it? India Today, 29 September 2020, https://www.indiatoday.in/india/story/explained-what-is-msp-and-why-farmers-are-protesting-over-it-1726658-2020-09-29. Accessed 29 Oct 2021

Iyer K (2021) India has launched a sharp assault on press freedom—but independent media is determined to resist. Scroll.in, 15 February 2021, https://scroll.in/article/986981/as-more-indians-turn-to-independent-media-for-news-press-freedom-faces-sharp-attacks. Accessed 12 Oct 2021

Kalamb S (2013) Black earth: poems of Shrikrishna Kalamb, Farmer-Poet. Translated by Amole Gupte, Penguin Books India

Kataria S (2024) Kites battle drones as farmers take on police during India protests. Reuters.com, 15 February 2024, https://www.reuters.com/world/india/kites-battle-drones-farmers-take-police-during-india-protests-2024-02-15/. Accessed 9 Apr 2024

Kumar A (2021) Farmers stir upsets political equations in Haryana. The Hindu, 19 November 2021, https://www.thehindu.com/news/national/other-states/farmers-stir-upsets-political-equations-in-haryana/article37583350.ece. Accessed 19 Nov 2021

Ministry of Finance, Government of India (2021) Economic Survey 2020–21, vol 2, Ministry of Finance, Government of India, 2021, https://www.indiabudget.gov.in/economicsurvey/ebook_es2021/index.html. Accessed 27 Oct 2021

Nagaraj K, Sainath P, Rukmani R, Gopinath R (2014) 'Farmers' suicides in India: magnitudes, trends, and spatial patterns, 1997–2012. Rev Agrarian Stud 4(2):53–83

Nair P (2021) Will Farmers' Muzaffarnagar meet change political equations in UP Polls?, Outlook India, 5 September 2021, https://www.outlookindia.com/website/story/will-farmers-muzaffarnagar-meet-change-political-equations-in-up-polls/393605. Accessed 28 Oct 2021

National Crime Records Bureau, Government of India (2019) Chap. 2 of the Accidental Deaths & Suicides in India – 2019. Government of India, 2019), https://ncrb.gov.in/en/accidental-deaths-suicides-india-2019. Accessed 15 Oct 2021

Nero's Guests (2009) Directed by Deepa Bhatia. Mistral Movies in association with ARTE, Oktober, and YLE

Press Trust of India (2021a) India slips to 101st position in the Global Hunger Index, down seven spots from 2020. Firstpost.com, 19 October 2021, https://www.firstpost.com/india/india-slips-to-101st-position-in-the-global-hunger-index-down-seven-spots-from-2020-10068841.html

Press Trust of India (2021b) Jai Kisan Andolan launches "MSP loot calculator" to show losses incurred by farmers. TheHindu.com, 18 March 2021, https://www.thehindu.com/news/national/jai-kisan-andolan-launches-msp-loot-calculator-to-show-losses-incurred-by-farmers/article34099726.ece. Accessed 30 Oct 2021

Press Trust of India (2023) Global Hunger Index 2023: India ranks 111th out of 125 countries; Pakistan, Bangladesh fare better.' The Economic Times, 12 October, 2023, https://economictimes.indiatimes.com/news/economy/indicators/global-hunger-index-2023-india-ranks-111th-out-of-125-countries-pakistan-bangladesh-fare-better/articleshow/104377651.cms?from=mdr. Accessed 8 Apr 2024

Roy D (2021) Farmer Suicides in India, 1997–2013: taking stock of data, arguments and evidence. Econ Polit Weekly 56(15):50–56

Sanyal K (2006) 'Report summary Swaminathan committee on farmers (October 2006).' PRS Legislative Research, 7 December 2006, https://prsindia.org/files/policy/policy_committee_reports/1242360972--final%20summary_pdf_0.pdf. Accessed 28 Oct 2021

Sainath P (1996) Everybody loves a good drought: stories from India's poorest districts. Penguin Books

Sainath P (2014) 'Maharashtra crosses 60,000 farm suicides. 21 July 2014, https://ruralindiaonline.org/en/articles/maharashtra-crosses-60000-farm-suicides/. Accessed 22 Oct 2021

Sen A (1980) Famine mortality: a study of the Bengal Famine of 1943 Peasants in history: essays in honour of Daniel Thorner. In: Eric JH (ed) Sameeksha Trust, pp 194–220

Singh G (2016) Alms in the Name of a Blind Horse. Translated by Rana Nayar, Rupa Publications

Suri KC (2006) Political economy of Agrarian distress. Econ Polit Weekly 41(16):1523–1529

Tacitus (2004) The annals. Translated by Woodman AJ, Hackett Publishing

The Wire Staff (2021) "Happened in US 40 Years Ago": 87 US Farmers' Unions Speak Out for Indian Farmers' Protest. TheWire.in, 21 February 2021, https://thewire.in/agriculture/usa-farmers-unions-msp-protests-reagan. Accessed 21 Oct 2021

Part IV
Activism, the limits of agency and the Pursuit of Social Justice in Asia and the Pacific

Chapter 13
Hunger's Cry: Bijon Bhattacharya's "Nabanna" and the Bengal Famine of 1943

Subhajeet Singha

Winston Churchill once infamously iterated that unlike many other great populace of the world, Indians were so effectively shielded from perils of the World War (Mukherjee xiii) This blatant disregard of actual history can be found aplenty when one reads brutish British prime-minister Winston Churchill's version of history of Second World War. Winston Churchill's messianic role as the chief antagonist to the global evil called Adolf Hitler earned him accolades worldwide as well as a Noble Prize in Literature! But the role he played as the chief architect of the slow genocide of millions of Bengalis through the worst engineered famine in history was never put to trial as perpetrator of heinous war crimes. His name was never linked to the Great Bengal Famine of 1943–44 or the infamous '*Panchaser Manwantar*' (Famine of Fifties, because according to Bengali calendar it was the year of 1350). Yet he arrogantly tried to rewrite history, citing the 'honorary' role British Empire played to protect its colonies from the carnage of war.

The colonial enterprises everywhere in the colonised world have effectively tried to efface the marks of their mindless malevolence, sweeping the dust under the carpet of such propaganda as Churchill claimed it, the role of the protector. The Great Bengal Famine of 1943 didn't only coincide with the trauma and eruption of fanatic mob-violence during the partition and independence of India in 1947, the annals of famine aggravated the situation. Which was once '*sonar Bangla*' (golden Bengal) in the pages of minstrels and folk-lore of the old, turned out to be the ravaged, famished skeleton of a well-nourished body. Churchill's 'Hindustan' might have not been involved directly in the Second World War, but it bore the brunt and the bloody aftermath like all other nations concerned. India went bankrupt as the Empire siphoned off the resources to fund the war of his own. India was always the crown jewel in the assembly of colonial coronet of the British Empire, but how much

S. Singha (✉)
Department of English, Deshapran Mahavidyalaya, Vidyasagar University, Midnapore, West Bengal, India
e-mail: subhajeet112singha@gmail.com

S. S. Ali and A. Basak (eds.), *Marginal Narratives and the Question of Human Rights in Asian Pacific Literature*, https://doi.org/10.1007/978-981-97-4544-9_13

resourceful was it? A glance over the economic as well as mercantile prosperity of Bengal delta during eighteenth century, just at the beginning of the exploitative expansion of East India Company, will prove that the sobriquet '*sonar Bangla*' was no hyperbole.

In her book "Churchill's Secret War: The British Empire and The Ravaging of India During World War II", Madhusree Mukherjee writes,

> For centuries, gold and silver had poured into Bengal; they now poured out. The East India Company no longer had to transport bullions to India to purchase goods for selling abroad. Instead, the tax revenues from Bengal supplied all the capital it had previously imported for investing in trade, and more. 'If a district yielded, as in the case of [Birbhum], pound 90,000 of revenue, the Council took care that not more than pound 5000 or pound 6000 were spent in governing it'. (xviii)

If we ponder over the figures here, we can have an estimate of the amount of profit the East India Company reaped from Bengal province from the example of only one district of Birbhum. The rest of the region can be imagined vividly. These are accounts from eighteenth century, after the Company defeated Nawab Siraj-ud-Daula in Battle of Plassey in 1757 A.D. So, we can only imagine the volume of resources and wealth that British plundered out of entire India. Beside Birbhum, there has been an account of the exponential growth of Company fortune, as the revenue collected from Bihar province was near about 200,000 pounds and it shot up to 680,000 pounds (Mukherjee xviii). Did the growth occur fortuitously? The answer was given by the author herself in petrifying words, the taxpayers were forced to "necessitated to sell their children in order to pay their rents, or otherwise obliged to fly the country (Mukherjee xviii)."

The wealth and resources accumulated throughout Bengal delta was more than enough to substantially accommodate all the material needs of the people here. It is not that the Bengali people had never witnessed a foreign invasion before. There were armies of Emperor Harshvardhan against King Shasanka of Gour Banga (Bengal in sixth century A.D.) or Bakhtiar Khilji attacking the last Hindu sovereign of Bengal, King Lakshman Sen (thirteenth century A.D.)—there are multiple incidents of foreign power conquering over the land of Bengal. But the British occupying and desecrating the lives here is unprecedented and nonpareil. The scale of the funnelling out and drying up the economic reserve of the land was such an eyesore that Mukherjee in her book cites about the report of a group of Armenian merchants, "A group of Armenian merchants…complaining that the lack of currency had brought virtually all business to a halt, so that not only a general bankruptcy is to be feared, but a real famine, in that midst of wealth and plenty (xix)."

The hint lies at the end of the quoted line here, 'that midst of wealth and plenty'. It refers back to the sobriquet of proficient and resourceful Bengal, the golden Bengal. The 'gold' is a figurative trope here, pointing at the agricultural abundance of the land. In his poem "*Sonar Tori*" (Golden Boat) Rabindranath Tagore writes,

> No room, no room, the boat is too small.
> Loaded with my gold paddy, the boat is full.
> Across the rain-sky clouds heave to and fro,

On the bare river-bank, I remain alone-
What had has gone: the golden boat took all. (Tagore)

In Bengal gold was often considered something of an intrinsic cultural value than a medium of bartering or economical standard. Being a land of fertile acres of irrigable land mass, Bengal delta was always an agricultural marvel. The crops, especially rice or paddy, mentioned in this poem is symbolic of our abundant agricultural product—a mark that bears the blessing of Hindu goddess Lakkhi or Laxmi, the presiding deity of prosperity, agriculture and resources. Even in Bengali language the word 'Lakkhi or Laxmi' connotes domestic bliss and amelioration and words such '*lakshmishree*' (graceful, blissful) is associated with our heritage of agriculture. The gold in the name of 'golden Bengal' refers to this perennial philosophy of plenty to produce and plenty to feed.

That philosophy is so pitilessly countermined when Bengal is laid to waste by a selfish and cruel mercantile policy of the empire. Famine was imminent. The staggering number of people who perished down the famished road in British India, is astounding. Between 1757 A.D. and 1901 A.D. India witnessed more over sixty incidents of acute starvations, and some of them are the worst famines in history. In between 1854 A.D. and 1901 A.D., within a span of forty-seven years, an amount of almost 3 crores of Indians were succumbed to famine (Pal 14). Now this is an estimate supported by the documents kept by the government alone. The actual number of victims may become more in number. Historian R.C.Majumdar in his book, "Bangladesh er Itihas" (History of Bengal) reminds us the fact that two of the most severe famines mark the beginning and the end of British dominance in Bengal. The earlier one is the infamous *Chiattorer Manwantar* (famine of seventy-six) which occurred in 1770 A.D., year of 1176 according to Bengali calendar, hence the 'seventy-six'. The fragments of that grievous time are documented in Bankimchandra Chattopadhyay's magnum opus, "Aanandamath". And the other one is the famine of 1943 A.D. These two events of perilous mass-starvation simply stand as the monuments of British exploitation of common Bengalis. *Panchaser Manwantar*' may have not been placed in such vivid colour in Bengali literature, but there are people living who remember the wounds of it (Majumdar 383).

R. C. Majumdar was probably not aware of the multitude of literary productions coming out from the anguished and distressed hands of Bengali people which commemorated these ghastly memories of the famine of 1943 A.D. Famous Bengali novelist Premendra Mitra composed a heart-rending description of millions of village-folks pouring in the streets of Calcutta for food, in his Bengali poem "Fyan" (drained water of cooked rice). The narrator witnesses some anomalies in the streets of the metropolis. They may have the shape of human long ago, but now they are haggard heap of bones. They are the mockery of human form, they are no different than the overflowing garbage in the city dumpsters, they are the remnants of human form. All they want is 'fyan', not even solid food. The poem reads like,

Human-like, yet, not quite human
Cruel caricatures of humanity!

Yet they move and speak,
Like debris they piled up by the road,
Sit, foraging food, on pile of garbage (Bhattacharya 11).

These victims portrayed here are step brothers of all humanity, whom the rest of the humanity has forgotten to show a little act of mercy. Like "Fyan", Amiya Chakrabarty's poem "Anna Dao" (give me food), Buddhadeb Basu in his poem "Shravan" (Bengali month roughly equivalent of July and August according to Gregorian calendar), Kazi Akram Hossein in his poem "Manwantar" (famine), Bishnu Dey's poem "Ek Pousher Sheet" (a winter in the month of Poush), Dinesh Das' poem "Bhukh Michil" (procession of hunger)—these poems are the etchings of abominable suffering of the famine victims, who were left to starve on the pavements of an affluent city.

Beside these poems, what afflicted our imagination more, were the dramas and street theatre productions that sprawled after the cruelties of the Famine of 1943. Most of these productions were enacted under the banner of I.P.T.A. or Indian People's Theatre Association. The easier way to pave the road straight to the heart of the mass was performative and visual art. Various socialist groups started performing translated versions of socialist plays like Clifford Odet's "Waiting for the Lefty". About the initial phase of IPTA and historical importance of the movement, Bhumika Agarwal writes, that veteran and renowned artists of the time like Prithviraj Kapoor, Bijon Bhattacharya, Ritwik Ghatak, Utpal Dutt, Khwaja Ahmad Abbas, Mulk Raj Anand, Salil Chowdhury,Pandit Ravi Shankar and others helped to shape I.P.T.A in 1942 (02).

To shape up the repertoire of the dramas of Bijon Bhattacharya, IPTA played an important role. Bijon himself was a communist and for the initial stage productions of IPTA, his "Nabanna" was selected among the others. IPTA ushered in new experiments in drama and performing arts, as it moved the theatre production from the commercial values to social contents. It revolutionized the medium of Indian theatre by making it a public funded affair and taking the theatre to the people, telling them their own stories, their own conflicts.

"Nabanna" was first performed at Srirangam theatre (now demolished) in Kolkata, on 24th October, 1944, as the entire country was set ablaze with 'Quit India' movement. The opening scene portrays predominance of red in the background, as well as the flags and banners of the people painted vermillion confirm the state of the agitated and beleaguered people's protest. Here we meet the character Judhisthir who can be best inducted as those firebrand Bengali revolutionaries of armed rebellion, like Surjya Sen or Prafulla Chaki or Jatindranath Mukherjee (Bagha Jatin). He is the representative of the wave of resistance against the Raj but he is only presented in the opening scene. Probably Bijon employed him only to situate the temporality of the action of the play, its proximity with the 'Quit India' movement. The leaders like Judhisthir stirs up the environment and it erupts in conflagration of dissent. Like the Yudhisthir from "Mahabharata", he is the leader in this war buthis role in this war is of a mere strategist. This scene may seem not aligned to the general narrative of the play, but it serves a pivotal purpose. It introduces us with Pradhan Samaddar, a native farmer of Aminpur, as well as the patriarch of the Samaddar household.

> Kunja: (to Judhisthir) The loss of the two sons has really driven him insane.
> Judhisthir: No, no. This is not insanity. This is what it should be. There is a need for
> this frenzy. This is not madness.
> Pradhan: No. No.
> Judhisthir; (to Kunja) You call this madness, but can you tell me Kunja, from where does this frenzy come? Why this madness? You are wrong, wrong Kunja. You are mistaken. Pradhan is not mad.
> Kunja: Not mad.
> Pradhan: No, no, no, no.
> Judhisthir: Our shortcomings can only be overcome by struggles within us (Bhattacharya 39).

What Pradhan's own nephew Kunja could not diagnose, Judhisthir's keen eye for human nature substantiates. Pradhan's loss of his two sons might be taken as a great tragic abyss from which none can escape unruffled. But Judhisthir believes that only in the face of gravest circumstances, one can bring out the most treasured virtue of oneself.

And the gravest circumstance was already upon the village of Aminpur, which can be assumed as the precise replica of Bengal itself, during 1943. The Samaddar household of Aminpur village is the centre of critical attention here. They are farmers for generations and they have withstood all the natural calamities, like dry spell of seasons or floodwater devouring paddy-fields. They are industrious, honest and altruist natives of the land, who cannot even gauge the warnings of a disaster.

> Kunja: Why? What about the old *aus* that I had kept away in the big black barrel on the roof?
> Radhi: (rebuking) Yes, that grain is still waiting for you up there. Do you have a clue of how many seers we need in a day?
> Kunja: (annoyed) No. I've never made the calculation. We've been surviving just like that.
> Niranjan: (intervenes) Come on now. Want and anguish are part of life. But there is no need for bitterness early in the morning. Don't fight (Bhattacharya 43).

The 'aus' referred here is a breed of rice which the farmers sow a plenty during monsoon in Bengal. These grow faster and can be harvested quicker than other breeds. The sheer availability of rice made Kunja saying "I've never made the calculation (Bhattacharya 45)." This doesn't reflect inefficacy of a man's pragmatic philosophy, rather this leads to a circumstance unforeseen. A famine is closing in on and Niranjan's words seem so ominous, when he says, "But there is no need for bitterness early in the morning (Bhattacharya 45)." The morning is definitely uneventful because even for seasoned farmers of Samaddar family, the gradual scarcity of food-grain in the market is no sign of apprehension. Death by lack of food was quite unheard of.

Without their knowing the famine was moving rapidly. Kalicharan Ghosh in his "Famines in Bengal" writes, "On May 13, 1943, the Hon'ble Sir Azizul Haque, Hon'ble Mr. Suhrawardy and Major General Wood, Secretary, Food Department, Govt. of India, tried to prove by elaborate statistics which had absolutely no relation to actual facts, that there was no shortage of foodstuffs in Bengal…(18)" The then Bengal govt. under Suhrawardy, which was no less than a puppet administration under British supervision, never cared to address the issue of famine as something crucial and threatening. They refuted any report of 'famine' and cited 'psychological factors' behind food shortage. But the reality showed the picture quite conflicting and incensing. Diya Gupta in her essay cites, "The most affected regions were largely in east Bengal, including the districts of Dacca, Faridpur, Noakhali, Mymensingh, Pabna and Khulna, while the sub-divisions of Contai and Tamluk in the district of Midnapur and Diamond Harbour in 24 Parganas were the main regions (02)." These are the worst hit regions of Bengal, but none of the regions has any shortage of irrigable land. She further cites historian Indivar Kamtekar, "In sheer scale, the tragedy of the Bengal Famine bears comparison with any other of the World War II, and dominates over other incidents in India. The dead outnumbered the entire Indian industrial working class (Gupta 2)."

From the historical point of view, as Kamtekar shows, the slow genocide of millions left the Bengal province paralysed. Aminpur felt the burn too. The mass exodus from their native birth-place became inevitable. Aminpur can no longer provide the food and the Samaddar family moved to the streets of Calcutta. Being the second most important city in British India, during 1943–44, Calcutta was the bauble in the economic roundabout of the world trade and commerce. Millions of starving village folks started to throng the streets and many of them were left to die without the lack of Govt. policies to counter the effects of famine. Food shortage and the hunger-stricken mob have been a recurrent trope in the Bengali literature that came out during 1940s and 50 s. "Nabanna" was no doubt the most brilliant representation of hunger and the transformation of human beings into regressive primal instinctive existence which was forced upon them by British Empire, a state of 'zoe'.

'Zoe' was an important critical term popularized by Italian philosopher Giorgio Agamben in his book "Homo Sacer: Sovereign Power and Bare life" (1995), where he formulated a new paradigm to understand the exploitive nature of the state power and its association with Foucauldian idea of 'biopolitics'. Michel Foucault in his "Will to Power", which happens to be the first volume of his "History of Sexuality" trilogy introduced the world with the idea of biopolitics. The sovereign state or autocratic power use various strategies and means to exert and establish domination over the mass. If we take the idea of panopticon, which Foucault owed from Jeremy Bentham, the British Utilitarian philosopher, we may see that Foucault analysed the way the community or the mass is governed by the sovereign power. The mode of surveillance and govern is collective here. But here an important issue is raised too. Besides the governing of population, Foucault wanted to enquire how the system of governance works upon individual subjects. How does the sovereign state indoctrinate the individual self? There he devises the notion of the rational mode of sovereign power, the idea of biopolitics or biopower. The biopower isn't regarded as authoritarian or domineering like other forms of discourse. Biopower has the guise of populist beneficial state policies, like population register, rate of mortality, percentage of vaccination completed and others. Through these pseudo-rationalist approaches to governance, biopower legitimises biopolitics and from the exterior of the biopolitical policies it always seems libertarian as Catherine Mills writes, "...it places the new political subject of the population at the centre of governmental calculations, and one of its key problematics is the fostering of life through the political conjunction of the individual and the population (22)."

Giorgio Agamben found the darker side of biopolitics when he applied and analyzed the theory to understand the Holocaust during Second World War in Germany. Stanley Milgram in his seminal work, "Obedience to Authority" observes, "Gas chambers were built, death camps were guarded...These inhuman policies may have originated in the mind of a single person, but they could only have been carried out on a massive scale if a very large number of people obeyed others (14)." And according to Agamben the original benevolent organism of biopower provided the necessary authorization to those 'large number of people' who were the accomplice of the genocide. The process of validating the authority of carrying out the order of mass-execution lies in Agamben's understanding of 'bare life'.

Agamben's idea of 'bare life' is intricately associated with his vindication of the terms, 'bios', 'zoe', 'Homo Sacer' and 'der Muselmann'. Agamben took the idea of civilized and disciplined life, anointed as 'bios', from the ancient Greeks. Both the terms 'bios' and 'zoe' refer to the state of life in general. Whereas 'zoe' appears to be the primitive, uncouth and pre-civilized state of being, wherefrom the term 'zoology' originate, the term 'bios' stands for the political, indoctrinated and civilized multitude which brings forth the term 'biology' Thus 'bios' is the manifestation of socio-political progression of life and its standard of excellence is meted out against the ever decomposing state of 'zoe'. 'Zoe' is always excluded as the marginal, bare-minimal identity whose sole existence proves the necessity of the 'being' of superior 'bios'. And according to Agamben, 'a state of exception' is always created at the heart of the state of sovereignty, where all the legal rights, jurisprudential privileges are suspended and an absolute authority over the 'zoe' is attributed and bestowed upon 'bios'. And through the lenses of Agamben's idea of 'biopower' the suspension of the rights of 'being' for 'zoe' is the basis of Nazi Germany's legitimization of Holocaust. Such heavy impetus Agamben binds with the idea of Foucauldian 'biopolitics', that he called it 'thanatopolitics'. Roberto Esposito in his book "Bios: Biopolitics and Philosophy" writes, "On the other hand, a growing superimposition between the domain of power or of law [*diritto*] and that of life; on the other, an equally close implication that seems to have been derived with regard to death. It is exactly the tragic paradox that Michel Foucault, in a series of writing dating back to the middle of the 1970s, examined. Why does a politics of life always risk being reversed into a work of death? (28)".

Now Agamben always wanted to understand the reason behind biopolitics' degradation into 'thanatopolitics'. Just like the Nazi sovereign state of Germany excluded the Jews from the realm of 'bios' to the realm of bare-minimal surviving of 'zoe', the same happens to the fateful populace of Bengal during 1943. British Empire did the same with the people here, turning them into 'Homo Sacer'. Agamben received the idea of 'Homo Sacer' from the pages of ancient Roman law, as he writes in his "Homo Sacer: Sovereign Power and Bare life", "The sacred man is the one whom the people have judged on account of a crime. It is not permitted to sacrifice this man, yet he who kills him will not be condemned for homicide; in the first tribunitian law, in fact, it is noted that "if someone kills the one who is sacred according to the plebiscite, it will not be considered homicide." This is why it is customary for a bad or impure man to be called sacred. (61)" 'Homo Sacer' is the sacrificial offal that shares its origin from religion but it is more like a condition that permeates sovereignty.

In order to conserve and accentuate the right of the living of privileged class, the state can impose an impromptu and spontaneous measure which is known as 'Homo Sacer'. During the emergency of Second World War the expenses of running a war become tantamount of exposing million of innocent Bengali lives to the brutal truth of slow, anguishing death by starvation. The people were left to starve on the streets, and the famine was not the only reason behind human casualty. As Arup Maharatna in his essay "The demography of the Bengal famine of 1943–44: A detailed study" writes, "Thus, the Famine Inquiry Commission's Report on Bengal almost certainly provides an underestimate of famine mortality of only 1.5 million excess deaths. According to the report the period of peak famine mortality was from the middle of 1943 to the middle of 1944. (170)" Although it can never be actually estimated about the human casualty, the cases of co-morbidity were never accounted inside the "Report on Bengal". Maharatna further writes, "It has been widely agreed that in the early phase of the famine most deaths were due to sheer starvation, but later the occurrence of multiple epidemics of cholera, malaria and smallpox accounted for the peak famine mortality…It recognises the role of widespread famine-induced starvation in causing these epidemics (171)." The British Government pushed the people of Bengal, just like the Samaddar family of Aminpur, into the domain of 'zoe' and subsequently into the abysmal, excruciating realm of 'Bare Life'.

Who were once farmers with land and steady flow of income upon agricultural produces; they have been reduced to 'der Muselmann'—the embodiment of 'Homo Sacer'. Bijon Bhattacharya painted the most reprehensible picture of 'Bare Life' among the stage directions at the beginning of 'Act Two', 'Scene Three' in 'Nabanna', it is shown that there is a ceremony of wedding is going on. Just at the entrance of the wedding feast, on one side of the stage, there is a dustbin overflowing with left-over foods and Kunja, Radhika and Pradhan are seen foraging and scraping for foods there and fighting with dogs. As Bhattacharya writes, "The master of household stands in front of the gate along with others. He is greeting the guests, "Please come in. Have a seat."… On the left corner there is a dustbin, barely visible. Radhika and Kunja search for food among the rubbish. It is dark and nothing is clearly visible…Suddenly, a dog starts barking ferociously near the dustbin. Almost immediately Kunja responds in screaming in bestial anger. In a few moments, Kunja advances towards the light holding up his wounded hand—bitten by the dog and dripping with blood (91)." This is the graphical representation of Agamben's 'der Muselmann', which refers as sub-human beings in German. It is a racial slur designed to discriminate the Jewish-lives in general and endorses the idea of killing "Homo Sacer" in the guise of benevolence of billions. Winston Churchill's government was never accused of this slow, engineered, brutal genocide in Bengal and Agamben exactly points this out as 'state of exception'.

'State of exception' is the axis on which the legitimization of such brutal policies of 'Homo Sacer' is rested upon. Agamben writes in his "States of Exception" (second volume of "Homo Sacer Omnibus"), "Indeed, according to a widely held opinion, the state of exception constitutes a "point of imbalance between public law and political fact" (Saint Bonnet 2001, 28) that is situated—like civil war, insurrection, and resistance—in an "ambiguous, uncertain, borderline fringe, at the intersection of the legal and the political (167)." The law that provides sovereignty the biopower to suspend even the right to live or right to feed the subjects of the state, it is the same biopower that excludes the sovereignty from any sort of legal proceedings or indictment. Why was the Samaddar family pushed to such extremes, and what gives the 'state of exception' such paradoxical stature, Agamben further writes, "The question of borders becomes all the more urgent: if exceptional measures are the result of periods of political crisis and, as such, must be understood on political and not juridico-constitutional grounds (De Martino 1973, 320), then they find themselves in the paradoxical position of being juridical measures that cannot be understood in legal terms, and the state of exception appears as the legal form of what cannot have legal form (Agamben 167)."

In "Act Two", "Scene Three" of "Nabanna" outside the wedding ceremony, Pradhan Samaddar wails,

> How much longer do I have to shout out for a little bit of rice! Have all of you become deaf? Can't you hear? Don't you have a heart? O Baba, o Babu- you waste so much of food, and throw away so much. But you are unable to give a fistful of rice to this old starving man. Don't you have any mercy O Baba, o Babu! (Bhattacharya 96)

All the people who were perished in this man-made famine to protect the empire, all of the people who walked down this famished road and never returned—they never believed that Bengal delta can run so dry that there would be death by starvation. People here are used to celebrate 'nabanna' the ceremony of rich harvest—the proper symbol of 'bios'. And at the end of the play, the Samaddar family returns to their rightful place, the village of Aminpur. They are distressed but not destroyed, bent but not broken. And their decision of celebrating the festival of 'nabanna' once again shows us the resilience and endurance of the people against the 'state of exception' or 'bare life' or 'Homo Sacer' of sovereign. The ceremony of 'nabanna' becomes a symbol of life at the end, where Dayal, Kunja and Niranjan rejoice at the prospect of celebrating the festival of Nabanna once again (Bhattacharya 145). They were the survivors of the worst ordeal they escaped, though not unscathed. The cycle of life is once again prevailed the negation of the bestiality of 'der Muselmann' is once more achieved.

References

Agamben G (2017) The Omnibus: Homo Sacer. Stanford University Press
Agarwal B (2013) IPTA's contribution in awakening nationalism. The Criterion 4:1–5
Bhattacharya B (2018) Nabanna: of famine and resilience: a play. Translated by Arjun Ghosh, Rupa Publications
Esposito R (2008) Bios: biopolitics and philosophy. Translated by Timothy Campbell, University of Minnesota Press
Ghosh KC (1994) Famines in Bengal: 1770–1943. National Council of Education, Bengal
Gupta D (2019) Bodies in hunger: literary representations of the Indian home-front during world war II. J War Cult Stud. https://doi.org/10.1080/17526272.2019.1644274
Maharatna A (1994) The demography of the Bengal famine of 1943–44: A detailed study. Indian Econ Social History Rev 31(2):169–215
Majumdar RC (1982) Bangladesh er Itihas, 4th volume. 2nd ed., General Printers and publishers
Milgram S (2009) Obedience to authority. Harper Perennial
Mills C (2018) Biopolitics. Routledge
Mukherjee M (2010) Churchill's secret war: the British empire and the ravaging of India during world war II. Tranquebar
Pal M (2019) (ed) Khudharta Bangla: Rashtra O Beniatantrer Ganahatyar Dalil. 4th ed., Publishing Plus
Tagore R (2021) Golden boat. all poetry, 26 Dec. 2021. allpoetry.com/The-Golden-Boat.

Chapter 14
Dalit Negotiations: Yogesh Maitreya's Perspective on University Spaces and Human Rights

Ambalika Biswas

> "The constitution has merely prescribed but has not given any description of the ground reality. We can make a dent only if we recognize the fact that the caste system is a major source, indeed an obnoxious one, of human rights violations" (Pal 23)

The caste system in India itself is responsible for the means and opportunities for the exploitation of Dalit communities. 'Caste' is a form of social stratification that allocates an individual's explicit permanent identities in arranged groups at birth. Ambedkar defined caste as a 'hoary institution which is familiar and unexplained in nature'(Ambedkar 32). Ambedkar in one of his most important works argues: Caste is a notion; it is a state of the mind. The demolition of caste does not mean the elimination of a physical barrier. It means a notional change. (Ambedkar 68). In the contemporary world violation of Human rights is rampant. Developing countries like India bear the most burden of this kind of violation despite many proclamations, declarations, conventions, and covenants. When a government, society, institution, or individual violates the rights of its citizens or its members or for that matter any human being then it is known as a Human Rights Violation. India is one country where the Dalits are deprived of their rights hence sharing a major burden of the human rights violation. People of the lower caste are discriminated against due to their caste even in recent times, which marks the violation of the human rights of the people of these communities. Even in institutes of excellence and higher education, caste-based atrocity is prevalent in the present times which indicates a shameful act of the violation of basic human rights of the people of specific communities within the space of the university.

University is supposed to be an inclusive and liberal space. John Henry Newman gave the title 'The Idea of a University Defined and Illustrated' to a series of lectures originally given in Dublin in the 1850s. Newman thought that knowledge should be

A. Biswas (✉)
Department of English, Rabindra Mahavidyalaya, Champadanga, Hooghly, India
e-mail: ambalikab8@gmail.com

S. S. Ali and A. Basak (eds.), *Marginal Narratives and the Question of Human Rights in Asian Pacific Literature*, https://doi.org/10.1007/978-981-97-4544-9_14

pursued 'for its own sake'. (Anderson). According to him the quest for truth was part of an educational ideal that transformed the personality of the cultivated man, and could not be separated from moral and religious education. Yogesh Maitreya presents his collection of short stories *The Flower in the Grave of Caste* where the idea of the Dalits being discriminated against and their human rights being violated is depicted. Despite the existence of Acts like the POAA 1989, the atrocities against the scheduled castes, scheduled tribes, and Bahujan have not ended rather the amendment of the Act in 2018 is a farce and fails to protect the Scheduled Caste and Scheduled tribes even in supposedly liberal spaces like that of a university.

Unfortunately, universities in contemporary India are upholders and defenders of caste privilege as the percentage of upper caste people, both in the teaching and student communities is consistently higher than their proportion in the general population. (Babu MT 217). This indicates that there is a lack of proper representation from different communities in the University Spaces and reflects that the upper castes have always occupied the higher educational institutions in India. (Babu MT 217). The university space in India has been observing differences in numerous fields and has been a failure in addressing the subjects regarding social inequality and exclusion. (Babu MT 217).

If we examine minutely, we will notice that underprivileged citizens are still fighting hard to attain equality and this struggle is not a matter of concern for those citizens who have already occupied positions of privilege. As Thorat puts it, the glitches of the lower castes (the scheduled castes- SCs, Scheduled Tribes -and the OBCs) are exclusive and different, and as such these communities should be understood from the perspective that they did not have equal rights in the 'past' also. These forms of exclusion, continue to disseminate themselves in the 'present'. (2432).

Although the legislature has made reservation mandatory, the implementation of the same has always been met with more resistance than eagerness. We witness this taking place at the undergraduate level, research level, and even in the case of teaching positions. Thus, "a right policy can be made entirely infructuous if there is inordinate delay in its implementation, or if it is implemented in a distorted manner". (Babu MT 220) There is silence about this in the media and public sphere even when reports of huge violations of reservation policy are reported in institutions like IIt's and Central universities like Delhi University this marks the violation of the equality clause ensured by articles 14,15,16. (Babu MT 220). The interesting fact is that the struggles of proper implementation of reservation do not fetch any support but rather give rise to political resentment. This is not astounding, considering that these movements are always against the preferences of the dominant classes of people who are in control of the administrative structure.

We have witnessed numerous stories of discrimination and suicides by Dalit students in higher educational institutions. When the reservation policy is violated, the upper-caste-dominated mainstream student groups never care to protest. The discrimination towards the Dalit students also hardly attracted any attention just like the caste atrocities of Khairlanji had done. (Babu MT 222). According to Johan Galtung who introduced the concept of structural violence in his article "Violence, Peace, and Peace Research" in 1969 structural violence is a form of violence wherein social structures or social institutions impair people by not allowing them to meet their basic needs. Structural violence is not very visible but it is one of the most lethal forms of violence which causes deaths that would not occur in more equal societies. (Lewis). Maitreya beautifully portrayed in his short story *Re-Evolution* the plight of Baliraja who was the first person from his village to opt for a Ph.D. in a University. He was fascinated by the idea of a university without realizing that "in this country dreams are filtered by a person's caste and class". (Maitreya 8). He further explains how in a liberal space of higher education like the University he was expelled from the institution for protesting against the perpetrators of the Khairlanji Massacre.[1] "The beginning of everything had no end, until I, along with several other Dalit students, was suspended by the university one day, for taking part in the protest that was demanding the arrest of perpetrators of the Khairlanji massacre in 2006." (Maitreya 8).

In *Re-evolution*, Maitreya successfully conveys that revolution for the lower caste starts by learning the alphabet and acquiring education this was the life message of Dr. Ambedkar. In this story, he has empowered the character of Baliraja to fight back against injustice. Maitreya in his story *Flower on the Grave of Caste* tells the reader that a human has no class and caste in real, that such labels are the work of humans. This can be seen through the lenses of the theory of intersectionality propounded by Kimberle Crenshaw, who in 1989 proposed the theory where in her paper "Demarginalizing The Intersection of Race And Sex: A Black Feminist Critique Of Antidiscrimination Doctrine, Feminist Theory And Antiracist Politics". It describes how race, class, caste, gender identity, sexual orientation, religion, and various other identity markers "intersect" and overlap with one another (What is intersectionality and what does it have to do with me?). Crenshaw took the example of 'black woman' and stated that to understand the oppression of black women it is vital to look at the intersection of blackness and womanhood. Similarly, to understand the oppression of an underprivileged Dalit one must consider the overlapping of caste and class. The main purpose of Crenshaw was to demolish the hierarchies altogether. (Coaston). The theory of intersectionality is portrayed here in Maitreya's story where he tries to reflect on the idea of intersecting caste and class which are treated as labels in the society and are markers of oppression.

The question of caste has always been neglected and suffered institutional denial. The state remains in constant denial of the fact that Brahminism is taking the lives of people of lower caste in the places they dwell, their work fields, and the educational institutions where they study like that of Rohit Vemula and Dr. Payel Tadvi. Yogesh Maitreya portrays this in his collection of short stories *The Flowers on the Grave of Caste* where his characters feel threatened in a Brahmanical environment. These incidences perpetuate systemic oppression which indicates disadvantaging a group of people intentionally based on their identity while giving an undue advantage to the dominant groups. The identity markers could be gender, race, class, caste, sexual orientation, language, and the like. In this case, the primary focus will be on Caste. Systemic oppression exists at the institutional level and its existence is visible across the structures like education, health, transportation, economy, and the like. These are not only interconnected but reinforced over time. Mistreatment is meted out through systemic oppression via tools such as racism, classism, casteism, sexism, or homophobia. This is more than just an amalgamation of individual prejudices but operates in a structured pattern. Systemic oppression is a tool used to oppress the Dalit students in the University Spaces. The characters portrayed in Yogesh Maitreya's stories face systemic oppression. Even the Dalit students who are reprimanded in real life because of their Dalit identity cannot escape the clutches of systemic oppression brought out on them by the authority of these institutions. However, the main trait of the characters present in Maitreya's stories is their consciousness of self-respect which infuses their identity, hence focusing on the individual notion rather than a collective claim an idea that Dr. Ambedkar articulately puts forward in the debates of the Constituent Assembly. (Adsule). Yogesh Maitreya emphasizes his place as one of the new voices in an age of populist and post-truth literature. (Adsule). The neo-liberal publishers in a country like India, which is considered the republic of caste, prefer promoting books on Hinduism and elitist, Savarna feminist Ideals, thereby denouncing Dalits and Dalit aesthetics.[2] Maitreya stands apart with his works which span across poetry and translations that reflect the subconscious prejudice of the society. (Adsule).

In this collection of short stories, he magnifies Ambedkar's ideas about gender, caste, and class echoing the theory of intersectionality as depicted by Kimberley Crenshaw where it is vividly shown how these aspects intersect. Maitreya's stories are defined by logical lucidity, vivid pragmatism, and a sense of determination and commitment. The characters in these stories dwell in a Republic of Paradox, which ensured them justice, liberty, equality,fraternity, and possibilities that were not fulfilled. And yet in the milieu, justice is served, thus keeping alive the hope of these broken people; they continue to celebrate songs of freedom. (Adsule). This is evident in the story *Life is Beautiful* where the chief character Nagaraj is a conservancy worker who attempts to fulfill his and his child's aspirations with the expectation that sooner or later, there will be justice.

In *Educate, Organise, Agitate* Maitreya creates two characters Gautam and Ashoka, and their parallel journeys in a casteist educational institute, which hampers Ashoka's life as he disappears mysteriously, with a probability that he may have been abducted. Later on, it was found that he committed suicide to assert his Dalit identity. The idea of a university being an elitist institution perpetuating a casteist atmosphere is reflected in this story as Gautam states "Here everyone tries to be something else, or someone distinct or superior to the common people. Here, everyone is made to think that only they are capable of bringing changes to the society, and not the people who contribute every day to it, such as carpenters, drivers, porters, sweepers, gardeners, weavers, municipality workers, tanners, farmer, daily wage workers, housemaids, etc. People in the university do not even think that such people must be thinking something." (Maitreya 69). During this critical juncture Gautam feels lost, he remembers Ashoka's words about how they can't afford to stop dreaming because dreams are their only asset. As embodied by the story's title, it is ultimately Babasaheb's words that serve as guiding principles to Gautam. The story of Siddhartha and Gautam deals with sexuality, the consciousness, and social pressure that caste identities inflict constant efforts to surpass caste through class imitation, and the prevalent nature of caste in classrooms of elite institutions where Dalit students, like Siddhartha who are vocal about their rights, are punished. This echoes the tragic death of Rohith Vemula and the grave instances of Human Rights Violations in the University spaces. It reflects oppression through Structural Violence. As Gaultang states any scenario in which a social structure spreads inequity as a result causing suffering is structural violence. One of the most potent forms of violence is Structural violence which includes homicides, suicides, mass murders, and war. (Lewis). The various ways in which social, economic, and political systems expose certain populations to risks and vulnerabilities resulting in increased morbidities and mortality is known as "Structural Violence" (Lewis). Those systems include income inequality, racism, homophobia, Islamophobia, sexism, and other means of social exclusion leading to vulnerabilities, such as poverty, stress, trauma, crime, etc. (Lewis). This is reflected in the case of Rohit Vemula and the other institutional murders of Dalit students across the country, as they are the victims of the nexus of caste which itself is a social structure harming people from the caste-based marginalized groups. His death is a classic example of structural violence meted out on a Dalit as his suicide marks how certain groups in this case the Dalits are exposed to risks causing morbidity and mortality.

Rohith Vemula dreamt of becoming Carl Sagan to write science but unfortunately, this dream came to an end. In *Life is Beautiful*, Maitreya challenges the arbitrary argument of "Merit" given by the Savarnas by bringing to light how poor people are not allowed to dream in this country because of the rigid and airtight box of caste and not "class" (Kamble). Hindutva gives rise to the philosophy of caste discrimination. Public spaces like universities have turned anti-Dalit and institutional discrimination that existed for ages was highlighted through the case of Rohit and other students in the Universities. Rohit's death exposes the crime against Dalits that takes place in institutions like HCU a Central University of Hyderabad. This indicates that Dalit students are the victims of systemic oppression and structural violence practiced in these institutions by the upper caste students, teachers, and administration of the so-called liberal spaces. The casteist, extremist, and anti-national activities in Central University have been exposed. This is not the only incidence of a Dalit scholar committing suicide at the HCU, nor is the HCU the only university in the country to have such incidents.

Dr. Payel Tadvi was a 26-year-old tribal Muslim from the Adivasi Bhil community, which is a Scheduled Tribe community. She was a gynecologist by profession and died due to suicide in Mumbai. She was mentally harassed by three upper-caste women doctors. She was the first doctor in eighty years from her community whom we lost to the pangs of institutional casteism. (Suchitra). Stretching from Rohith Vemula to Payel Tadvi, caste discrimination followed by suicides is a continuing spectacle in Indian educational institutions, including medical schools. Protests are being organized in Mumbai, Pune, and Delhi today, in memory of Dr. Tadvi and against caste harassment in educational institutions in various parts of the country. Payel Tadvi was the first woman in their community to pursue post-graduation and the first in their family to become a doctor. (Bhuyan). This incident can also be interpreted through Crenshaw's theory of intersectionality where a woman is harassed and oppressed to the extent that she commits suicide because of her caste, gender, and religion and she is trebly marginalized because of these intersecting factors.

It is proved by several surveys that the caste venom inflicts the country, the number of such incidences has been rising in recent years according to the National Crime Research Bureau (NCRB) atrocities against scheduled castes have risen from 50,291in 2020 to 45,961 cases in 2019. The crime rate had increased from 22.8 per lakh population to 25 per lakh population in 2020. (Crimes against SC's, ST's). The strategy of the Hindutva camp is to Brahminise common folks of the Dalits. As dissenting Muslim youth are termed as branded terrorists, Dalit Activist youth are being stamped as extremist casteists and anti-nationals. Maitreya in his short story *The Sense Of The Beginning* through the portrayal of the character Siddhartha challenges the popular illusion about the so-called liberal educational institutions. Siddhartha describes the premier institute in Mumbai as a Brahmanical place and states that the Dalits do not belong there "People like us do not belong to such Brahmanical places (Maitreya 36). The narrator was under an illusion that the institute was a liberal place and he would be accepted but failed to fit in "People here looked different; they smelled different. I wanted to smell like them, I wanted to fit in their world, secretly" (Maitreya 28). Feeling unaccepted he wanted to be invisible on the campus "My time after classes was spent in searching for corners in the campus where I could sit and read and make myself feel invisible." (Maitreya 28). The narrator understood Siddhartha's stance of calling the institute a Brahmanical place only when he committed suicide "For a long time, I did not know why he said that a campus is a Brahmanical place. After a month, it was only his death that unveiled the dark side of the campus. Siddhartha was highly disappointed with the attitude of the professors of the institute and he mocked them and called them names "creatures with big belly, narrow mind, and weak stomach" (Maitreya 36). As we read the story, we find the reference to how a Brahmin professor supports the caste system in the classroom and Siddhartha opposes this idea. He explained to the other students that the idea or explanation of the professor was casteist, which the accused never accepted. "It was only through one of his classmates I was told that during one of the classes, his Brahmin professor implicitly supported the existence of a caste system to which Siddhartha not only opposed but explained to other students in the class that how professor's explanation was casteist and thus, in support of long prevailed caste-oppression. This made the professor furious but he manipulated Siddhartha's explanation as rhetoric". (Maiterya 37).

The task of investigating caste, gender, and class is simplified through the usage of Ambedkarite and humanistic frameworks in Maitreya's *Flowers on the Grave of Caste* Maitreya differs from the Savarna writers of the past as he does not satiate the appetites of the upper castes in his stories. Another interesting fact about Maitreya is that he writes his stories in English, which is considered the language of the Upper caste, thereby using language as a weapon against a privileged community owing to their birth. (Kamble). "There was only one Dalit student in his class apart from him who, from the first day, made to feel inferior in English-speaking, jargon-based environment of the class and grappling with assignments compulsory to write in English. Siddharth went to the dean to discuss this issue but nothing was done. Instead,

The Dean mockingly suggested him to learn English first because that was a basic requirement to learn the course in the institute." (Maitreya 37). Maitreya explores various facets of caste barriers through its stories like accessing basic necessities to a vision of emancipation via education, the cobwebs of chaos and confusion in the lives of Dalits, and also the hypocrisy of the Marxists. The major characters in Maitreya's stories echo Babasaheb's idea of egalitarian Utopia although the characters were defeated by circumstances and failed miserably in life yet they were bound by one common thread that was hope. His stories also explicitly deal with the various instances of human rights violations of the people of the marginalized communities in this case the students of an elite university in Mumbai. Through the different stories in his collection, he repeatedly tried to focus on the various facets of the violation of Human Rights of the students inside the campus by the professors, students, and administration. It is also portrayed that how a university disappoints the students and members of the marginalized communities and how equality is but a myth in reality.

Through his stories, Yogesh Maitreya not only portrays the life of Dalits across the country, but he has also tried to bring to attention the reality of the Indian caste system prevailing still today emphasizing its practice in institutes of higher education. The problem with fiction writing in English is that the problems of the marginalized and the oppressed never find expression in the stories, Maitreya's stories break the ceiling. In the story *Caste*, Maitreya confronts the privileged class through his narrating character. (Kamble) When he takes Gargi to the house of Sumedh Sapkal the poet, Gargi begins to grow uncomfortable with the noise, the mosquitoes, the smell and asks "How do people live here?' the narrating character replies, "Not by choice, obviously. In your comfort, lies the history of their discomfort." (Maitreya 25). Through this story, Maitreya subtly exposes the hypocrisy of the left where the left liberals talk about revolution and socialization of the country propounds the theory of classlessness, and on the other hand, are unenthusiastic about eating food prepared by a lower caste or on the communist term a "Labour class" (Kamble). This is indeed ironic as the character referred to was stated to be a bright young individual from a liberal university. This attitude also indicates the various basic human rights violations practiced within the university campuses where even the workers deny service to the Dalit students as they are from a lower caste, for example, they are denied food in the mess, called names, and deprived of other services even by the workers of the University.

Maitreya's story *Educate, Organise, Agitate* is the lengthiest story in the book. In this story, the protagonist reaches Mumbai, and suddenly his life changes as he becomes influential. Here Maiterya exposed how the judiciary is lame and inaccessible to the poor and henceforth fails to give justice. Maitreya emphasizes human rights violations of the Dalit students by highlighting the atmosphere of central universities and also shows that the students have corrupt educated minds. In reality, when the Dalit Bahujan student groups engage themselves in issues regarding the freedom of expression, the groups of upper-caste students support them halfheartedly as they are not totally apathetic about the struggles of Dalit Bahujan to attain equality. (Babu MT 227). The upper caste minds are unable to understand the pangs of discrimination because equality to them is a given concept. (Babu MT 227). Hence, these citizens fail to see the struggle of unequal students to attain equality. Even though the struggles of the various student groups seem to converge their basic interest diverge. Unless the upper caste dominant student groups take an active part in making the University an inclusive place and represent the social diversity uniformly the university will reproduce the social discrimination and prejudice (Babu MT 227). As the universities fail to be inclusive spaces and are exclusionary therefore the social mobility of Dalit Students is restricted (Babu MT 227).

The social mobility of Dalit students is constrained due to the rampant exclusionary methods prevalent in higher education. Hence, right from their school days to higher education Dalit students face tangible or intangible methods of exclusion (Neelaknandan and Patil 9). There are terrible practices of exclusion that are being practiced for example non-Dalit teachers do not supervise Dalit students and put the blame that they are not fluent in the English Language. With the ideology of caste structures and the reference to the sense of pollution, even the workers are reluctant to serve the Dalit students in the mess. (Neelaknandan and Patil 8). Dalit students are not allowed to sit with the upper-caste students while writing exams, they are called by caste names, various comments are made based on their habits, color, and culture, they are excluded from birthday parties, farewells organized by the non-dalit students, thus practicing social exclusion and hence marginalizing, discriminating them and violating their basic human rights. Sukumar also maps the derogatory language used by non-Dalit students using terms such as 'pigs', 'governments son-in-law's (this term signifies that Dalit students avail the benefits of reservation and get special privileges from the government by the virtue of reservation), "bastards", "son of god" (translation of the Gandhian term used 'Harijan'), 'beggar' and so on. They also wrote 'bastard' on a poster of B.R. Ambedkar (Sukumar 17). It portrays that higher caste students have a huge aversion towards Ambedkar for providing revolutionary potentials to Dalits. The Dalit students face discrimination while they seek jobs after the completion of higher education. Dalit students and teachers face threats from the emerging groups of anti-reservationists. Media in our country which is supposed to be a part of the democracy also supports such non-democratic, authoritarian, caste-based political groups. Educational institutes have internalized caste-based oppression and miscellaneous aspects of education systems that eliminate others as the caretakers of the upper-caste hegemony in India (Tharu et al.2702).

The Hindu religion is based on a caste system and hierarchy, according to Sukhdeo Thorat, it challenges the universal human rights framework. A conflict in the discourse of human rights is created due to the Hindu religious and social order. According to the constitution, there is legal support for the Dalits such as the anti-untouchability Act 1955, the protection of Civic Rights Act 1975, and the Prevention of Atrocities Act-1989. It is stated that constitutional privileges have changed the lives of Dalits and tribals. (Sriniwas 154). However, Sukhdeao Thorat argued that 'caste discrimination' and untouchability' exist outside the realm of 'non-legal process'. By using the category of 'non-legal process', he refers to the mainstream Hindus who control the religious and economic spheres in India and it is also permeated into state machinery such as the police and executive who are preordained to practice the law (Thorat 4). The government of India also passed the scheduled caste/tribes Prevention of Atrocities Act which prohibits atrocities against Dalits and scheduled tribes. This Act was passed to prevent atrocities such as 'forcing them (Dalits) to eat human excreta, dumping carcasses or other waste matter in their (Dalits) premises, polluting the drinking water used by them (Dalits), implicating them (Dalits) in false cases' (Commission for Scheduled Castes/Scheduled Tribes, 1998, cited in (Thorat 6).

Human Rights Watch (HRW), is an NGO whose main objective is to conduct advocacy on human rights, in one of the reports published by HRW in 2016 the Scheduled Castes and Scheduled Tribes (Prevention of Atrocities) Act 1989 as a law that confines freedom of expression. (Babu, MT 226). The report states that the 2015 amendments in the Act have banned an expression that "promotes or attempts to promote feelings of enmity, hatred or will against members of the Scheduled Castes or Scheduled Tribes" and that "disrespects any late person held in high esteem by members of the Scheduled castes or Scheduled tribes",(Failure to Meet). According to this respect Prevention of Atrocities Act and Sedition law are considered under the same category. Interestingly, the former is meant to protect the marginalized sections of society, and the latter is intended to uphold the might of the state and is often used to further crush the vulnerable sections of society a large number of Muslims and tribals are charged under the sedition law at regular intervals.

It is sad to witness that the state of human rights of a certain section of people namely the marginalized people of the Dalit and Bahujan communities are violated despite enjoying independence for 72 years. The Dalits are still vulnerable and their rights are unprotected or under-protected. The Scheduled castes or Scheduled tribes are denied other basic human rights, they are deprived of their right to life, and right to dignity. The marginalized people of the Dalit communities are disgraced and treated as second-grade citizens or even lower than that. The Dalits have become the main victims of oppression, humiliation, and harassment. The existing caste system offers a glaring example of a violation of Dalit rights through centuries of hegemony, oppression, and exploitation. Sadly enough, the same is practiced in the institutes of higher education and the Universities are no exception.

The government of India implemented the Scheduled Castes and Scheduled Tribes Prevention of Atrocities Act in 1989 to provide protection to the Dalits, safeguard their rights, and eliminate the atrocities meted out by the upper caste people against these communities and in the process eradicate social discrimination. Still, the condition of these communities is miserable, it is highly alarming that there is a drastic increase in violence against the people of the Dalit community especially Dalit women despite having such Acts.

The POA Act was enacted to protect the SC/STs from atrocities committed against them by non-SC/STs because the normal provisions of existing laws like the Protection of Civil Rights Act 1995 and the Indian Penal Code were found insufficient to stop or eliminate the offenses against the members of the SC/ST communities. The provisions of the SC/ST Prevention of Atrocities Act (1989) and Rules can be broadly divided into three parts. The first category establishes criminal liability for several specifically defined atrocities and for penalizations given in the Indian Penal Code (IPC). The second category contains provisions for relief and compensation for victims of (All You Need). The third category contains provisions that establish special authorities for the implementation and monitoring of the Act (India: Non-implementation). Subsequently, the National Human Rights Commission also stated that SC's/ST POA Act, 1989 was not properly implemented by the state and central mechanism. As per the report on the prevention of the Atrocities Act, the Act failed to protect the Dalits.

There are various reasons which indicate the failure of the implementation of the POA Act, of 1989. According to the sixth report of the National Commission for Scheduled castes and Scheduled tribes says that the police in a very systematic and organized mechanism are rejecting the SC/ST atrocities cases because the members of these communities lack awareness. The cases registered under this Act show a downward trend but in reality, we see that this reduction is not the real picture of the actual scenario. From the reviews of the state government and the National Commission, we can understand that a large number of cases go unregistered, mainly because of the reluctance of the police to register these cases and also because of the lack of awareness of the members of these communities about the tenets of the provisions of the Act. (Failure to Meet).

The main crux of my argument reflected in this paper is the portrayal of various forms of human rights violations meted out on the socially underprivileged and marginalized groups in the university spaces. This argument is justified through various examples from the collection of short stories by Yogesh Maitreya *Flowers on the Grave of caste.* It is also evident from Bourdieu that society is nothing but a gathering of various people with unequal proficiencies, and such proficiencies are socially or historically built or inherited as per their capacity to accomplish various forms of social, cultural, and symbolic capital. These capitals are unequally distributed in a society with a lop-sided social structure (KV). Attributed identities will be a privilege for the upper castes to attain and exchange dissimilar forms of capital no matter how anti-caste, or how secular they are. On the other hand, never becomes a negotiable form of capital for Dalits and hence their situations are different from those of the advantaged community (KV). Hence, despite having various Acts to protect the human rights of the marginalized in the University Spaces and institutes of Higher education the rights of the Dalit Bahujan Students are desecrated. Unless the Universities become a more inclusive place for students ignoring the social hierarchies in terms of caste, race, class, and gender the social mobility of the Dalit students is not possible.

Notes

1. Kherlanji Massacre- The murder of four scheduled caste citizens by the villagers of Kherlanji on September 29, 2006, is referred to here. The brutal killings took place in a small village in India named Kherlanji. This village is located in the Bhandara district of the State of Maharashtra.

2. Dalit Aesthetics: By aesthetics, we mean pleasure and beauty. This is imparted by the mainstream works of art and literature. However, Dalit aesthetics talks about the pain and sufferings of a large section of the Indian population namely the Dalits.

References

Adsule N (2019) Flowers on the grave of caste review: new short story collection depicts hope Amid Dalit struggles. First Post, November 24, 2019. firstpost.com/living/flowers-on-the-grave-of-caste-review-new-short-story-collection-depicts-hope-amid-dalit-struggles-7673691.html

Ambedkar BR (1989) Annihilation of caste, in V. Moon (compiled) Dr. Babasaheb Ambedkar Writings and Speeches. Education Department: Government of Maharashtra, pp 25–85

Ambedkar BR (2006) Castes in India: their mechanism, genesis and development. In: Mohanty M (ed) Class, caste and gender: reading in Indian Government and Politics, vol 5. Sage Publications, New Delhi, pp 131–153

Anderson R (2010) The 'Idea of a University' today. History & Policy, 1st March 2010, historyandpolicy.org/policy-papers/papers/the-idea-of-a-university-today

Babu H (2019) The convergence of unequals, Struggle for rights in the university space. In: Debaditya B (ed) The Idea of the University Histories and Contexts, Taylor &Francis group London And New York, Routledge, pp 217–227. routledge.com/The-Idea-of-the-University-Histories-and-Contexts/Bhattacharya/p/book/9780367733483

Bhuyan A (2019) Even After Payal Tadvi's Death, Doctors' Body Unconvinced of Caste Discrimination. Analysis Caste, 28 May 2019, thewire.in/caste/payal-tadvi-doctor-caste-discrimination

"Constituent Assembly Debates" (1949) Part I i, indiakanoon.org/doc/708184

"Crimes against SCs, STs went up in 2020; UP, MP top charts: NCRB data" (2021) Business Standard, September 16, 2021, business-standard.com/article/current-affairs/crimes-against-scs-sts-went-up-in-2020-up-mp-top-charts-ncrb-data-121091601048_1.html

Coaston J (2019) Intersectionality Wars. Vox, May 28, 2019, vox.com/the-highlight/2019/5/20/18542843/intersectionality-conservatism-law-race-gender-dicrimination

"Failure to Meet Domestic and International: Legal Obligations to Protect Dalits" Human Rights Watch.hrw.org/reports/1999/india/India994-13.html

Kamble D (2019) Yogesh Maitreya's flower on the grave of caste gives space and voice to Dalit Struggles. Two circles. net, Nov 25, twocircles.net/2019nov25/433457.html

Lewis E (2021) What is structural violence? Anthropological definition and examples. Thought Co, February 16, 2021, thoughtco.com/structural-violence-4174956

Mohanty M Class (2004) caste and gender: reading in Indian Government and politics, Sage Publications, New Delhi, pp 256–267, April 30, 2004

Maitreya Y (2019) Flowers on the grave of caste. Panther's Paw Publications, Nagpur

Mukherjee A (2016) Stifling Dissent' the Criminalization of Peaceful Expression in India. Human Rights Watch, May 24, 2016, hrw.org/report/2016/05/25/stifling-dissent/criminalization-peaceful-expression-india

Neelalandan SM, Margeshwar SM (2012) Complexities of Inclusion and exclusion: Dalit students and higher education in India. J Social Inclusion 3(1):89–100

Pal RM The caste system and human rights violations. In: Human rights from the Dalit Perspective. Dalit Liberation Education Trust, Madras, p 23

"Rohith Vemula: Foregrounding Caste Oppression in Indian Higher Education Institutions" (2021) Engage, Sept 7, 2021, epw.in/engage/article/rohith-vemula-foregrounding-caste-oppression

Srinivas MN (2006) Caste in modern India. In: Mohanti M (ed) Class, caste and gender: readings in Indian Government and politics-5. Sage Publications, New Delhi, pp 154–182

Suchitra (2020) Institutional Casteism: 4 Years After Rohith Vemula, Has anything changed? Feminism in India, Jan 17, 2020. feminisminindia.com/2020/01/17/institutional-casteism-4-years-rohith-vemula/
Sukumar N (2008) Living a concept: semiotics of everyday exclusion. Econ Pol Wkly 43(46):14–17
Sukhadeo T (2004) The Hindu social system and human rights of Dalits. Critical Quest, New Delhi
Sukhadeo T (2006) Paying the social debt. Econ Pol Weekly 41(24):2432–2435
Syamprasad KV (2016) Rohith Vemula: The antecedents and aftermaths of his institutional murder". March 19, 2016, academia.edu/24013824/Rohith_Vemula_The_antecedents_and_aftermaths_of_his_institutional_murder
Tharu S, Poduval S, Kumar P (1998) Higher Education, New Agendas, New Mandates. Econ Polit Weekly 33(42/43):2701–2702
"What is intersectionality, and what does it have to do with me?" Eliminating racism empowering women YW Boston Blog.ywboston.org/2017/03/what-is-intersectionality-and-what-does-it-have-to-do-with-me/

Chapter 15
On the Margins of Respectability: The Disempowered *Devadasi* in Muvalur Ramamirthammal's *Web of Deceit*

P. Muralidhar Sharma

This paper is an attempt to identify patterns of cultural displacement in the lives of temple ritual performers like the *devadasis* and their representations in fiction. The paper focuses on the changing destinies of the *devadasis* in the context of colonialism and nationalism, with an added emphasis on the emergence of novel notions of cultural modernity in the early decades of the twentieth century. More importantly, it seeks to locate the cultural displacement and shifts in the status of the *devadasi* in relation to her body. In the early decades of the twentieth century, the body of the dancing woman and her corporeality became the site of a decisive shift in indigenous performance practices. Her corporeality embodied the change in ethos which also led to corresponding changes in her status. Ideological debates surrounding the conflict of values with the onset of colonial modernity were staged in relation to the body of the *devadasi.* As Lakshmi Subramanian observes,

> Nineteenth century social reform in south India was fixed firmly on the body of the devadasi who became the site of multiple definitions, imaginings, and contestations. Viewed as both the bearer of artistic skill and tradition, and as the purveyor of immorality and dissolution, deified as the servant of god who never bore the stigma of widowhood and, at the same time, reviled as the common whore whose powers of seduction snared the misguided householder, the devadasi became the principal site for the debate between tradition and reform. (115)

In his influential book *Unfinished Gestures,* Davesh Soneji attempts to understand the body of the *devadasi* as a rich repository of memory, one that contests the archive. The body, as a site of memory, offers radically new insights into the movements of social reform and dance revival, which disinherited the *devadasi* of her sanctioned status.

> The memory of bodily habitus, in the form of a repertoire allows us to perceive connections between history, language, and gestures of the body that would be invisible otherwise, and are impossible to house in the archive.

P. M. Sharma (✉)
School of English, Gangadhar Meher University, Sambalpur, India
e-mail: pmsharma@gmuniversity.ac.in

S. S. Ali and A. Basak (eds.), *Marginal Narratives and the Question of Human Rights in Asian Pacific Literature*, https://doi.org/10.1007/978-981-97-4544-9_15

> [...]
>
> But how can we convincingly account for the place that aesthetic experience holds in the lives of devadasis without reducing our interpretations to mere aestheticizations? The music and dance repertoire of devadasi courtesans, I argue, far from being incidental to the larger issue of their economic and political disenfranchisement, is essential to the question of their identities. Indeed, their art is not an ahistorical artifact, it is an embodied form of memory. (16)

A critical perspective like this, which acknowledges the inextricable link between the corporeal and aesthetic experiences of the *devadasis*, is crucial to the study. The paper seeks to read the figure of the *devadasi* in a set of texts which are embedded in the debates on her status in the early and mid-twentieth century. It thus explores the ways in which her troubled corporeality assumed centrality in these debates and influenced literary constructions. It also attempts to focus on the manifold ways in which aesthetics featured in these debates and how a radically new aesthetic modernity was envisaged which attempted to purge itself of the pernicious influence of the *devadasi* and her pathologized, unchaste body.

15.1 Contextualizing the *Devadasi*

A hereditary performer who used her performance to express her devotion and substantiate a set of highly specialized rituals prescribed by a temple, the *devadasi* remained an indispensable part of the community of temple servants. It is a well-established fact that some of the most illustrious kingdoms in the southern part of the subcontinent could boast of patronizing a huge number of *devadasis* associated with their temples. The practice of patronizing women dancers and singers by temples and the court attained a high watermark during the reign of the Cholas (985–1013 AD.), when about 400 *devadasis* were maintained by the Brihadeeshwara temple of Thanjavur. The practice also prevailed extensively during the Vijayanagar Empire, especially under the generous patronage of Krishnadeva Raya who ruled from 1509 to 1529 AD (Sriram xii-xiii). Thanjavur continued to be the cultural centre of the *devadasi* institution in the south, and many eminent *devadasis* trace their lineage to some or the other dancer or singer associated with the Thanjavur court. Other places which boasted of legendary dancers include Tiruvarur, Srirangam, Mysore, Kanjee-varam, and of course, colonial Madras. In the east, the Jagannatha temple of Puri had patronized a whole community of *devadasis* who were instrumental in the performance of the daily as well as special rituals of the presiding deity, Jagannatha. The dancing women of these temples have been epitomized in poetry, songs, and literary works, and projected as figures that demanded veneration as hereditary performers and erudite litterateurs.

The *devadasis* constituted a community of performers with a unique lifestyle of their own. They were mostly women who were 'dedicated' to a certain temple in infancy as part of the family practice or as a means of fulfillment of a vow. Once dedicated, they received intensive training in the arts of dancing and singing. It was also customary for a *devadasi* to receive education in classical Sanskrit literature and language. The *devadasi* was perhaps the most educated woman at a time when women were confined to the domestic sphere. Legendary *devadasis* like Muddupalani from the court of King Pratapsimha are evoked even today for their proficiency in the arts and matchless erudition. The late nineteenth and twentieth centuries saw the rise to fame of a number of distinguished performers from the community, among whom, mention might be made of M.S. Subbulakshmi, Veena Dhanammal, Bangalore Nagaratnamma and Balasaraswati.

Beginning from the nineteenth century onwards, the extraordinary lifestyle and cultural practices of the *devadasis* became the focus of a number of journals, diaries, travelogues, reform-oriented books and novels penned by the evangelical missionaries, administrators, and the *memsahibs.* Amy Wilson Charmichael's *Lotus Buds* (1905) and Marcus Fuller's *Wrongs of Indian Womanhood* (1909) engage in a rather detailed exploration of the institution of the *devadasis.* Carmichael reductively understands the practice as a euphemism for the flesh trade. Her book details the exhaustive efforts of the missionaries in rescuing the girls from a life of 'sin'. Consider, for instance, the following passage, which evaluates the profession in moral terms.

> As to her education, the movements of the dance are taught very early, and the flexible little limbs are rendered more flexible by a system of massage. In all ways the natural grace of the child is cultivated and developed, but always along lines which lead far away from the freedom and innocence of childhood. As it is important she should learn a great deal of poetry, she is taught to read. The poetry is almost entirely of a debased character; and so most insidiously, by story and allusion, the child's mind is familiarised with sin; and before she knows how to refuse the evil and choose the good, the instinct which would have been her guide, is tampered with and perverted, till the poor little mind, thus bewildered and deceived, is incapable of choice. (255)

However, the government's attitude to the *devadasis* was characterized by ambiguity and indecisiveness. The British policy of non-interference in native customs and religion forestalled them from involving themselves directly in the formulation of laws preventing the custom of dedicating minor girls for services in the temples. On being consistently pestered by the evangelical missionaries and the native elite, the government began seriously considering the moral standards of the *devadasis.*The aggravation of the demands made by the missionaries with regard to the institution prompted the government to devote serious attention to the practice. However, concrete initiatives in relation to the abolition of the custom were taken only after the involvement of Indian social reformers in the legislature in the second decade of the twentieth century. In this respect, Jordan observes,

> The colonial government perceived the *devadasis* as immoral women, but recognized their religious status mandated by dedication to a deity and temple service. It hesitated to interfere with their customs. As the structure of the government changed, the Indian westernized elite became progressively involved in the legislative process… These reforms were often supported by appeals to modern values. (194–5)

15.2 The 'Anti-Nautch' Campaign and the Criminalization of the *Devadasi*

Initiated by the missionaries as a form of collective condemnation of the *devadasis* and their cultural practices, the 'Anti-Nautch' campaign was a strong move to hasten the prohibition of public performances of the *devadasis.* The movement was aggravated by the participation of Indian social reformers, who, through their extraordinary eloquence, wrote extensively on the subject. By the early decades of the twentieth century, the Anti-Nautch movement was at its peak, as the *devadasi* question was vigorously debated in the Madras legislative Council. The issue solicited responses from many a reform-minded nationalist from both the centre and the provinces, prominent among them being Pandit Madan Mohan Malviya, who believed that "not a man in the country will be able to put forward one single text which will justify a thing which is so irreligious and sinful as the dedication of minor girls in a position where they must be compelled to lead a life of sin and shame" (qtd. in Jordan 176). The campaign also attracted the attention of M.K. Gandhi, who denounced the performances of *devadasis* in no uncertain terms. He went to the extent of proclaiming that the custom can only be eradicated by bringing discredit on it. "We must rob it of every vestige of respectability. That we shall do by mercilessly condemning the custom" he says in speech delivered at Pudupalayam in 1925 (118). For nationalists like Gandhi, the practice was synonymous with prostitution, and there is no ambiguity about its disreputable status. The language of denunciation underwent intensification with the upsurge of nationalism as a potent ideological force in the subcontinent. The *devadasi* question was embedded in a larger nationalist framework, from which it derived its world view. In the words of Teresa Hubel, "To elite men and women who had the greatest say in what constituted the new Indian nation, the *devadasis* were an embarrassing remnant of the pre-colonial and pre-nationalist feudal age and, as such, could not be permitted to cross over in to the homogeneity that the nationalists hoped would be postcolonial India" (161).

Although both the *tawaif* and the *devadasi* came to be collectively condemned with the rise of nationalism, the participation and active involvement of women reformers is a unique attribute of *devadasi* reform. Early Indian feminists took great amount of interest in the condemnation of the practice. Women reformers and feminists like Dr. Muthulakshmi Reddi, Yamini Purnatilakam and Muvalur Ramamirthammal were deeply interested in the *devadasi* debate for reasons of their own. These middle class, upper caste women (Reddi and Ramamirthammal came from *devadasi* families) privileged women's roles as mothers and dutiful wives in their speeches and writings, and their discourse of an 'enlightened' womanhood completely erased the identities of the *devadasis* as women. They saw the *devadasis* as embodying an aberrant sexuality, and took it as a moral responsibility to 'reform' the degraded *devadasis.* Women activists like Annie Besant and Dr.Muthulakshmi Reddi, who were the founding members of associations like Women's Indian Association (WIA) and All India Women's Conference (AIWC) were instrumental in voicing the need for *devadasi* reform in South India through their initiatives to uplift

Hindu women. Annie Besant, in particular, approved of the divine origin of the *devadasis*, and believed that there was a time in the distant past when the *devadasis* were synonymous with religious piety:

> There was a band of pure virgin devotees attached to the ancient Hindu temples. They used to preach religion like any other religious teacher to the common people that resort to the temple for their daily worship. In those days they were held in high esteem and respect and were very well looked after. They would spend their time in doing religious service to the Gods and the devotees of the temple as the word 'dasi' itself signifies. They would follow the procession of Gods dressed in the simplest sanyasi garbs and singing pious hymns suitable to the occasion. This is the history and the origin of the Devadasi class. (qtd. in Reddi, *Autobiography* 141–42)

This description of the *devadasis* fits in to the narrative of the 'lost glory' of the country, one which also acknowledged and lamented the present 'fallen' state. The description hovers around certain important markers which were recurrent motifs in the *devadasi* debate in the Legislative Assembly and in newspapers like the *Hindu* and the *Madras Mail*. The *devadasis* were once 'pure' virgins, a marker that at once absolves them from the claims of sexual depravity. They were mostly servants of Gods, performing religious duties, a claim that negates their more mundane functions like entertaining their clientele in a secular setting. They were dressed in the simplest of robes as *sanyasinis*, without any display of flamboyance in their gestures and the colourful clothes and rich jewelry for which they were consistently criticized by the utilitarian lot. They would be singing only devotional hymns, not the *padams* or erotically charged love poems which fuelled the Anti-Nautch movement.

It is interesting to note that while Muthulakshmi Reddi addressed the issue of *devadasi* reform and proposed legal measures to be taken for them, she dismissed the agitations of *devadasis* themselves as meaningless demands made by prostitutes. In the year 1927, Muthulakshmi was instrumental in passing a bill for the abolition of the institution. It was she who for the first time redirected Gandhi's attention to the *devadasi* system prevalent in the temples of Southern India. Her untiring efforts paved the way for the Madras *Devadasis* Prevention of Dedication Act of 1947 which prohibited them to continue the practice of dedication in temples. Muthulakshmi Reddi's views on the *devadasis*, expressed eloquently and elaborately in her lengthy addresses on the issue, offer interesting study of the ways in which the narrative of ancient Indian glory, subjected womanhood, and medical discourse coalesced with each other to construct the *devadasi* as the subject of moral reform. In most of these comments, Brahminical orthodoxy is pitted against European scientific modernity. Vehemently dismissive of the *devadasis* as a "slur on Indian womanhood" and "a great wrong and injustice done to the innocent young of the country", she calls for a reform "by which we can rescue thousands of young innocent children from a life of immorality and vice, from life-long invalidism, suffering, disease and death resulting from infection with venereal disease" (Reddi, *Autobiography* 138). A discerning reader can notice the parallels between Amy Wilson Carmichael's condemnation of the practice and Reddi's terminology, which is derived from the former. She appears to have been influenced by the missionaries in her adoption of the rhetoric of 'rescue'. Her influential recommendations made in her address entitled "Why should the Devadasi Institution in the Hindu Temples be Abolished?" remains a central text of the Anti-Nautch campaign, where she approaches the question of reform from different perspectives, prominent among them being the question of immorality affecting the nation at large.

> One more point I like to impress upon the attention of the Hindu public is that this practice, though prevalent only among certain sections of the Hindus in Southern India, but as it affects the morality, health and well-being of the Hindu society at large, loses its communal nature and becomes a question of national importance and interest. Now the appellation 'dasi', as everyone of us here knows, whatever the original meaning might have been, stands for a prostitute. None of us who are too familiar with their customs can dispute that fact. (138–39)

Such views were further strengthened by various political alliances which foregrounded themselves at about the same time. The *devadasi* debate got aggravated further through its alignment with the Self-Respect movement. The Self-Respect movement in Tamil Nadu, which aimed at introducing certain reforms in the domestic sphere, articulated the need to base family life on the principles of comradeship and companionship between the husband and wife. It saw the 'reformed' family as the foundation of the Dravidian nation and thus became instrumental in projecting conjugality as the ideal to be emulated (Sreenivas 138). The sexuality of the *devadasis* represented a deviation from the conjugal norm which the Self-Respecters publicized, and therefore they could not be accommodated in the newly created 'ideal' social order.

An ardent Self-Respecter and a *devadasi* herself, Muvalur Ramamirthammal supported and indeed borrowed her arguments from Muthulakshmi Reddi's demand for abolition. However, there were significant points of departure between the two. For Ramamirthammal, the *devadasi* system was a take off point in her critique of Brahminical Hinduism, and she saw the *devadasis* as victims of orthodoxy. Muthulakshmi had a firm faith in a glorious Hindu past in which the *devadasis* who served in temples were pure and chaste and lived simple lives. Muthulakshmi's critique of the institution never contested its roots in a Brahminical patriarchy.

15.3 The Disempowered *Devadasi* in Ramamirthammal's *Web of Deceit*

Muvalur Ramamirthammal's Tamil novel *Dasigal Mosavalai* (1936), translated as *Web of Deceit*, is a text that propagates social reform and projects the *devadasi* institution as corrupt. Written in a decade when the debates on the social and political status of the *devadasis* were actively pursued in the Madras Legislative Council, the text constitutes an insider's perspective of the debates. Whereas *devadasis* appeared as minor characters in novels written by men in the early twentieth century, *Web of Deceit* is unique in that it incorporates the subjectivity of the victimized. Ramamirthammal's take on the *devadasi* question marks a paradigm shift, as she was herself a reformed *devadasi* who was actively involved with the Self-Respect movement. This was also the time when, in popular perception, the contempt for the community witnessed an unprecedented rise. In conformity to the opinion of the educated, reform-minded elite of the time, Ramamirthammal perceives the *devadasis* as money-hungry prostitutes who ensnare young men by their deceptive ways only to rob them of their wealth and turn them to utter penury.

In *Web of Deceit,* the *devadasis* Kamalapuram Kantha and Ganavathi are daughters of the ageing Boga Chintamani, a shrewd intriguer who promotes her daughters and arranges suitable clients for them. On their way to Chennai for a concert, they encounter the Tiruchi Minor, who succumbs to their deceptive ways and presents them his watch in anticipation of their favours. They deceive him by directing him to a wrong address, where he meets Gunabusani, a reformed *devadasi* and her husband, who reveal the secrets of the profession of the *devadasis* and attempt to transform him. He leaves their house as a changed man, who is interested in reform. Meanwhile, Somasekaran, son of a reputed *zamindar*, who attends the "enchanting sisters' concert" falls for them. He is also misled in a similar fashion, after which he returns to his hostel. Meanwhile, his father fixes his marriage with Gnanasundari, the model of enlightened womanhood in the novel, who is educated and thinks rationally. Somasekaran meets Kantha and Ganavathi at his wedding, where they have been invited to perform. Fearing his downfall, the Tiruchi Minor promises to help him in making an alliance with the *devadasis,* even as he actually intends to rescue him from their trap. The Minor, disguised as a *Mama,* or a middle-man, accompanies Somasekaran to Kamalapuram, where they live with the sisters Kantha and Ganavathi for some time. Gnanasundari, the newly-wed bride, sets out on a mission to bring her husband back with the help of the Minor. The Minor plans things in a way that Somasekaran is brought back to his normal state, and is able to accept his wife. The novel ends with a Social Reform Conference where the *devadasis* and their arts are condemned and legal measures for the abolition of the custom are proposed as part of the resolutions.

The novel has been studied as a 'radical' text that allows the 'voices' of the *devadasis* to enter the narrative (Anandhi 743–44). The element of radicalism in the novel, it has been argued, is a strategy to unsettle the stereotype that the *devadasi* debate attempted to create:

> What is important about this novel is not merely its story, but the fact that it allows multiple voices of the devadasis to echo within the text and thus violates the process of stereotyping them into essentialist categories to represent issues other than themselves. This is exactly where the novel acquires its distinctive radicalism compared to the devadasi debate. (Anandhi 103)

There has also been a tendency among scholars to view the text as embodying the politics of the Self-Respect movement and the propagation of normative conjugality as the norm. Through a condemnation of their non-conjugal sexual practices, this view establishes, the text prescribes conjugal relationships as the only corrective to the wayward lives of the *dasis.* Kalpana and Vasanth Kannabiran, the translators of the text, argue that the text facilitates "the re-location of the language of love from non-conjugal "free-unions" to egalitarian, inter-caste, monogamous conjugality, and the re-inscription of marriage from an extended/joint family norm to nuclear, monogamous marriage as the ideal" (18–19).

Whereas one can hardly deny the fact that the text is overtly propagandist in form and is an explicit plea for the abolition of the *devadasi* institution, one cannot undermine its critical intervention with the discourses that legitimized the status of the *devadasis* as embodiments of religious authority and the hereditary propagators of performance traditions. The analyses of the novel attempt to over-emphasize the centrality of reform to the over-all structure, thereby undermining the cultural shifts that are obliquely engaged with in the text.

Ramamirthammal's unequivocal advocacy of the abolition of the *devadasi* system is clearly evident in the authorial comments: "This caste can act like great saints when they are certain that the goods will not slip out of their hands. If they see them slipping then they start talking humorously and seize hold of the goods. These dasis can size up a man's character and his aim at first sight" (57). The author's abolitionist stance is firmly premised on two grounds—that the *devadasis* are not divine damsels but the unfortunate victims of Brahminical orthodoxy, and that their expertise in music and dance is just a camouflage for prostitution. Interestingly, the *devadasis* in the novel have little or nothing to do with temple rituals; they are projected as prostitutes trained to trap men by their wily charms. The narrative of divine origin of the community is punctured in the novel. In a conversation between the Tiruchi Minor and Gunabusani, the latter questions the foundations of this institution:

> Minor: "... Dasis are from heaven and have that divine quality. Their music is proof of that quality...."
> Gunabusani: "What a mad world! And you think dasis are from heaven and have divine qualities. You are familiar with dasi houses you say. Don't you know that dasis who have no daughters buy girls from different castes and train them? If dasis were all born of dasi wombs then you can say that they are all god's gifts from heaven... What is the reason for the title devadasi? There was a caste of people called Thevar in those days. These women must have served them. Trained as they are for prostitution as livelihood it is small wonder that they charm you completely. (64)

The Minor justifies his association with *devadasis* by evoking their divinely sanctioned status, but Gunabusani contests the belief with her rationally informed arguments. Ramamirthammal perceives the unquestioned perpetuation of the practice as strongly rooted in Brahmanical orthodoxy, which uses religion to justify the 'vice' of prostitution. "It is because our forefathers built temples and set up dasis there for worship and invited them to weddings that future generations have been ruined" the Tiruchi Minor says as a reformed man (76). Later in the novel, when Vivekavathi, Karunakaran's daughter and Kantha's niece, is sold to Kamavardhani, a *devadasi*, by her mother, she resists her attempts to teach her the art of seduction and requests her to get her married instead. An enraged Kamavardhani retorts,

> You are preaching morals. Don't you know the truth? You ask me to get you married. Will god not be angry? Can you live with someone after being married to another? After being

> married to god can you hanker after marriage with a mere human being? It is generations of *punyam* that has made you the bride of god. How many can claim such a title?... Pray to god asking forgiveness for the sin of talking about marriage. (181)

Rituals in the community of *devadasis*, including the *pottu-kattu* ceremony, where the young girl about to be dedicated to the deity is 'married' to the idol through the tying of the sacred knot by the chief priest, legitimize the religious status of the *devadasi*, and are therefore the butt of ridicule in Ramamirthammal's critique of the institution. She disproves the claim of the religious association of the *devadasis* by taking recourse to the newly available discourse of scientific modernity. This view treated the practice as obscure and baseless, without any scientific or logical reasons to support its continuation. Seen from this perspective, such practices have ceased to be viable in a rapidly changing, 'modern' world. The authority of religious texts that affirm the perpetuation of the pre-modern, 'evil' practice is also questioned. This is particularly evident in the last chapter of the novel, where Gunabusani delivers a lecture on the abolition of the institution.

> In this twentieth century when we are speaking of the progress of science and civilization it is disgraceful that some *sastris* and leaders claim that an abolition of the devadasi system is against the arts (cries of Shame! Shame!). First we must destroy the foundations on which the devadasi system rests namely-god-religion-*Smrithis*-sacred texts, *Puranas*. If these go there will be no justification for the devadasi system to remain in existence. (202)

In addition to the discourse of scientific modernity that is employed to de-legitimize the *devadasi* system, the novel effectively uses the rhetoric of subjugated womanhood to develop a narrative of victimhood and helplessness. The *devadasi* system, a remnant of a pre-modern, feudal past, is also an evidence of the subjection of women. This view, popular with the self-styled 'feminists' of the early twentieth century like Dr. Muthulakshmi Reddi also fits into the larger nationalist anxiety about the symbolic value of womanhood. Exposing the moral, scientific/rational, and religious baselessness of the continued existence of the *devadasis,* Ramamirthammal simultaneously invokes a variety of discourses to condemn the hateful practice. These discourses, perfectly timed and contrived, collaborate with each other in formulating a collective invective against the community as a whole.

15.4 Sacred or Profane?: The *Devadasi* and her Dance

The movement for revival in Indian classical dance, which gained momentum in the 1930s was energized by the efforts of prominent innovators like Rukmini Devi Arundale, E. Krishna Iyer, Vallathol, Rabindranath Tagore and Madame Menaka. Inspired by the newly emerging Orientalist discourse on Indian performing arts, they set out to modernize different regional performance traditions. Innovators like Rukmini Devi Arundale and E Krishna Iyer realized that in order to reconstruct dance as a symbol of national heritage, it had to be purged of its associations with the troubled corporeality of the *devadasis*. The contribution of Rukmini Devi Arundale to this process of redefinition of art forms merits attention. She was instrumental in reviving '*Sadir*', a dance form associated with the *devadasis* as '*Bharatanatyam'*. This initiative classicized *Sadir* and purged it of its associations with the body of the *devadasi*. This refashioning pointed to the textual origins of the dance in Bharata's *Natyashastra*. Rukmini Devi also introduced certain changes in the repertoire of the *devadasis* by undermining and completely obliterating the prominence given to the depiction of eroticism in dance. She persuaded her students not to perform on erotic love songs like the '*padam*' and the '*javali*', which formed an indispensable part of the *devadasi* repertoire. "Indian dance being spiritual, it is suited only for spiritual expression" she argued (194). In place of erotic love songs, devotional items like '*kirtanams*' became the base on which dance items were choreographed. Rukmini Devi also introduced the practice of using Sanskrit texts for performance, a practice by which she pointed to the scriptural precedents of dance.

Along with "ritualized prostitution" sanctioned by Hinduism in the case of *devadasis*, their status as performers became another eye-sore for the reform-minded nationalists. First censured by the missionaries, the continued condemnation of performances by *devadasis* constituted a central aspect of Indian social reform. Their performances, it was believed, gave an added impetus to their immoral influence in the public sphere. Ramamirthammal's stringent criticism of performance traditions fostered by them constitutes a significant strain in *Web of Deceit*. Here the author is in conformity with the established discourses which hold that music is a mask that provides aesthetic legitimization to the carnal desires of the *devadasis*. This view, common to the reformers, attested to the evil influence of their performances on the nation's youth. In the face of the intensification of debates on their status in the public realm, the supporters of the institution and the *devadasis* themselves consistently asserted their status as 'protectors' of art and performance traditions. The reformers dismissed these claims as strategies for defense of the institution. In most of their exhortatory writings and speeches, the reformers considered music itself to be lowly and debased because of its association with the body of the *devadasi*. In opposition to the view that the performing arts were ancient expressions of civilizational refinement and that they should be promoted as part of a national culture, *Web of Deceit* adopts a largely denunciatory tone for the depiction of performing arts. Ramamirthammal also attempts to invalidate the narrative of the spiritual origin of music in the episode delineating Somasekaran's downfall. The novel charts the emergence of a modern, middle-class, enlightened public that views public performances by *devadasis* as detrimental to social health.

In *Web of Deceit*, one of the major refutations of the *devadasi* system emerges from the idea that *Bharatanatyam* encourages promiscuity in young girls. The novel establishes an indispensable link between the performing arts and moral degeneration. The last chapter of the novel, which records the effervescence of social reform activity by both respectable women and reformed *dasis*, denounces *Bharatanatyam* in no uncertain terms: "First of all Bharatanatyam should be abolished. Bharatanatyam is the lifeline that encourages the growth of prostitution. Prostitution is the creation of Bharatanatyam" (210).

Although the text promotes social reform, it also signals the beginning of the historically simultaneous movement for dance revival, which was equally responsible for disinheriting the *devadasis* of their traditional performance practices. It propagates an Anti-Nautch sentiment, but also demonstrates the ways in which it aligned itself to the project of cultural regeneration and dance revival that collectively disinherited the *devadasi* of not just her social stature as an economically powerful and autonomous woman, but also her artistic repertoire and claims to age-old performance traditions.

References

Allen MH (1997) Re-writing the script for South-Indian dance. TDR 41(3):63–100. JSTOR, www.jstor.org/stable/1146609

Anandhi S (1991) Representing Devadasis: Dasigal Mosavalai as a radical text. Econ Polit Weekly 26(11):96–107. JSTOR www.jstor.org/stable/4397430

Arundale RD The spiritual background of Indian dance. Soneji, Bharatanatyam, pp 192–197

Avanthi M (2005) (ed) Rukmini Devi Arundale. Motilal Banaridass

Balasaraswati T "Bharata Natyam". Soneji, Bharatanatyam, pp 198–207

Carmicheal AW (1909) Lotus buds. Morgan and Scott

Fuller MB (1990) The wrongs of Indian womanhood. Caxton Press

Gandhi MK "Fallen Sisters". Joshi, pp 84–86

Gandhi MK "Fallen Sisters". Joshi, pp 126–27

Gandhi MK "Speech at Ashram, Pudupalayam". Joshi, pp 118

Gandhi MK "Our Unfortunate Sisters". Joshi, p 123

George TJS (2004) MS, a life in music. Harper Collins

Hubel T The high cost of dancing: when the Women's movement went after the Devadasis. Soneji, Bharatanatyam, pp 160–81

Jordon KK (1989) From sacred servant to profane prostitute: a study of the changing legal status of the Devadasis, 1857–1947. U of Iowa P

Joshi P (1988) (ed) Gandhi on women. Navjivan Trust

Kannabiran K (1995) Judiciary, social reform and debate on 'Religious Prostitution' in colonial India. Econ Polit Weekly 30(43):175–85, JSTOR, www.jstor.org/stable/4403368.

Marglin FA (1985) Wives of the God-King: rituals of the Devadasis of Puri. Oxford UP

Meduri A (2005) (ed) Rukmini Devi Arundale. Motilal Banaridass

Muddupalani (2011) The Appeasement of Radhika: Radhika Santwanam. Translated by Sandhya Mulchandani. Penguin

Raghavan V "Bharata Natya-Classic Indian Dance". Soneji, Bharatanatyam, pp 182–190

Ramamirthammal M (2003) Web of Deceit. Translated by Kalpana Kannabiran and Vasanth Kannabiran, Kali for Women

Reddi SM (1965) Autobiography of Dr. (Mrs.) Muthulakshmi Reddi: a pioneer woman legislator. M.L.J. Press

Reddi SM Why Should the Devadasi Institution in the Hindu Temples be Abolished?. Soneji, Bharatanatyam, pp 136–147

Soneji D (2010) (ed) Bharatanatyam—a reader. Oxford UP

Soneji D (2012) Unfinished gestures: Devadasis, memory, and modernity in South India. Permanent Black

Sreenivas M (2008) Wives, widows and concubines. Orient Blackswan

Srinivasan A (1985) Reform and revival: the Devadasi and Her dance. Econ Polit Weekly 20(44):1869–76. JSTOR www.jstor.org/stable/4375001.

Sriram V (2007) Introduction. The Devadasi and the Saint: The life and times of Bangalore Nagarathnamma. East West, pp ix–xxiii
Subramaniam L (2006) From the Tanjore Court to the Madras music academy: a social history of music in South India. Oxford UP
Subramaniam L (2009) Veena Dhanammal: the making of a legend. Routledge
Viswanathan L (2008) Women of Pride, The Devadasi heritage. Roli
Whitehead J (1998) Community honour/sexual boundaries: a discursive analysis of Devadasi criminalization in Madras, India, 1920–1947. In: James EE (ed) Prostitution: On Whores, Hustlers, and Johns, Prometheus Books, pp 91–106

Chapter 16
Telling, Writing and Translating: Narratives of Reclaiming People's Rights

Mrinmoy Pramanick

16.1 Introduction

The intersection of literature as a form of creative expression and political engagement revolves around the concept of universal humanism. In his various literary works, Tagore extensively addresses the concept of universal humanism, assuming the roles of a poet, philosopher, and political theorist. Particularly noteworthy is the concept of "Visva Sahitya", put out by the individual in question, which might be seen as a fervent advocacy for universal humanism and the profound significance of literature. Literary methodologies have undergone a transformation following the incorporation of subaltern perspectives into historical narratives. This shift has prompted a reevaluation of the values inherent in these approaches, particularly as critics and practitioners from diverse social strata have begun to engage with more authentic forms of literature. This endeavour aims to document the historical experiences of marginalised sections or classes that were historically ignored or silenced. The endeavour of chronicling historical events by literary means is not merely a singular undertaking of post-subaltern literary compositions, but rather it exemplifies the inherent propensity of literary interventions within the space of storytelling. In the post-subaltern era, a notable shift occurred as authors from diverse social backgrounds began to assert their own voices and narratives, rather than depending solely on exogenous representation. The utilisation of third-person representation of characters in literature serves as a significant literary intervention in contemporary times, as it allows for the historicization of the first person or the author. Identity-based movements, both social and political in nature, have made significant contributions to the sphere of narratives. These movements have played a crucial role in raising awareness among individuals from diverse communities about their marginalised

M. Pramanick (✉)
Department of Comparative Indian Language and Literature, University of Calcutta, Kolkata, India
e-mail: mpcill@caluniv.ac.in

S. S. Ali and A. Basak (eds.), *Marginal Narratives and the Question of Human Rights in Asian Pacific Literature*, https://doi.org/10.1007/978-981-97-4544-9_16

status and have empowered them to voice their own experiences and perspectives. Furthermore, the extensive history of literary labour, particularly following the formation of the Progressive Writers' Association, has also played a significant role in unearthing alternative narratives within the fields of history and literature. The assertion regarding human rights, as well as the rights of labourers and peasants, has been a focal point of political movements spearheaded by communist parties and labour or peasant organisations. This motivation has also prompted authors to delve into the experiences and perspectives of these social classes, with some emerging as writers from within these communities. This essay examines the impact of diverse identities and their narratives on academic scholarship, specifically highlighting the influence they have on the study of literature and its organic development.

The act of writing is inherently privileged and holds significant power. It serves as a political tactic for preserving one's memories for future generations. Consequently, regardless of its specific content, writing itself can be considered a form of historical documentation. Conversely, the act of verbal expression, commonly referred to as orality, can serve as a potent approach to assert one's personal position and shape a narrative including one's life and historical experiences. Only a select few individuals possess the privilege of recounting their narratives, as the act of storytelling necessitates the presence of a receptive audience. A limited number of individuals possess the privilege of encountering attentive listeners for their narratives. Hence, the acts of verbal communication and written expression hold significant value for marginalised people considering the limited documentation, recognition, and reception of their words. Oral tradition, commonly seen as a viable means of documenting the narratives of individuals and interpreting them as works of literature. This study posits that the acts of storytelling, writing, and translating serve as significant modes of expression and strategies for preserving one's memory. The process of narrating one's experiences is a fundamental step in safeguarding and conceptualising the fundamental human rights necessary for marginalised people and communities.

16.2 Writing as Epistemic Justice

> "He [Abhay Xaxa] highlighted that when Adivasis write, it is such an arduous process to establish oneself... Sometimes the writings don't get published for months. One needs contacts in important places. In these circumstances how does one even go ahead telling their stories?" - Jacinta Kerketta, a Jharkhand-based Poet (Shushmita)

A limited number of individuals in our global society hold the belief that they possess the entitlement to engage in written expression. The act of writing is a complex cognitive activity that requires a comprehensive understanding of social dynamics. The sentiment towards the act of writing is closely intertwined with the acknowledgment of one's own inherent worth. Without a sense of self-dignity, individuals may find it challenging to assert their entitlement to express themselves through writing, sharing their personal experiences and opinions. Hence, the act of an individual from a marginalised group assuming the role of an author, or emerging as an author from a marginalised background, can be seen as a transformative process with significant social, cultural, and historical implications. The act of granting an individual the authority to engage in written expression pertains to conferring human rights within a certain organisational/social framework. Abhay Xaxa, a sociologist, and tribal poet, offers substantial critique of non-tribal scholars over their tendency to objectify tribal communities. Xaxa argues that even impartial research conducted by non-tribals is often tainted by unconscious pity towards the tribal population. This study represents the culmination of a deliberate endeavour to document the experiences of marginalised communities such as the Dalit and Adivasis, which has been undertaken over the past few years.

The current era can be characterised as a period of literary democracy when the act of writing has become more accessible and widespread among the general population. Authors, publishers, and translators across different linguistic backgrounds are actively endeavouring to shift the focal point of literature through their collective efforts in writing, publishing, and translation. The central position of literature exhibits a notable resistance to change, enduring over epochs despite diverse endeavours. However, it is indeed accurate to acknowledge the inclusion of novel literary forms within the broader sphere of literature. The term "literature" in this context refers to the body of work that explores the concept of new identity. This discourse pertains to emerging social collectives, novel ethnicities, evolving gender identities, recently formed nations, evolving cultural expressions, and emerging geographical areas. The period during which literature is being practised represents a pivotal juncture for the development of a novel literary identity. A recently emerged author, whose works have the potential to be translated, analysed, and studied in conjunction with renowned and established authors of our day, may have garnered limited readership thus far. Despite maybe having authored only a single book, this author also holds promise as a subject for scholarly investigation. The phenomenon of individuals' self-perception and inclination to align themselves with the discourse of rights based on shared identification with a specific collective has contributed to the emergence of pluralism within the realms of literature and consciousness. Identity politics, like other political perspectives, may possess certain limitations. However, the significance of these limitations is diminished in a world characterised by a one-dimensional sociocultural awareness. In such a context, the primary value of identity politics lies in its ability to maintain a sense of diversity and establish a conducive environment for the collective mobilisation of various groups.

Bengali literature is mainly written by upper caste people and great characters of literature come from upper class or upper caste. Bengali cinema, heroes and heroines of the soap operas/TV serials and supporting characters in these popular visual arts also come from Brahmin, Vaidya or Kayastha families. As a result, the cultural milieu of Bengal is dominated by an upper caste Hindu culture. Bengal's festivals, events and religious patronage by the government also show indulgence, loyalty and encouragement of upper caste Hindu culture. In a group context, society, politics, literature, culture do not function separately and independently, but are interrelated. Government funding to religious festivals like Durga Puja of the majority, promotes a certain kind of mainstream monolithic culture of the community. Due to over-representation of the upper caste Hindus in movies and serials, upper caste citizens in Bengali literature, many people from different under-represented social categories are supposed to wake up in this situation very naturally. From various parts of the Bengali language region, the words of small people are coming out through various newspapers and publications. This is the democracy of writing, the era of common writing. Publishers, translators, and researchers continue to resist the majority culture through their small powers and efforts to build a pluralistic space. Many people from different parts of the world are trying to explain that a linguistic, cultural, geographical range does not consist of one type of people only.

Writing about one's own life-story, one's group, or one's own society is very necessary and effective for representatives of those societies whose words have not been much spoken in literature or recorded in the memory of the larger human group. Our age is the age of life stories. The biographies of individuals are narratives of continuous dialogue between individuals and groups. In a society where the tradition of writing literature is not very long, it is easy for the people of that society to start writing with their own vocabularies. Because the person will have the highest right to their own words. Their daily reality sounds like a story to another class of people, because the connections between different classes of people are so small that the extent of knowing about each other is also less. Other than the mainstream culture, rest remains unknown in the world of knowledge, which is an epistemic crisis and injustice to the communities. Therefore, the testimonies or life writings in one's own words are an uttered claim of one's right within a given political system, as it offers epistemic authority to the community.

Kannada poet Siddalingaiah wrote his autobiography into Kannada and titled as *Oru Keri* but when it was translated into English the publisher of English translation S Anand of Navayana suggested that title should be *A Word with You, World* (2013), which is a line translated into English from one of the Siddalingaiah's important poem (Siddalingaiah 11). The very essence of the poem talks about the essence of the autobiography in general. As Western philosopher John Locke suggested, the mind of a human being is like "Tabula Rasa" and the experience marks on it and then people gather knowledge about the world. Siddalingaiah argues if one must know the world, they have to have continuous conversation with the subject of any matter or any human being and through these continuous conversations people come to know about the world. A marginal human need to know the world with continuous conversations. Therefore, Siddalingaiah's philosophy of writing his autobiography is craftily captured in the title of the English translation of the book with Anand's suggestion. This autobiography like most of the life narratives of the margins suggest how one earns epistemic authority and affects the community with their writings by offering vocabularies of the political. Thus, such literature in general is literature of the affectives, which proves the role of literature as confirming human rights to a certain extent. Writing about the community from within the community is also about engaging with the questions of direct claim of human rights required and deserved by the people with authority, which may be understood as authority of human rights without being represented by others. As Abhay Xaxa mentioned in his poem, by critiquing the elites (including the civil society and the state), about the politics of representation which may stereotyped the community, should be resisted and rejected. He says,

> "I am not your data, nor am I your vote bank,
> I am not your project, or any exotic museum object,
> I am not the soul waiting to be harvested,
> Nor am I the lab where your theories are tested,
> I am not your cannon fodder, or the invisible worker,
> or your entertainment at India habitat center,
> I am not your field, your crowd, your history,
> your help, your guilt, medallions of your victory,
> I refuse, reject, resist your labels,
> your judgments, documents, definitions,
> your models, leaders and patrons,
> because they deny me my existence, my vision, my space,
> your words, maps, figures, indicators,
> they all create illusions and put you on pedestal,
> from where you look down upon me,
> So I draw my own picture, and invent my own grammar,
> I make my own tools to fight my own battle,
> For me, my people, my world, and my Adivasi self!" ("I Am Not Your Data - Agitate")

16.3 Telling the Tales

This section delves into the comprehensive analysis of testimonies procured through meticulous field research endeavours undertaken amongst Dalit women living in different parts of West Bengal, with a particular focus on those actively engaged in a myriad of livelihood pursuits. The women who articulated their personal narratives, mostly except few, possessed no previous background in literary composition. A considerable proportion of these women exhibited a notable deficiency in fundamental literacy skills and possessed a restricted level of familiarity with formal education, as only a minority had the opportunity to partake in scholastic endeavours. The compiled narratives, which have been authored by the interviewers, are predominantly composed by individuals who maintain a significant level of familiarity with the speakers or are situated within proximity to them geographically. Following the events, succinct written representations of their chronicles were devised. Every individual has eloquently recounted their narratives in a manner that is distinctly their own. The narratives articulated by these individuals offer valuable insights into their personal experiences within the realms of both domestic and outer spheres. When referring to the concept of "home and world", I am alluding to the various encounter individuals have within the domestic sphere, as well as their experiences that extend beyond the physical boundaries of their residence. This encompasses their routine personal and professional efforts in a comprehensive manner. The narratives proffered by the individuals serve as a manifestation of their idiosyncratic viewpoints on existence, situated at the confluence of their domestic and external surroundings.

In the project, I am talking about in this section, we tried to collect and serve women, who are victims of various oppressions in terms of gender identity, on the one hand, and marginalised women, who are victims of various oppressions in terms of social identity, on the other hand. As a result of the project, me and Asish Heera edited a book entitled *Bratya Narir Atma-Katha* (Testimonies of Out Caste Women), published by the Gangchil in 2023(Heera and Pramanick). We tried to represent people from different castes, races, and religions from across West Bengal in this book. Many are writing for the first time, some are not in the habit of writing regularly, so their words are written by their relatives, in most cases sons or daughters. Most of the writing in this book is autobiographical, some writing is in transcription, one-half writing must be written in second person as the author felt strongly to share the stories of their closest one, instead of telling their own stories.

In this project we targeted to get people from across the geographical varieties, as we know different geographic regions speak differently with different empirical narratives. West Bengal like many other places has significant diversity of human life, human society, from north to south, on the hills, on the plains, in the forests, at the river valleys or at the seashores. Nature of inequality is different, stories of oppression, and experience of marginalisation are also quite different. This book contains the story of a Rajbanshi Muslim woman, Moumita Alam, her ideology, political position, along with the society of North Bengal and the cultural life of that region. Shyamali's life is a story of tragic and harsh reality, sexual-oppression, gender-based oppression, life of slavery, life of being torn apart—Shyamali has told us many things. The simple truth and destiny of a middle class or lower middle class Indian woman's life is revealed in Veenapani's story, this story can be the story of any girl in our country. In Badli Haldar's story, the border-barbed wire-river has come up. The story brings everyday experience of a woman beginning from the idea of 'home' to a woman, her father's house and father-in-law's house, daily domestic life, poverty, and women's life in a family. In "Nonapari" Jogmaya narrated the history of an island in the Sundarbans, the story of people's struggle there, the story of their struggle, the story of their establishment, the construction of their sense of selfhood, their village life and society, their working life etc. In her words Padma Guha narrated the memories of the terrible experience of the Bangladesh Liberation War, camp life, story of her own marriage etc. Not only during the Partition of Bangladesh Liberation War, but emigration of people from Bangladesh is still going on, as people say. The long history of partition and Bangladesh Liberation War is spread among these emigration events. Shefali Swarnakar's story contains a piece of this history, and the stories of people becoming people within this history. Ila Das talks about her literary life, newspaper editing, her coming of age, neighbourhood and society in general. Pramila Dhali Halder told the story of a *Desh,* language, and everyday life of East Pakistan (Bangladesh), about the importance of education in the society, about the power of culture and how education and culture are rooted in the context and memories of the Bangladesh Liberation War and the kind of atrocities of the Pakistani army committed against women there. Deepali Biswas tells us the story of her working life, fish-cutting profession in a small market in the district of north 24 Parganas of West Bengal. Kumkum Naiya tells the story of Savitri Naiya, the story of a woman's promise, the story of bringing up her granddaughters, the story of women's male-dependent identity in the society etc. In the story of Puja Valmiki, we hear about caste-based humiliation faced by her in the academic institution she studied, and the story of her helplessness as a minority Dalit oppressed woman. Swasti Sardar Bhowmik narrated the life struggle of Indumati, the ups and downs of the family, the story developed with the relation of Indumati with her family members and so on. The family is not just a family, the story of the family is like a novel, an epic; that is the hint we get in the story of Indumati's life. Rabi Prabha Sarkar's story is also the story of the atrocities of Pakistani Khansena, her own school life, their migration into India and beginning of a new life as a citizen of India. In the story of Ujjwali Samaddar, there is the experience of crossing the country on foot during the Bangladesh Liberation War, riots, terror, and genocide, and also about the society divided by caste identity. In the writings of Umarani Sarkar, various stories about her education and personality building, the story of her working life, as well as the story of her family and life outside the family have come up. Pital Mandal of Padui community also tells the story of Bangladesh Liberation War, border issue, her financial crisis and frustration with the government.

Bengali Dalit literature is mainly dominated by the narrative of the Namashudra community, this collection along with another unpublished project of collecting testimonies of the Dalit communities from West Bengal, bring out the voices from silence into words in the field of literature in the domain of Dalitism. All the marginal communities carry the culture of the roots and those are in indigenous or transformative forms represented as national culture of a community or nation. So, the community cultures through story-telling and performances are very much alive and continued from one generation into another generation through memory and practice. So, the community narrative and history is always visible in community practices. But when in this paper I am talking about silence or wording, it is purely from the perspective of Dalit literary politics. A similar, and a larger project was envisioned and carried over by me with a team of young researcher with the generous funding from the Dalit Sahitya Akademi from the September 2021 to August 2022, for one year and we surveyed different Dalit communities of West Bengal to collect testimonies of the people belong to various communities, professions and regions of the state. The project should be published soon entitled as *Dalit katha*, which includes polyphony of the voices of differences, diversity and autonomy of the community existence. This project is especially important for the same reason our aforementioned book is important, but in this project of *Dalit Katha*, we covered communities at large. It helped us not only to understand the people to a little extent otherwise which were unknown in our literary academic practices, but also to re-conceptualise and reshape the Dalit literary spaces.

16.4 Publishing and Rights of the Margin

> "I am a Dalit (not a fact that I wish to emphasise, but I want to make my position clear as a publisher). I am a first generation university-goer in my family, the first person to get a doctorate. I have been working in English language publishing for four years now and I know what it means to publish stories, especially those which were deliberately erased from public consciousness." (Maitreya)

Like the authors from the community who represent authentic voices of the community or can have authority to debate on the authenticity of the words they use, publishers, if coming from within the community, can put forward their favourable messages as claim of rights to the recorded history of the time. Publishers like "adivaani", "Panther's Paw" in English publishing in India and publishers like "Chaturtha Duniya", "Gangchil", in Bengali are few such examples. As I personally worked with Gangchil, I had a chance to observe it very closely, the way the publishing editor Adhir Biswas continuously engaged himself with the marginal issues to reconstruct the epistemology of the margins from the very central location of the intellectual culture of Kolkata, that is College Street. His self-assertion with writing about his life and selecting the texts for publishing and also making the authors work on such unheard areas is a strong political statement towards empowering various marginal communities. As a member of a Dalit community and once a refugee Adhir Biswas lived with the life of discrimination and sufferings. Adhir Biswas has been writing his own memoirs, editing Doyal Shishu magazine and Gangchil magazine, etc., besides regularly working on various topics with new writers. This book project of ours is also full of thoughts of Adhir Biswas. He has produced books on many subjects, which have guided the direction of later college-university curricula, research, and seminars. The book project *BratyaNarirAtmaKatha* is also a part of the larger project of Adhir Biswas about making history of the margins. Chaturtha Duniya, even before Adhir Biswas's intervention into publishing, appeared as the first Dalit publishing house in Kolkata and started forming a conscious category of Dalit literature into Bengali. Other than decaying Chaturtha Duniya as publishing and Adhir Biswas's Gangchil there is no such publishing house in Bengali publishes Dalit literature as a genre or category of literature with continuity. Few publishing houses have been publishing Dalit literature in Bengali, but the number of titles is hardly more than one. Yogesh Maitreya's assertion as publisher with his Panther's Paw, a significant name with historical and political contexts, is a strong message in our contemporary time that marginal people should occupy even their little space in the world of publishing.

A publishing house completely focusing on publishing tribal literature adivani writes about itself on the website as,

> "adivaani (the first voices) is a platform for indigenous expression and assertion, founded in 2012. It is an archiving, chronicling, publishing, and disseminating outfit of and by the 104 million indigenous peoples of India (Adivasi). Our intervention through multiform and multimedia is about literary, socio-cultural-politico and identity engagements and inquiries with and within our lived-in wisdom, lived in knowledge and our everyday realities. The adivaani mediation work is an ongoing inter-generational knowledge, heritage, memory, and

legacy project, which serves as a wellspring of the authentic Adivasi voice, as recounted by us". ("About Adivaani")

Ganesh Devy's Bhasha Research is also such an initiative by the remarkable and unique academic and cultural activist, who with grand sound tried to awaken the nation about the lives and human resources of the nation. The objective of the research centre as mentioned on the website,

> "Bhasha is engaged in bringing a greater appreciation of the cultures of these two social sectors [Adivasis and Nomadic and Denotified] and ensuring their entitlement to constitutional guarantees and social security. It needs to be stressed that this work is of huge proportion and involves not just the question of reducing the economic deprivation of the Adivasis and DNT's but also of social attitudes beset with stereotypes, Besides, the question of restoring their access to resources such as land, water and forest, and shaping the structural instruments such as policy and regulations, have been of high-priority in Bhasha's activities. Bhasha tries to pursue all these lines of action for a social transformation by activating the energy and imagination of the young and the educated among the Adivasis." ("About").

Similarly, as bhasha's objective adivani is also to serve the largest silent human resource of the nation. Their project is wording the silence to ensure rights to live and express.

Literary practitioners in academic institutions by engaging themselves with new course curriculum and academic programmes such as workshop, seminar and so on in collaboration with such houses or by incorporating literature published by them and with critical engagements with the print and publishing history as resistance extend and may extend their solidarity with the activists and thus with new epistemological intervention, they can put forward their efforts towards humanity.

Dalit and tribal literature from different parts of India initiated dialogues amongst them due to the translation culture initiated in the last three decades. New publishing houses and growing demand of marginal literature into English is a significant part of the political economy of literature which insists new contents into the market as well as reading culture. Importantly this age is the age of life writing like autobiography/ memoir/testimonies. Hence every utterance is important to the history and literature of both the disciplines. Emergence of Public History and Oral History as a discipline after the Subaltern intervention into history and literature gave significance to the small voices of history. These small voices as the marker and source of alternative history/historical narratives also provoked new writings from marginal sections of a society into print. The English publishing house, as their market strategy, celebrates the book more than any other Indian languages publications in India. Such power of publishing along with the prestige and privilege of English brought Dalit consciousness and Dalitality in both the Dalit and non-Dalit literary canon.

16.5 Collaborative Translation as a Method of Margin

Translation of literature of the marginal communities is always organic as it is a living issue of the society and people often speak about their experiences which are represented otherwise in the literature. For example, social Dalit as an organic entity is associated with literature and consecutive translations, and the literature and translation is associated with the cultural and political Dalit, therefore with the social Dalits too. Translation of Dalit literature into English brings an organic Dalitality in the socio-cultural and political sphere of the society and both the Dalit and English are interdependent to the greater political cause.

India is a multilingual country and most of the languages are unrecognised in academic studies, therefore, the knowledge tradition of those languages remains unrecognised and becomes endangered with the migration and displacements of people of the community. I argue that the Organic Collaborative Translation (OCT) is the most potential method for literary documentation of marginal and endangered linguistic communities and for introducing knowledge in academic studies in higher education institutions. OCT involves speakers and experts of the Source Language (SL) and a group of translators together, ideally in a chosen space which is the origin of the language or the literary texts (oral and/or written). Such a method fills the gap of knowledge that translators have about the source text and culture as those are not well documented as knowledge sources and reduces the lack of opportunity and expertise the community requires for translation and documentation of literature. The methods and outcomes of such organic collaborative translation practised as an experiment through workshops organised by a trust Calcutta Comparatists 1919 across the Indian state of West Bengal and the similar initiatives taken by the Department of Comparative Indian Language and Literature, University of Calcutta. This part of the essay is about the experiences gained through such translation activities. The languages which were taken for organic collaborative translation are Sadri and Sundari languages of the islands of Sundarban of West Bengal, Shershabadia, a language of Bihar and West Bengal border, Subarnaraikhik, the language of Subarnarekha riverbank of West Bengal–Jharkhand–Odisha, and Toto, an endangered language with approximately 1645 speakers residing at the valley of the Himalaya in India and Bhutan border. I argue that the OCT method is a remarkably effective method to document the literature, culture and knowledge of the languages which are hardly recorded and critically endangered.

Glossaries, dictionaries, and a few anthropological elements—tools essential for translating lesser-known languages—have also been developed through these workshops. The literature of the Sundarbans, which was developed through constant interactions between humans and nature in their everyday vocabularies, is the specific focus of the workshop organised between 21st and 23rd March 2022, at the Department of Comparative Indian Language and literature, University of Calcutta. As a claim to distinguish the literature of the regions from other canonical literature of the geo-cultural space, we attempted to bring issues like how the forest, rivers, sea, animals, natural disasters, and migration in the Islands of Sundarbans make people's lives distinct, and therefore their mode of expression. We contend that the relocation of a literary category or genre inside the source cultural space occurs due to the translation into a language of power, which likewise reshapes the source culture. One approach to promote literary inclusiveness in the institutions that directly influence the formation of literary history is through translation, which enables a dynamic literary interaction in academic institutions.

Calcutta Comparatists 1919's initiative of documenting, translating, and publishing Toto language already received significant response across the nation and some parts of the world too. *Toto Shabda Sangraha*, a trilingual dictionary made by Bhakta Toto and published jointly by the Calcutta Comparatists 1919 and Bhasha Samsad, Kolkata in August 2023, widely received and appreciated. Leading newspapers in English in Bengali published from India and Singapore covered the news with their own initiative and great enthusiasm. The community itself for getting first such popular and well circulated coverage is very much enthusiastic to respond to the academic initiatives taken for archiving the language and literature and making those living for the present and future generations. With such personal experiences of working with the marginal communities I found that the collaborative translation is the only potential method of giving importance to both the community and the academic and of having a consensual dialogue for the benefit of the community and to fulfil the academic responsibilities. This is how our literary practices in academics can be extended beyond regular and traditional study of literature by engaging greater society with the academics, that is about the academic-social responsibility. As the University Grants Commission (UGC), India mentioned in their policy,

> "Higher educational institutions (HEIs) can play an important role to achieve the objectives of socio-economic development of New India through their active community engagement. This approach will also contribute to improvements in quality of both teaching and research in HEIs as they will develop better understanding of issues confronting the society. Therefore, it would in the fitness of things, if HEIs bring in social responsibility and community in their vision and mission itself. It is also important that institutional mechanisms are developed to adopt a holistic and functional approach to community engagement, encompassing all the three functions of HEIs-teaching, research, and service" (Singh).

16.6 Curriculum of Rights

Department of Comparative Indian Language and Literature, University of Calcutta, introduced a course in its post-graduate programme, entitled as "Language Situation of India and Other Literature of West Bengal". This course was designed with the philosophy of not only reshaping the canon of literature in academic culture within the scope of regular literary studies but also engaging with some serious questions about the lives interrupted by different power causing violation of people's rights. This course was aimed at making the literary invisible visible to the group of students imagining new literary geographies.

I believe that Comparative Literature as a discipline is always locally defined, it should be locally defined. Geo-cultural location should ideally define the curriculum of the discipline. Comparative Literature never should have the same syllabus across the regions even in the same nation. Hence, there is no universal curriculum of the discipline. This scope of diversity within the discipline makes Comparative Literature significant to the context of different geo-cultural regions. Comparative Literature in India is much different than the Comparative Literature studied in any other part of the world. Multilingual and multicultural contexts of Comparative Literature drive it towards a philosophy of responsibility to understand the literariness of the locale. Now let us understand the rationale of making a curriculum of the discipline to understand a local. Hence, each local must find a suitable literary structure for its own. The method of preparing a literary structure might go in a upended pyramid which means the closest linguistic locality of the academic institution will be the first unit of Literary study. Hence, literary concentration should be focused on the people visible with direct contact, the physical man of literature, primary producer, subscriber, and receiver of literature.

The Department of Comparative Indian Language and Literature at the University of Calcutta believes in such philosophy of localising Comparative Literature. It believes that each single literature department also needs comparative methodology to have adequate understanding of connection between literature and people, a text and history and also for transcending linguistic boundaries to find extra geo-linguistic life of a literary text. Our objective is to practise an alternative Comparative Literature which is in India having a centre with Indian literature. Our study is within Indian Literature and studying other literature of the world with reference to Indian literature. Indian students of literature are supposed to conceptualise a literary spectrum with their own position being at the receiving end. It happens to most of the single Indian Literature departments that except the exceptions most of the students are participatory observant of literary study. Therefore, they appear as potential contributors in the literary system from their own very existential experiences. Our primary responsibility is to anchor our discipline in the history we inherit, and we share in our beingness.

Literature produced by the people of hill Bengal is historically and culturally comparative. Literary traditions of hill Bengal comprised both the oral and written culture and multiple ethnic, linguistic, and cultural groups have been staying together there. The locale is very much cosmopolitan, and each ethnic culture has cross-cultural interactions with other communities which make their creative expressions necessarily comparative. The academic exploration of the Indian Nepali's identity struggle, the Lepcha community's efforts to preserve their memory through digital script development, the Toto's fight for linguistic existence, and the Rajbanshis/Kamtapuri's struggle for linguistic and political identities can be effectively examined and understood through a Comparative Literature perspective in the department. Even the literature written in different linguistic variants of dominating Bengali seemed as 'other' to the urban and economically represented Bengali culture, also may be studied together to have a peaceful coexistence and to decrease the differences among the communities within the greater Bengali identity. Introduction of such literary discipline in the universities and colleges of such areas is an affirmative action to know the 'other/s', archiving the knowledge and establishing the peace among the communities. None of the single literature departments can serve the purpose; even if those are studied under the same roof cannot erase the difference until and unless those are included in a single curriculum, and thus become comparative.

Taking such initiative in politically and culturally marginal areas is always a part of literary activism. The curriculum of such a Comparative Literature department may include digital humanities, translation studies, practical translation, technical and machine translation, creative writing, lexicography, linguistics, dictionary preparation, performance studies, fieldwork, preparing online archives etc. which will result in an academic discipline to relate to people. Such literary discipline, in my understanding, is solidarity with the people living in margin, people whose voices are not widely heard, people whose memory is not well recorded. Therefore, our curriculum included the language debate that happened since the time of independence, and the various linguistic contexts of the margins in India and the literature of various Adivasi and other marginal communities of West Bengal. The curriculum is quite flexible as we can accommodate from time to time newly emerged texts in our curriculum. The collaborative translation workshops so far conducted in the last few years by the department as well as the Calcutta Comparatists 1919, also accommodated in the curriculum to make literary engagement livelier, and contemporary with continuous engagement with the communities.

16.7 Conclusion

This paper connects mainly two different enquiries, one is about the writing, translating, and publishing Dalit/Adivasi or marginal narratives from a particular geo-cultural space and other one is about crisis of languages in a multilingual nation where only too few languages are designated as official language and the language of right to the knowledge. Apparently two different areas brought together as two different case studies led by the author from the institutional infrastructure completely or partially. And the outcome of both the studies is publishing and archiving the narratives, texts or vocabularies of the marginalised communities or the community who is critically endangered. Thus, the role of academic departments in bringing those in the curriculum to understand the history and other narratives of the people. The primary aim of this study was to examine the function of the academic discipline within its defined scope to actively interact with previously overlooked narratives, contributing to the historical understanding of marginalised subjects and ultimately promoting human rights for a broader population.

References

"About Adivaani." WordPress.com, 21 Mar. 2019, https://adivaani.org/about

Bhasha (2021) About. https://bhasharesearch.org/about, Accessed 21 Mar 2024

CC1919 (2023) https://www.calcomps.org/. Accessed 18 Nov 2023

Heera A, Mrinmoy P (2023) (eds) Bratyanarir Atmakatha. 1st ed., India, Gangchil

"I Am Not Your Data - Agitate". Agitate, 1 Feb. 2022, https://agitatejournal.org/article/i-am-not-your-data

Maitreya Y (2021) How Panther's paw publications is publishing its Dalit books during, and against, the pandemic. Scroll.in, 20 Oct. 2021, https://scroll.in/article/969353/how-panthers-paw-publications-is-publishing-its-dalit-books-during-and-against-the-pandemic.

Sushmita (2020) Remembering scholar and activist Abhay Xaxa, whose death is an irreparable loss to Adivasi movements. The Caravan, 27 June 2020, https://caravanmagazine.in/communities/remembering-abhay-xaxa-whose-death-is-a-loss-to-adivasi-movements. Accessed 18 Nov 2023

Siddhalingaiah (2013) A word with you, world: the autobiography of a poet. Translated by S. R. Ramakrishna, Navayana Pub.

Singh DP (2020) Fostering social responsibility and community engagement in higher educational institutions in India. UGC, India, 16 Jan. 2020, www.ugc.gov.in/ebook/UNNAT%20BHARAT%20ABHIYAN.pdf

MIX
Papier aus verantwortungsvollen Quellen
Paper from responsible sources
FSC® C105338

If you have any concerns about our products,
you can contact us on
ProductSafety@springernature.com

In case Publisher is established outside the EU,
the EU authorized representative is:
Springer Nature Customer Service Center GmbH
Europaplatz 3, 69115 Heidelberg, Germany

Printed by Libri Plureos GmbH
in Hamburg, Germany